This book examines the characteristics of political power in the cities of the colonial Spanish Empire between the 1740s and 1780s, based on a detailed study of the mining city of Oruro in Alto Peru (present-day Bolivia).

Oruro, after Potosí, was the second most important colonial center of silver production in the southern hemisphere. The fluctuations in the volume of this activity, as well as its financing and production, were important cultural and political factors in this colonial city.

Special emphasis is given to the specific forms of the exercise of power, assessing the judicial process and the material opportunities that the various bureaucratic positions made possible. From this, it can be seen how these public activities were to a large extent of a private nature, and how the resources available to each official greatly determined his scope of action.

Toward the end of this period, the analysis focuses on the particularities of the important Indian uprisings of the 1780s (the rebellions of Tupac Amaru) and the causes of the alliances or confrontations between the members of the distinct bands, either white or Indian.

CAMBRIDGE LATIN AMERICAN STUDIES

General Editor
Simon Collier

ADVISORY COMMITTEE
MALCOLM DEAS, STUART SCHWARTZ, ARTURO VALENZUELA

76

POWER AND VIOLENCE IN THE COLONIAL CITY

For a list of other books in the
Cambridge Latin American Studies series,
see page 229

POWER AND VIOLENCE IN THE COLONIAL CITY

ORURO FROM THE MINING RENAISSANCE TO THE REBELLION OF TUPAC AMARU (1740–1782)

OSCAR CORNBLIT

Social Investigations Center of the
Torcuato Di Tella Institute, and the
Center for Studies in Applied Public Policies

Translated by
ELIZABETH LADD GLICK

CAMBRIDGE
UNIVERSITY PRESS

Published by the Press Syndicate of the University of Cambridge
The Pitt Building, Trumpington Street, Cambridge CB2 1RP
40 West 20th Street, New York, NY 10011-4211, USA
10 Stamford Road, Oakleigh, Melbourne 3166, Australia

First published 1995

Printed in the United States of America

Library of Congress cataloguing data applied for.

A catalog record for this book is available from the British Library.

ISBN 0-521-44148-X hardback

Contents

Figure, maps, and tables

Figure

Maps

Tables

Preface

History books often contain the implicit assumption that the events of the past can be interpreted in only one way, and that this vision of history underlies the book in hand. This is not my point of view. I believe that there are many ways to explain history, and furthermore that they are not necessarily mutually exclusive. In certain cases one kind of explanation might even require elucidation from one or several of the others.

The choice of a style of explanation or a combination of several styles depends closely on the author's purposes – purposes that might be predictive, rhetorical, narrative, expressive, or pedagogical, among others. Moreover, underlying all of these is a system of ontology, whether explicitly stated or not.

Philosophically speaking, this means that our conceptions of the nature of the world may be different. In historical interpretation, one crucial issue is our conception of the nature of past events. Are they simply there waiting to be told, or does our description alter them? Further, do historical events repeat themselves with some degree of similarity or not?[1]

It is not my intention in this preface to discuss problems that would require a great deal more space than I have available here.[2] I will indicate only that the predominant explanatory mode in this book is a narrative one. There are discrete kinds of narratives; each contains different combinations of rhetorical conceptions about the course of events, hypotheses about the causal links between them, and overall views about social reality.[3]

1 See Louis O. Mink, "Narrative Form as a Cognitive Instrument," in R. Canary and H. Kosicki, eds., *The Writing of History: Literary Form and Historical Understanding* (Madison, University of Wisconsin Press, 1978), p. 140.
2 See on these topics Oscar Cornblit, "Acontecimientos y leyes en la explicación histórica," *Análisis Filosófico*, 8, no. 2 (1988), 141–59. For another view, see Hayden White, *Metahistory* (Baltimore, Md., Johns Hopkins University Press, 1975).
3 In my work *Cambio político en Cuzco y Oruro a fines del siglo XVIII: un estudio comparado de simulación* (Buenos Aires, Instituto Torcuato di Tella, 1970), I tried to formulate mathematically some hypotheses that would permit an explanation of the different political coalitions that arose in the cities studied.
   In "La formalización teórica en las ciencias sociales," Torcuato Di Tella defends a "modelistic" conception of explanation. This article was published in Oscar Cornblit, ed., *Dilemas del conocimiento*

The work presented here is, accordingly, only one account of events that took place in Oruro between 1740 and 1780. One of many cities in the Spanish colonial empire in America, Oruro had several peculiar features that place it within the at-once imaginary and real category of "mining cities" of the period. In the book I have occasionally used this category in an attempt to achieve a better comprehension of certain events; and although an understanding of its history does not depend exclusively on this classification, it does to some extent.

The history of Oruro during this forty-year period can be viewed as the story of a colonial city within the power system of the Spanish crown. In my step-by-step tracing of different kinds of events that overlapped within a certain time frame, I have tried to emphasize the concrete connections between them. It is possible (and perhaps probable) that these connections were representative of similar ones in other colonial cities of Spanish America. This too is one of the assumptions of this book, supported by examples from comparable places.

The narrative revolves predominantly around events that occurred in Oruro during the period discussed, events that were naturally linked to other occurrences influencing life in the city, and also to places and persons over which Oruro, in turn, cast its influence. I have made a special effort to examine the actual power (as opposed to the theoretical power conferred by law) that individuals exercised through their jobs. To this end, again, I have relied not only on what happened in the city but also on events in other cities of the same epoch.

I have not drawn any general conclusions from this account, but prefer to let history speak for itself. Nevertheless, the repetition of some themes might be interpreted as an emphasis on causal links. I think it is difficult to avoid such assumptions, but I also believe that the narrator can cogently argue a different position: that he is recounting these events without implying that they have any causal weight. In this case, I presume that the particulars I chose to relate influenced one another. Thus the history of the old Oruran families – the Herreras and the Rodríguez – the personalities of the family heads, their political ambitions, and their economic vicissitudes, cannot be ignored if one is to understand the life of the city. These things help us understand the events in many other colonial cities, and perhaps in those of later epochs.

My approach was different in my earlier work, cited in note 3 (*Cambio*

histórico: argumentaciones y controversias (Buenos Aires, Editorial Sudamericana, 1992). Several other articles in this collection examine related questions. Tulio Halperín Donghi addresses the results of the efforts at quantification in recent decades; Ezequiel Gallo, inevitability and accident in history; Manuel Mora y Araujo, the possibilities of verification; Guido Pincione, generalizations and explanation; Osvaldo Guariglia, narration and comprehensive reason (Dilthey); and Roberto Cortés Conde, economic history.

político en Cuzco y Oruro . . .). There I tried to use mathematical relationships in order to strictly deduce the formation of certain political coalitions rather than others. The same is true, to lesser extent, of my work *Society and Mass Rebellion* (1970),[4] which provoked a stimulating discussion about the causal roots of the Tupamarist movement of the eighteenth century, and was in many ways the point of departure for the present book.[5]

Perhaps another virtue of a narrative style that is less dependent on underlying preconceptions is that it permits various interpretations to be imposed upon it, thus allowing readers to make their own choices. If readers, using their own insights, end by constructing a mental panorama of life in the city, of the relations among its inhabitants – their way of thinking and feeling, their hopes and ambitions – framed in the material context of the conditions in which those people lived their daily lives, the book will have accomplished its goal. It is true that this picture will vary according to each reader's subjective responses, but this is the way it ought to be until new facts narrow the parameters of speculation, or until the way of looking at the world changes for the narrator, the reader, or both.

It was not my intention to recount events in such a manner that the last chapters would constitute the culmination of all that came before. The story can, however, be read in this way and there is no reason it should not be, since there is an assumption in history that later events are causally linked to earlier ones. At least this is so in our times, when the gods do not intervene directly in the daily actions of human beings, as they did in the days of the Iliad. In this volume, however, there is an emphasis on the symmetry of some aspects of the beginning and the end, although events posterior to the components of this symmetry may be sharply dissimilar: in one case – the last – blood, desolation, destruction, and death; in the other, negotiation and accommodation, although highly unstable.

Here I would like to express my thanks for the generous assistance I received during this long labor. Institutionally I had the opportunity to work in the stimulating research atmosphere of the Instituto Di Tella, with the matchless support of its library and the people who work or used to work there. Among others I wish to mention Nelly Pesce de Kay, Baby Destuet, Raúl Romero, and Ricardo Rodríguez Pereyra. I am also grateful for the fellowships awarded me by the Social Science Research Council and the John Simon Guggenheim Memorial Foundation. It also gives me pleasure to

4 Oscar Cornblit, "Society and Mass Rebellion in Eighteenth-Century Peru and Bolivia," in Raymond Carr, ed., *Latin American Affairs* (Oxford University Press, 1970), pp. 9–44. Several translations of this work have been published in Spanish.
5 See Steve J. Stern, "The Age of Andean Insurrection, 1742–1782: A Reappraisal," in Stern, ed., *Resistance, Rebellion and Consciousness in the Andean Peasant World, 18th to 20th Centuries* (Madison, University of Wisconsin Press, 1987), pp. 34–93, and the bibliography cited therein. See also Scarlett O'Phelan Godoy, *Un siglo de rebeliones anticoloniales* (Cuzco, Centro Bartolomé de las Casas, 1988).

acknowledge the open cooperation extended to me in all the archives mentioned in the book.

In addition, during the more than two decades I devoted to this topic, time spent gathering the data and publishing articles and monographs, I had opportunities to discuss my ideas with many colleagues. At Oxford University in England those who attended the seminar at the Latin American Center of St. Anthony's College in 1968 and 1971 made many observations that contributed to my revisions of the concepts I presented there. I would especially like to thank Sir Raymond Carr, Ezequiel Gallo, Tulio Halperín Donghi, Alan Angell, Malcolm Deas, and Laurence Whitehead. I also wish to acknowledge my discussions with many others with whom I had the opportunity to exchange ideas during my stays there as a visiting fellow in those years.

In Buenos Aires, I especially recall the stimulating and pointed conversations I had with Torcuato Di Tella; the chance to meet again with Ezequiel Gallo and continue the conversations we began at Oxford; my collaboration with Nicolás Sánchez Albornoz, with whom I had the satisfaction of working simultaneously at the Archivo Nacional de la Nación in Buenos Aires; and for more general interaction with Natalio Botana, Roberto Cortés Conde, and Manuel Mora y Araujo.

I also wish to mention the help of the late Leandro Gutiérrez and Laura Golbert (who is now busy with her own history project) in the early stages of my research, and the very central role of Liliana Lewinski before she went to Paris to finish her doctorate. Later, Eva Balbina Fernández, among others, was very helpful to me.

It is important to mention the generous bibliographical assistance offered by Enrique Tandeter, who placed at my disposal his broad knowledge and extensive library. And I wish to thank Magnus Moerner, who sent me works of his own that were relevant to my topic.

My greatest recent debt, however, during the crucial days as the work was being brought to a close, is to Olga Weyne. Her irreplaceable and energetic participation in every aspect of my book, her identification with the spirit of and the distinct problems presented by the arguments, the exposition, and the editing of it, made her contribution essential.

Buenos Aires, August 1994

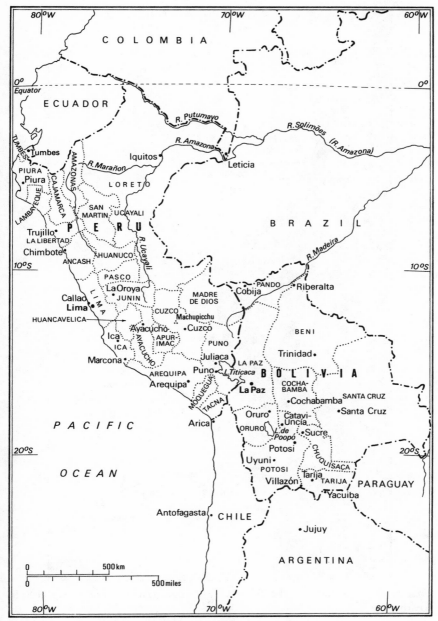

Map 1. Present-day Bolivia and surrounds

Source: *The Cambridge History of Latin America,* Vol. VIII, Ed. Leslie Bethell. Cambridge, 1991.

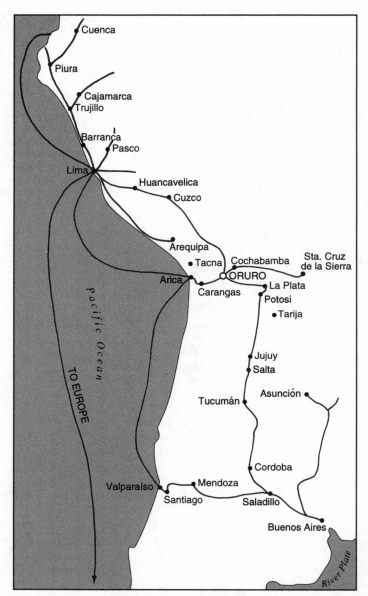

Map 2. Principal routes of the Viceroyalty of Peru (second half of the eighteenth century)

Source: Guillermo Céspedes del Castillo, "Lima y Buenos Aires – Repercusiones económicas y políticas de la creación del Virreinato del Río de la Plata," *Anuario de Estudios Latinoamericanos*, Vol. III. Seville, 1946. Redrawn by Cambridge University Press, 1995.

1

Oruro between two epochs: a mining cycle

In the forty years between 1741 and 1781, Oruro was not a sleepy little town. On the contrary, its inhabitants zealously pursued a variety of goals: they wanted to become wealthy, to hold public office both municipal and royal, to receive honors, and to wield power.

Judging by the information available to us, harmony did not reign among these people. Reading between the lines – and seeing the express words – of the documents analyzed here, we may well suspect that the so-called colonial siesta of the era was not as quiet as has been supposed. The opinions expressed by neighbors about one another were often so insulting that it is difficult to imagine how people who hated each other so intensely could coexist on a day-to-day basis within the narrow confines of a town of a few thousand inhabitants.

Of course, we are not speaking of an all-out war. Nevertheless, even taking into account that two clearly differentiated factions had formed, the actions of these Capulets and Montagues – and others as well – seem excessive for this relatively short span of time. None of them had the slightest trouble finding opportunities to launch fierce attacks against each other, as we will see in the chapters that follow.

It is to be expected that in a city whose principal activity was silver extraction, most of the energy would revolve around the mines: their possession, exploitation, financing, and provisioning. During these forty years, the town subsisted fundamentally on the mines. Nevertheless, the fact is – and this is pertinent to a great deal of the conflict we shall discuss here – that mining had ceased to be sufficiently profitable well before this period came to an end.

Because the intense social and political crisis of 1781 was accompanied by a pronounced reduction in the production of silver, it is hard to avoid the conclusion that the crisis was caused by this decline in the Oruro region. Such a conjecture would, of course, have to be corroborated by pertinent data.[1]

---

1 The cycle of prosperity continued until 1776, when a slow decline commenced.

As we shall see, it is impossible to undertake a history of Oruro – of its residents and their desires, fears, and passions – without a prior understanding of the role played by the *cabildo*, or municipal government, and its members. This municipal milieu was an important source of lucrative positions that were relatively accessible to the residents.[2]

The proprietors of the mines and mills were not necessarily – in all the periods covered here – the most prominent political personages. Nor were positions in the *cabildo* the only ones to which a citizen had access. Evidently, however, there were advantages to be gained from the (theoretical) annual rotation of some jobs that supposedly permitted a more equitable sharing of honor, privilege, and power. Later we will take a closer look at how far this sharing went and what advantages each of these positions conferred.

I will, then, try to reconstruct the social and economic situation of the city of Oruro and its role in the uprisings of 1781, as well as the specific history at certain moments of some of its inhabitants. The research concentrates especially on the manner in which the inhabitants exercised power on a day-to-day basis, not only through the central power hierarchy, but also through their customary conduct, and the forms and networks within which they readied their potential for action.

In the 1740s and 1750s a highly controversial figure lived in Oruro: Don Melchor de Herrera y Medrano. The documents rarely mention his complete name; rather, he nearly always appears as Melchor de Herrera and sometimes simply as "Don Melchor." He was clearly the leader of one of the factions, indefatigable in his passions and the defense of his interests, obdurate in his dislikes. His figure neatly embodied the antagonisms felt by the citizens of Oruro, and his opponents sometimes managed to diminish his influence but never to eliminate it completely. Melchor de Herrera died in the early 1760s. In the 1770s another person achieved similar notoriety: Juan de Dios Rodríguez.

Both leaders left their mark on the history of the town during the forty years covered by this study. It is impossible to know if this history would have followed another path if these men's personalities had been different.

---

2 Furious competition for these posts did not seem to be present – at least not to such extremes – in many other colonial *cabildos*. In this respect, it would be interesting to compose a typology to clarify which of them really corroborated the idea of "colonial enervation" and which did not. The specific bibliography, unfortunately, centers around an analysis of different functions and jobs, and one cannot obtain material for a comparative work from it.

A case similar to Oruro, for numerous reasons, is that of Potosí between 1622 and 1625 (about which we fortunately have several comparative references). See Alberto Crespo Rodas, *La guerra entre Vicuñas y Vascongados* (La Paz, Juventud, 1975).

In other places where there were no outstanding tensions, there were still some conflicts over jobs in the *cabildo*. For example, see the elections of 1757 in the *cabildo* of San Luis (present-day Argentina) and also those of 1761, 1762, and 1765, among others. See *Actas capitulares de San Luis* Academia Nacional de la Historia (Buenos Aires, 1983), pp. 67, 135, 137, and 151–2.

They did not give rise to the reasons for which the inhabitants struggled among themselves, but there is no doubt that their presence lent an unusual amount of force and violence to the events that took place.

Both Herrera and Rodríguez served as *alcalde ordinario*, or city magistrate, several times, and coveted this position for themselves or for the members of their respective factions. They did outrageous things in order to control both these positions and others available in the *cabildo*.

Alongside them – or opposite them, depending on the state of alliances – governed the most conspicuous representatives of royal power in the city: the *corregidores*, or district officers appointed by the king. The personalities of these officials also had a bearing on the course of events.

One of these *corregidores*, Juan de Landaeta, was one of the outstanding figures of the first part of this history; he possessed a rare aptitude for moderating antagonisms, as well as a degree of personal disinterest unusual in functionaries of those times. In fact, the behavior of all these men – *corregidores*, *alcaldes*, *regidores* (city councillors) or simply citizens – was generally characterized by extreme greed, thinly disguised by solemn protestations of love for the sovereign. Juan de Landaeta, however, seems to have been different, at least judging from the documents that record his term in office. The opinion of his contemporaries also conveys this view; in a society whose members never hesitated to denigrate their rivals, not a single voice was raised in criticism of his conduct. Unless documents from a later period prove the contrary, Juan de Landaeta remains the most sympathetic and moderate figure of all those who acted out their passions during this initial stage of our story.

In the last part of the book, the figure of another *corregidor* is silhouetted – this time pathetically – against the bloody background of the uprisings of 1781–2. Don Ramón de Urrutia, who was opposed to the rebel band and was the object of the joint attacks by the Creoles and the indigenous people, never managed to find the means to avert the chaos that overwhelmed the city. His integrity, like Landaeta's, cannot be called into question, but his leadership was sorely lacking.

In this period, several incidents in which the inhabitants raised arms against one another will be described. Nevertheless, it is clear that during these years, the inhabitants of Oruro struggled resolutely to obtain positions in the *cabildo*. Even in the face of the imminent danger presented by the indigenous uprisings of 1781, the factions once again battled each other for municipal jobs during the traditional New Year elections. The time and energy wasted in the eternal struggle between adversarial families damaged the city's ability to defend itself against the indigenous attack.

According to some authors, this situation was not like the experience of other places in the same period of the eighteenth century in Spanish

America.[3] One student of the topic, J. P. Moore, says that tumult and disorder were permanent characteristics of the mining towns because they attracted adventurers, speculators, and prostitutes in much higher percentages than was usual in other urban centers.[4]

Perhaps this observation is more applicable to Potosí, where for long periods of time the migratory population constituted a high proportion of the total. As for Oruro, there is no indication of any large population growth during the years under consideration here. In any case, those who competed for jobs in the *cabildo* were by no means socially marginal. Although they were not at the other extreme of the social ladder either, by the time they were elected to municipal office they had already made something of a name for themselves, whether through wealth, good marriages, or connections to important people inside and outside the city.[5]

As for the interpretations mentioned earlier – which identify decadence with conflict in city government – the struggle for positions within the municipal institutions in Oruro certainly cannot be conceptualized in this way, or else corruption in the fulfillment of the public obligations inherent in these positions would have to be the keynote for two centuries of government. This seems a little farfetched. With all its pros and cons, the colonial system had managed to sustain itself, and it is interesting to note that the crown had to confront its worst difficulties at the moment of its broadest attempts at administrative reform.[6]

Apropos of this, the following statement by C. H. Haring is illustrative:

3 Several authors think that the golden age of the *cabildos* was the sixteenth century and that they declined during those that followed, particularly after the second half of the eighteenth century. They offer as evidence the inhabitants' growing uninterest in holding public office in communities with a *cabildo*. See J. R. Fisher, *Government and Society in Colonial Peru: The Intendant System, 1784–1814* (London, Athlone, 1970), pp. 174–5. Also, John Preston Moore, *The Cabildo in Peru under the Bourbons* (Durham, N.C., Duke University Press, 1966), p. 61. Moore quotes opinions about the situation in several cities of Peru such as Arequipa, Lima, Trujillo, and Cuzco, throughout the eighteenth century. In his work *The Cabildo in Peru under the Hapsburgs: A Study in the Origins and Powers of the Town Council in the Viceroyalty of Peru, 1530–1700* (Durham, N.C., Duke University Press, 1954), he devotes a whole chapter to the decline of the *cabildos* during the seventeenth century. In fact, this decline is inferred from contradictory evidence. For example, the author sees both the residents' lack of interest in buying positions as *regidores* and their acute conflicts over the possession of jobs in the *ayuntamiento*, especially those of *alcalde*, as evidence of decline. Another sign of decline, according to these interpretations, was the misuse of judicial office and the corruption in the public functions assigned to it.

4 J. P. Moore, *The Cabildo in Peru*, p. 266.

5 See the list of names of the founders in this chapter.

6 Oscar Cornblit, "Levantamientos en Perú y Bolivia durante el siglo XVIII," in Tulio Halperín Donghi (ed.), *El ocaso del orden colonial en Hispanoamérica* (Buenos Aires, Sudamericana, 1978), pp. 57–119. Also, Scarlett O'Phelan Godoy, "Las reformas fiscales borbónicas y su impacto en la sociedad colonial del Bajo y Alto Perú," in Nils Jacobsen and Hans Jurgen Puhle, eds., *The Economics of Mexico and Peru during the Late Colonial Period, 1760–1810* (Berlin, Coloquium Verlag, 1986), pp. 341–56. In the same book, see Manfred Kossok, "Commentary," pp. 357–60.

It was a government, as someone has said, not intolerably bad, but not thoroughly good either. And, given the conditions . . . a territorial empire that covered two continents, whose focus of authority was located six, eight, or ten thousand kilometers from the Metropolis, governed by an absolute sovereign, jealous of his authority and disposed to examine and determine every aspect of the life and government of the colonies. In an epoch in which communications were extremely slow and uncertain, in which there were neither steamboats nor telegraph, and the ships were small and difficult to sail, this was probably the only type of government imaginable that would be capable of attending equitably to all these things and at the same time possess the necessary elements of permanence and security. As a system, however, it was troublesome and expensive.[7]

Origins of the mining city of Oruro

The economy of Oruro and the surrounding region was based from antiquity on the production of silver. Mining in the area began several decades before the city was founded; indeed, by 1557 there was talk of the existence of silver mines in the hills that surround Oruro. In that period the region formed part of a royal land grant, or *encomienda*, to Lorenzo de Aldana, given as a reward for his participation on the side of the king's forces during the rebellion of Francisco Pizarro. The abundance of the mines swelled the fortunes of Aldana, who, although a recent arrival, amassed a considerable fortune.

On his death he left several of his properties to the Indians whose villages had been granted to him in the localities of Santo Tomás, Caricari, Burguillos, Guancarama, and Querejani. He also left money to endow a convent of Augustan monks in Challacollo, located on the outskirts of Oruro on the Desaguadero River. After Aldana's death in 1573, the mines ran out and were abandoned. A few years later, however, exploitation was renewed with considerable vigor after the rediscovery of several abandoned deposits.[8]

The founding charter of the "very noble and loyal city of San Felipe de Austria de Oruro" mentions that one year earlier – 1605 – the mining population of the place, which was by now substantial, requested that the settlement be elevated to the rank of *villa* after considering the advantages of this for its activities:

Having presented before the *licenciado* Alonzo Maldonado de Torres of our Royal Council of the Indies and President of our Court and Royal Chancery who resides in the city of La Plata, province of Charcas in Peru, a petition in 1605, last year, by Diego de Medrano,

---

7 Clarence Haring, *El Imperio Hispánico en América* (Buenos Aires, Solar/Hachette, 1972), p. 130.
8 José Mesa and Teresa Guisbert, "Oruro: origen de una villa minera," in Condarco Santillán, collection ed., *Documentos Orureños*, vol. 2 (Oruro, Pregor, 1977), p. 61. In this work – as in that of Alberto Crespo Rodas, "Fundación de la villa de San Felipe de Austria," in the same collection – there is abundant information on the early periods of settlement.

in name and with the power of several gentlemen and persons who have come to the site of the Oruro mines, of the mayoralty of Paria, which he described as having a large number of mines rich in silver, which began to be worked in times of the Incas, and which as they are still being mined and are substantial, it is very appropriate to our royal service that there be apportioned Indians to work in them and profit from them; and that they be provided with quicksilver and be given aid.[9]

In the official visit made by Manuel Castro y Padilla, who was sent by the *audiencia*, or royal court, of Charcas to evaluate the possibility of founding a new city, we read that

[one could see that the mines were] rich and permanent and of high quality [and that they could] continue to work them [and thus] settle and found a town in the name of his Majesty with the people who are present at these mines.[10]

Due to this productivity, a considerable number of miners and laborers had settled in the region by this time. During his visit, Castro y Padilla listened to the assessment – and of course to interested advice as well – of many of these settlers as well as to others who planned to move there or invest in local deposits:

These visits were made with the aid of the owners of the mines and by many disinterested persons who were miners and had practice and experience, having worked the mines of Potosí and with other minerals in these kingdoms, each of whom had himself informed (Castro y Padilla) in public and in secret and he asked them to tell him about the basis and quality of the mines, and all unanimously and in agreement told him and certified them to be the richest, stablest, and firmest that had been discovered in the Indies.[11]

After these guarantees, following the accustomed steps and rituals observed in founding towns in South America, the public pronouncement was made accordingly and on Wednesday, November 1, 1606 – All Saints' Day – the solemn act of foundation was carried out by the judge of the *audiencia* of La Plata, Manuel de Castro, who then swore in all the first members of the *cabildo*. Their names were: Gerónimo Ondegardo and Francisco de Medrano (*alcaldes ordinarios*); Alonso de Mendoza Hinojosa (royal standard-bearer, or *alferez real*); Manuel de Torrez Villavicencio (*alguacil mayor*, or head bailiff); Juan Bilbao (*fiel ejecutor*, or inspector of weights and measures); Pedro de Lequí, Francisco de Alzedo, Hernando de Alvarez Rubiales, Francisco de Encinas, Martín de Butrón, Francisco Marmolejo, Julián de la Carrera, Andrés Vela de Escobar (*regidores*, or city councillors); Bartolomé

9 *Diccionario geográfico de la República de Bolivia*, vol. 4, "Departamento de Oruro," by Pedro Aniceto Blanco (La Paz, Sociedad Geográfica, 1904), pp. 25–6.
10 Ibid., p. 27.
11 Ibid., p. 25.

Perez de Larrea (*escribano*, or clerk); Bartolomé Rubio de Bivero and Juan de Segovia Batallanos (*alcades de la Santa Hermandad*, or rural magistrates); Diego de Medrano (*procurador general*, or attorney general) and Alonso Alvarez de Nava (*mayordomo*, or steward).[12]

In the year of the founding, a group of settlers named a commission to petition the viceroy or the *audiencia* at Charcas to provide *mitayos*, or Indian forced labor, for the various occupations necessary for the extraction and production of silver.[13] The productivity of the mines had bestowed affluence on the miners and laborers, who earned more than those at the Potosí mines.[14] The request for *mitayos* indicates the favorable development of silver extraction as well as the growing competition with Potosí, which already enjoyed this prerogative. The request was based on the abundance and richness of the silver ore in the Oruro region, whose two principal hills were San Miguel and San Cristóbal.[15]

Among its other advantages, the city of Oruro had a scanty water supply. Although in another settlement this could bring poverty, it was a blessing for a mining town, for flooding of the mines was one of the most frequent disruptions to mineral extraction.

Of course, the shortage of water had its drawbacks, not only for the supply and health of the settlement but also for the output of the mines. Less water power from the rivers was available to operate the ore-processing mills; but even here Oruro was fortunate, for it was able to make up for this by utilizing a rushing stream in Las Sepulturas, about eight kilometers from the mines. There were also other usable streams a little farther away in Paria.

The energy from the rivers was sufficient when there was abundant rainfall. When rain was scant, the flow diminished and the normal functioning of the hydraulic mills in Sorasora, Paria, and Poopó was affected. However, the mills located on the banks of the Sepulturas continued to function without setbacks because the water came from several reservoirs. These required constant maintenance and repair, and a special tax was imposed to cover the associated expenses.

12 Ibid., pp. x–xv.
13 Crespo Rodas, *Fundación*, pp. 24, 31–3. The *mitayo*, according to law, was obliged to work during specific periods for a salary established by the viceroy. Later I will make some observations on the significance of forced labor in Oruro and Potosí. On this subject, see Cornblit, "Levantamientos," pp. 80–8. Also, Alberto Crespo Rodas, "La mita de Potosí," *Revista Histórica*, 12 (1955–6), 169–82, and "El reclutamiento y los viajes en la mita del cerro del Potosí," in *La minería hispana e iberoamericana*, vol. 1 (VI Congreso Internacional de Minería, León, Spain, 1970), pp. 467–82. Also see Jeffrey A. Cole, *The Potosí Mita* (Stanford, Calif., Stanford University Press, 1985) and Enrique Tandeter, "Forced and Free Labour in Late Colonial Potosí," *Past and Present*, 93 (November 1981), 98–136.
14 Indications on receipts in Mesa and Guisberg, op. cit., p. 64.
15 The receipt figures were not really very high. The vein called "Pie de Gallo" produced between three and four pesos per *quintal* of ore, that is, around four ounces per *quintal* (of 200 marks),

Geographical advantages of the town

The town's importance was not limited to its mining wealth; Oruro's location had decisive importance for its evolution. In fact, it reaped large profits from its privileged situation when it became the only route between Arica and Potosí; it was even necessary to pass through it to reach the road from Buenos Aires to Lima.[16]

The Arica–Oruro connection was crucial because Arica was the port of entry for the mercury required throughout the Peruvian highlands for silver production. The commercial routes for its transport therefore took on special importance.[17]

which would yield about twenty-five marks per *cajón*. These figures are approximately appropriate for mines with ore of low silver content in the eighteenth century. Thus one reads, for example, in the report of the *corregidor* of Chichas, August 18, 1778 (Archivo General de la Nación, Intendencia de Potosí, leg. 6; IX-6-3-3 6). There it mentions fifteen to thirty marks per *quintal* as typical for metal of low silver content. See also, Daniel Santamarina, "Potosí entre la plata y el estaño," *Revista Geográfica*, 79 (1973), 132.

One might see a difference, perhaps, in that the veins of ore in the region were very close to the surface. It is reported, in fact, that a *mingado* Indian (that is, one hired as a free laborer), could extract with his hammer nearly five *quintales* of ore in one day of work – that is, a case and a half.

According to the calculations of W. F. C. Purser, *Metal-Mining in Peru, Past and Present* (New York, Praeger, 1971), p. 319, a miner extracted five *quintales* a day. Basing his work on different documentary sources, this author estimated that for each miner with a hammer, it was necessary to have two or three additional workers. Using a daily wage of four *reales* – which is doubtful because a free laborer earned considerably more – this would imply that the cost of labor (assuming three additional workers per miner-with-pick) was sixteen *reales* to extract five *quintales* of ore. A case (fifty *quintales*) cost ten times more, that is, 160 *reales* (equivalent to twenty pesos). In addition, the value of a case of ore with a yield of twenty-five marks per case could be estimated at 156 pesos 2 *reales* (valuing the common silver mark at fifty *reales*, according to Barba). See Purser, op. cit., pp. 310, 319 and following. Therefore, the cost of direct labor was nearly 13 percent of the value of the product.

Purser establishes a formula for determining the level of return per case that would make a mining operation profitable. This is: $X > (17,600 + 4,000P) / (5,000 - 8N)$ marks per case. Where P = the number of additional workers per miner and N = the price of mercury in pesos per *quintal*. Given a value of $P = 2$ (two additional workers per miner) and $N = 90$ (ninety pesos per *quintal* of mercury), the ore was profitable at a return of six marks per case. If the number of additional workers were three ($P = 3$), the equilibrium value of X is 6.92 marks per case. This formula could be refined, taking into account different labor costs. To these costs others, fixed and variable, must be added, and these varied a great deal according to the characteristics of the mine, its location, etc. All in all, these estimates might explain why a return of twenty-five marks per case was considered excellent in the seventeenth century.

The yield from the ore was thus not very high, taking into account cost per *quintal*. In the example given, the settlers stipulated that from a *quintal* of ore it was, in fact, possible to obtain around twenty-five marks of silver. See Crespo Rodas, *Fundación*, p. 25. We can conclude that the large difference was due, then, to the quantity of ore that could be extracted by a miner.

16 Guillermo Céspedes del Castillo, "Lima y Buenos Aires: Repercusiones económicas y políticas de la creación del Virreinato del Río de la Plata," *Anuario de Estudios Americanos*, 3 (1946).
17 Ibid.

The mercury used was produced in two places: Huancavelica in Peru, and Almadén in Spain. Occasionally mercury was also imported from Istria (Austria).[18]

The mercury produced in Huancavelica was used preferentially in the viceroyalty of Peru – which until 1776 included the present countries of Peru and Bolivia – whereas the mercury produced in Almadén was consumed primarily in Mexico.

Nevertheless, this pattern was not rigidly adhered to. On numerous occasions the Mexican mines received mercury from Huancavelica, and the Peruvian ones used mercury from Almadén. As Huancavelica mining declined substantially throughout the eighteenth century, especially in the second half, the consumption of mercury from Almadén increased sharply.

Mercury from Spain was shipped to Lima and then carried overland to the port of Chinchas. From there, it was transported by ship to Arica, then carried to Oruro. When it reached the town it was distributed to all the users in the region of the *audiencia* of Charcas, primarily to Potosí. Although there was an alternate route from the port of Arica to Potosí, the easiest, because of its better condition, passed through Oruro.[19]

Oruro between two epochs

Oruro had reached its apogee at the end of the seventeenth century, when, according to some estimates,[20] its population climbed to eighty thousand. Later there was a period of sharp decline in local production, which continued through a long depression during the first decades of the eighteenth century. But in 1740, due to the discovery of new veins in Sepulturas, Sorasora, and Poopó, the area saw a recovery that lasted more than three decades, ending with the nearly definitive collapse of the last years of the century.[21]

In 1787, the description of Oruro offered in the "Geographical – Historical Dictionary of the West Indies" bears no resemblance to the prosperous profile of its beginnings as a mining city:

18 Arthur P. Whitaker, *The Huancavelica Mercury Mines* (Cambridge, Mass., Harvard University Press, 1941). See also J. R. Fisher, *Silver Mines and Silver Miners in Colonial Peru, 1776–1824* (University of Liverpool, Centre for Latin American Studies, 1977), pp. 74–89. This work gives production figures for Huancavelica and Almadén for various years (1759 the earliest and 1816 the most recent), as well as for mercury imports to Peru from the mid-eighteenth century.
19 Mesa and Guisbert, op. cit., p. 62.
20 José M. Dalence, *Bosquejo estadístico de Bolivia* (Sucre, Imprenta de Sucre), 1851.
21 See Chapter 7 for the development of the *caja real* of Oruro. There one can see the comparison with production at Potosí, as well as the level of production in Oruro between 1740 and 1780.

. . . a cold dry place subject to storms; the crops produced there are potatoes, quinine, and a little barley. They raise small livestock and game, and produce a lot of gunpowder because the land is very nitrous, although not as much as in the past when its gold and silver mines were flourishing: today it is in a state of extreme decline and most of it is washed out and difficult to remedy because of a lack of slope to the land. Thus the population is dwindling, and the whole province has only about 8,000 inhabitants . . . In the time of the Incas . . . the so-called Pie de Gallo was outstanding for its richness, but today is abandoned and only Poopó and a few other places are still being worked.[22]

This interim period of recovery from 1740 to 1780/1 embraces the conflicts and political development analyzed in the following chapters, a period that witnessed a struggle among its inhabitants for municipal posts and culminated in the bloody events of the great Indian rebellion of 1781.

---

22 Antonio de Alcedo, *Diccionario geográfico–histórico de las Indias Occidentales o América: es a saber de los reynos del Perú, Nueva España, Tierra Firme, Chile y Nuevo Reyno de Granada*, 5 vols. (Madrid, 1786–9).

2

Under Spanish law

Before we become enmeshed in the details of the history of Oruro in the second half of the eighteenth century, it is a good idea to review the normative and institutional framework of the age. It is also useful to compare the general functioning of Spanish colonial structure – using the most representative works on the theme – with the specific case of a Spanish American city that, like many others, reveals a past rich in historical detail that at times corroborates accepted opinion but in some cases presents contrasts and exceptions worthy of reflection.

According to Clarence Haring, the two primary characteristics of the Spanish imperial government in America were the division of authority – with the consequent allocation of responsibility in the functions of government – and the profound jealousy of the crown with respect to the initiatives of colonial officials. Thus, the government was not founded, as modern states are, on the division of the legislative, executive, and judicial powers, but rather divided authority among individuals or institutions who generally shared the same powers. The problem lay in the imprecise delineation of functions. This situation, with its great number of superimposed jurisdictions was, one assumes, created directly by the crown.[1]

In any case, the policy had its risks. The lack of direct control from Spain, a result of its great distance, bestowed a high degree of independence on the colonial powers, who were often ignorant not only of many royal mandates but also of general laws and regulations.

At the head of local administration was the viceroy or captain general, assigned to his particular geographical zone. The viceroys were the highest authorities in their jurisdictions as they were the direct representatives of the king. They held both civil and military authority and controlled the judiciary, the treasury, and some aspects of governance relating to the clergy. The administration of the royal income was their responsibility as well as the welfare of the Indians. In addition, they appointed most of the lesser colonial officials, both lay and ecclesiastical.[2]

1 Haring, op. cit., pp. 129–30.
2 Ibid., p. 127. With the priests there were other peculiarities.

The game of "checks and balances" was evident in the relations the viceroys and captains general had with the rest of the officials. For example, any of the latter had the right to carry on direct correspondence with the central authorities in Spain. One can see in this system – which was rigidly enforced, by the way – the intentions of a paternalistic monarchy that did not place much trust in the delegation of power. In the opinion of one official of the age, the consequences of the system of reciprocal control among officials were frequently anarchical. Pedro V. Cañete y Domínguez mentions the case of an order given in 1732 to the viceroys of Lima instructing them to appoint a minister of the *audiencia* of Charcas every two years, who would handle all the matters pertaining to *mita*, or Indian labor drafted for public works, and who would also act as superintendent of the town of Potosí for extra pay. What followed was "a multiplication of commands, a discrediting of the authority of the *corregidor*, or district officer, due to the ostentatious power of the robed ministers, and a kindling of new allegiances and factions in the town."[3] This situation also gave rise to distinct parties among the populace who were wooed by the leaders in their efforts to maintain the power of their own faction at all costs.

With the passage of time, the functions of the viceroy or captain general diminished. By the eighteenth century they had become simply the executors of royal orders; they no longer retained even the right (which was rescinded by the centralist, fiscalist regime of the Bourbons) to hand out favors and rewards.[4]

Every viceroy was simultaneously the captain general of his jurisdiction, with the entire military justice system in his charge. In the eighteenth century, these functions of the viceroy increased in importance, especially after the Seven Years' War (1756–63), when a decision was made to create a permanent army in the Spanish colonies.[5]

In the early days of colonization, the viceroys belonged to distinguished noble families, in spite of the prejudice in this regard shown by the Council of the Indies, who preferred candidates with legal training. In the eighteenth century, under the Bourbon dynasty (and especially in the century's second half), viceroys began to be appointed who came from the lower nobility and even the bourgeoisie. Value began to be placed on aptitude for military service or administration, and in these new criteria the concepts of enlightened absolutism can be seen. Examples of this new approach in Peru are represented by the viceroys Manuel de Amat and Francisco Gil y Taboada.[6]

---

3 Pedro Cañete y Domínguez, *Guía histórica, geográfica, física, política, civil y legal del gobierno e intendencia de la provincia de Potosí*, 1787, collection ed. Armando Alba (Potosí, 1952), vol. 1, 338.
4 Haring, op. cit., pp. 128–9.
5 Ibid., p. 132.
6 Richard Konetzke, *América Latina: la época colonial* (Madrid, Siglo XXI, 1974), p. 121.

Over the course of three centuries, Peru had forty-one viceroys, most of whom were of noble birth. Although many of them tried to purge public administration and the judiciary, founded colleges and defended arts and letters, a large number seem to have governed with indifference and, in more than a few cases, venality.

An important privilege of the viceroys was to fill vacant posts in the judiciary system. J. Juan and A. Ulloa criticize this prerogative:

[This privilege] would be very just because with such judgment one could remunerate the services that some residents would render to the king, not having in those parts anything else with which to satisfy those who distinguish themselves in royal service, but it is not executed anything like this, because all the positions, when they do not go to those who acquire them through their own interests, then they go to others who by force of flattery find the door open to them on the basis of favoritism.[7]

One of the questions that used to give rise to abuses was that the vacant positions for *corregidor* were frequently assigned to relatives of the viceroy. The same thing happened with nearly all official royal occupations; and if one believes Juan and Ulloa, with political, civil, and military ones as well. The only exception seems to be the jobs of ministers of the *audiencia*, whose positions could be neither created nor filled on an interim basis.[8] As for the viceroys known for their irreproachable public conduct, it appears that many of their efforts came to nothing in the face of the bellicose tendencies of the inhabitants, the arrogance of the high clergy, and the jealousies of other royal officials.

The prohibition against engaging in business was theoretical, and was disregarded by royal officials. Leaving aside the viceroys – among whom there were no notorious cases of transgression, perhaps because they did not need to resort to this in order to enrich themselves – the rest "all engaged in trade as freely as if it were their primary occupation."[9]

In the history of Peru there were only three ecclesiastical viceroys: of the forty-one who governed the viceroyalty, nine had previously been viceroys in New Spain during the Habsburg era. During this period the famous Francisco de Toledo stands out; to him we owe some of the government ordinances that remained in force even into the later period.[10]

In the period covered by the chapters that follow, the viceroys of Peru were:

1736–45   José Antonio de Mendoza Caamaño y Sotomayor, Marqués de Villa García;

1745–61   José Antonio Manso de Velazco, count of Superunda;

7 Juan and Ulloa, *Noticias secretas de América*, Ediciones Mar Océano Buenos Aires, 1953, pp. 346–7.
8 Ibid., p. 349.
9 Ibid., p. 357.
10 Haring, op. cit., pp. 135–6.

1761–76   Manuel Amat y Junyent y Santa Pau;
1776–80   Manuel Guirior;
1780–4   Agustín Jáuregui.

The *audiencias* were the royal high courts of appeal within their respective districts, and acted simultaneously as counsel to the viceroy or captain general. In the entire Spanish empire, the *audiencias* shown in Table 2.1 are those whose jurisdictional boundaries sometimes became tacit frontiers, anticipating the present republics.[11]

There were differences in rank among the *audiencias*. Those in the same city in which the viceroy had his court were the most important, because they took charge of the government in case of his inability or death. Those in a city that was a seat of government or a captaincy general were called *praetoriales*, and were second in rank. Finally, there were the subordinate *audiencias* whose president was a *letrado* (legal expert), subordinate to the viceroy or captain general in administrative matters.

Although faithful copies of their Castilian counterparts, the *audiencias* in America had broader legal authority. For example, they had full power to send judges of instruction, they could have the final say in disputes about the right of royal patronage, and they could verify the legality of measures taken by other local authorities. One could appeal to them against decisions made by viceroys and governors. On the municipal level, they confirmed decrees and exercised certain rights of inspection in cities. One of their most important functions was to tend to the application of the laws protecting the indigenous population. The decisions adopted by the *audiencia* in its sessions were *autos acordados*, or a kind of supreme court decision: that is, they had the force of law.[12]

These *audiencias* were one of the principal checks against the arbitrary power of the viceroy or the captain general. Because of their collegial character, they shared many functions of government with these officials. The number of members depended on the rank; before the eighteenth century in the most important *audiencias* – Mexico and Lima – there were only four judges, plus a president. At the end of the century the number had increased to ten, plus five criminal magistrates (*alcaldes de crimen*) and three public prosecutors (*fiscales*). The less important *audiencias* never had more than five judges. There was, of course, a large number of lesser officials: a chancellor, a head bailiff, a chaplain, court reporters, notaries, guards, a lawyer, and a public defender.[13]

Laws stipulated that sentences passed on crimes of falsehood, and on similar infractions, must be reviewed before they were executed by the *audiencia*

11 Konetzke, *América Latina*, p. 127.
12 Ibid., p. 124.
13 Haring, op. cit., pp. 137–8.

Table 2.1. Audiencias *in the Viceroyalties of New Spain and Peru*

Audiencia	year of creation
Viceroyalty of New Spain	
Santo Domingo	1511
Mexico	1527
Guatemala	1543
Guadalajara	1548
Viceroyalty of Peru	
Panama	1538
Lima	1543
Santa Fe de Bogota	1548
La Plata (Charcas)	1559
Quito	1563
Chile	1563
Buenos Aires	1661
Caracas	1786
Cuzco	1787

of the district, and that the case must be examined there. The *audiencias* were prohibited, however, from hindering the ordinary courts from carrying out the sentences in the cases where no appeal was allowed.[14]

The viceroy or captain general had no say in the judicial decisions of the *audiencia*, though theoretically he was its president when he lived in the same city. The exception might be a viceroy with previous experience as a lawyer, which was unusual.

Nevertheless, the viceroys were generally responsible for justice. They were helped by the right to visit the courts at the beginning of cases; they also had the power to pardon in criminal cases. It is nevertheless evident that with the passage of time the viceroys and captains general became less and less interested in routine judicial matters.

Beneath the *audiencia* was a large department for the administration of justice, which expanded especially in the eighteenth century. Institutions such as the royal treasury, the tribunal of accounts, the banking superintendent, the post office administration, and the boards of merchants, miners, shepherds, and physicians each had a separate code of law in civil suits. This large number of special tribunals led, obviously, to increasing administrative and judicial confusion. One must keep in mind that the boundaries of legal jurisdictions were not clearly defined in practice in every court case, even though they were spelled out in the regulations.

14 Cañete y Domínguez, op. cit., p. 538.

In general, the use of Castilian law was imposed without obstacles in America, since there was no formal legal tradition preceding it with which it had to coexist. In addition, the Spanish crown wanted to be tolerant of the indigenous habits and even to carry them out in cases where they were not in conflict with Spanish law.[15] But even when the laws destined for the Spanish Indies were compiled in 1680 and later in 1791, they had a supplementary character. The codes were considered definitive only in administrative or constitutional questions; even in these cases, however, customary practice was often cited as a way of avoiding some regulation or other. In civil, criminal, or commercial matters there was much more confusion: a judge might cite the code of the Indies as well as six other Spanish codes in deciding a case.[16]

To this ambiguity must be added the confusion resulting from the multiplicity of possible judgments, the form of execution of judicial resolutions, and the extent of the police power available in different legal situations.

This volume will emphasize the different kinds of situations that, over and above the law, created a power struggle among the parties involved. This power cannot be discerned through the codes or the compilations; it must be sought in the everyday activities of individuals and in the concrete manner in which differences among them were played out.

Having expressed these reservations and described the functions and characteristics of government, we must still ask who had more power in Spanish America, the viceroy or the *audiencia*. Here the ambiguities become immediately apparent. Clearly the *audiencia* was supreme as the highest court of appeal before the king or Council of the Indies. In other situations – especially administrative questions in which, according to Indian legislation, the *audiencia* must be subordinate to the viceroy – nothing was entirely clear. In the last analysis, harmony in their joint functioning depended on the character and personalities of both the viceroy and the members of the court. Whenever viceroyal intervention became too energetic, the *audiencia* governed subject to his commands, but with constant friction and conflict. If the chief executive lacked leadership qualities, however, the collegial body took charge of political control in practice, without any circumspection, especially if one of its members showed a talent for leadership.

---

15 *Recopilación de leyes de los reinos de las Indias, mandadas imprimir y publicar por la magestad católica del Rey Don Carlos II*, 4 vols. (Madrid, Boix, 1841), book 5, law 24.

16 José María Ots Capdequí, *Manual de historia del derecho español en las Indias y del derecho propiamente Indiano* (Buenos Aires, Facultad de Derecho y Ciencias Sociales, 1943), pp. 87–104. See also Colin MacLachlan, *La justicia criminal del siglo XVIII en México* (Mexico City, Septetentas, 1976), pp. 7–48.

In the last analysis, theoretically at least, the viceroy was supreme because he was the direct representative of the king; furthermore, the prerogative to fill vacant positions did much to consolidate his base of support.[17]

The *audiencia* was probably the most important and complex institution in the government of the Spanish realms in America. It became the center of the administrative system and the principal check against abuses of power by the viceroys. It also maintained a kind of continuity as a collegial body that the viceroys could never achieve. The viceroys succeeded one another, but the governing tradition of the court offered a guarantee of permanence.[18]

The lower administrative units in Spanish America were the *corregimientos* (royal mayoral districts), or *alcaldías mayores* (town magistrateships). In practice, the two administrative jurisdictions did not always coincide, and the *corregidor* generally had broader powers than the *alcalde mayor*.

In the viceroyalty of Peru there were seventeen Spanish and fifty-two indigenous *corregimientos*.[19]

The *corregidores* carried out diverse functions, not all of them specified. They intervened in judicial matters, were the superior judges of appeal of the *alcaldes ordinarios* of the towns,[20] and (one assumes) had to provide military assistance when necessary. They were considered representatives of the king in the provinces and thus their power was considerable.[21]

The *corregidores* had theoretically to provide "protection" to the Indians. Earlier this function was the duty of another state official, the "protector of Indians," but this position was abolished in the villages. In both cases, the most important task, with respect to the Indians, was the collection of tribute and the organization of the dispatching of *mitayos* to work sites. All this was carried out with the assistance of the *caciques*, or village chiefs.

While some *corregidores* had jurisdiction only over Indian villages, others were in charge of Spanish settlements and cities. Even in the second case, however, the office often had Indians under its jurisdiction.[22] In this way,

17 Ibid., pp. 139–42.
18 Haring, op. cit., p. 144.
19 Konetzke, op. cit., p. 125. In reality, aggregating Bajo and Alto Peru (incorporated in the viceroyalty of Rio de la Plata since 1776), the indigenous *corregimientos* reached seventy-six by the end of the eighteenth century (see Scarlett O'Phelan Godoy's map, *Un siglo . . .*, in Chapter 12).
20 Ots Capdequi, op. cit., vol. 2, 162.
21 Guillermo Lohmann Villena, *El corregidor de Indios en el Perú bajo los Austrias* (Madrid, Cultura Hispánica, 1957), p. 222. Also, J. M. Ots Capdequi, *Instituciones* (Barcelona, 1969), pp. 469–71, and Alfredo Moreno Cebrián, *El corregidor de Indios y la economía peruana en el siglo XVIII* (Madrid, Instituto Gonzalo Fernández de Oviedo, 1977).
22 In reality, all the *corregidores* had Indians under their jurisdiction, but their numbers varied markedly. While Cajamarca recorded 42,187 Indians in 1754, for example, Arequipa had only 1,699 in the same year. Trujillo had even fewer: 739. See Juerguen Golte, *Repartos y rebeliones* (Lima, Instituto de Estudios Peruanos, 1980), pp. 104–5.

the residents of each province – whether Indian, mestizo, or Spanish – came under the jurisdiction of the *corregidor*, who could choose to reside in any of the province's cities or villages, which then automatically became the capital of the *corregimiento*.[23]

In Peru the post of *corregidor* was introduced in the sixteenth century; one of the crown's purposes in creating it was to counteract the installation of a landed nobility in America with lordly rights over its vassals. Through the *corregidores* the power of the landholders was gradually diminished.[24]

Another feature of this position later had profound social consequences: because he was an officer of the crown, the *corregidor* was entitled to a salary linked to the tax base of the province. The annual salaries of *corregidores* varied from 1,200 to 4,800 pesos.[25] The *corregidor* was permitted neither to engage in business nor to participate in any kind of private activities – as stipulated in his oath of office – in order to avoid conflict with local businessmen.

Nevertheless, it soon become apparent that it was not possible for *corregidores* to live on their salaries.[26] Thus they were authorized to practice something called *repartimiento*, that is, a monopoly on the obligatory trade with the Indians of the villages. The *corregidor* could sell them a certain quantity of products during the five years of his term in office, and the Indians were obliged to purchase these goods.

This procedure was highly criticized by nearly all sectors of society.[27] One argument against it was that *repartimiento*, in reality, was a way of unloading surplus products, since the articles that the Indians were obliged to buy were generally of no use to them and the prices were much higher than they would have paid in the marketplace.

23 Oscar Cornblit, "Levantamientos de masas," pp. 94–5.
24 R. Konetzke, "Die Entstehung del Adels in Hispanisch Amerika waehrend der Kolonialzeit," *Viertel jahrschrift fuer Sozial-und-Wirtschaftgeschichte*, 39 (1952), 224.
25 Salaries have been stated in pesos of eight *reales*. Amounts are generally expressed in the so-called *peso ensayado* (an imaginary unit worth approximately 65 percent more than the peso of eight *reales*, or ordinary peso). Guillermo Lohmann Villena, *Los americanos en las órdenes nobiliarias, 1529–1900* (Madrid, 1942), pp. 595–600, provides the salaries of all the *corregidores* of Peru in the middle of the seventeenth century. These salaries, with a few exceptions, stayed at the same level throughout the eighteenth century, until the abolition of the office; see *Archivo general de Indias*, Audiencia de Lima, legajos 633–7. Moreno Cebrián, op. cit., p. 563, reproduces a list of salaries of *corregidores* from 1778, drawn up by Miguel Feijóo de Sosa.
26 The reader can consult the expenses in the budget of Manuel de Elcorrobarrutia, *corregidor* of Chancay, in Melchor de Paz, *Guerra separatista* (Lima, 1952), vol. 2, 307. He estimated that in a five-year period these reached 59,700 persons. See also the somewhat cynical defense of the *corregidores* by the probable author of the "Lazarillo de ciegos caminantes," Alonso Carrió de la Vandera, *Reforma del Perú* (Lima, Pablo Mancera, 1966), pp. 30–1. Moreno Cebrián, op. cit., pp. 106–11, provides the account of expenses and resources of *corregidores* (besides Elcorrobarrutia). These accounts were prepared by *corregidores* who wanted to demonstrate the risks incurred by the post and the possibilities for losing money while exercising it.
27 Juan and Ulloa, op. cit., pp. 198–9, did the same.

Repartimiento involved not only the Indians and the *corregidor*. The *corregidor* would usually acquire the products using credit extended by merchants from the cities, with whom he ran up large debts. Since he was not able to easily collect the money to repay these loans, there was constant potential for conflict. In fact, there were not many businessmen who were in a position to take the necessary risks; those who were charged exorbitantly high interest rates.[28]

These problems aside, clearly *repartimiento* was a way of increasing consumption since it forced demand on a community whose cultural patterns had very little relation to the Spanish market. This explains why it was supported not only by the *corregidores* but also by many businessmen. In debates over eliminating *repartimiento*, the fear was that this would curtail economic activity.[29]

The crown knew of the complications generated by *repartimiento*, but it was also aware that abolishing it would increase the costs of administration, since they would then have to raise the salaries of the *corregidores*; thus they adopted a variety of measures to curb abuses.

Each *corregidor* was allowed a maximum amount of money, and was not permitted to sell products to the Indians in amounts that exceeded this limit.[30] Nevertheless, one of the usual criticisms against them was their failure to observe the law. The Indians, for example, brought many suits against the excesses perpetrated by the *corregidores*.[31] In any case, even if these

---

28 See, for example, "Representación de la ciudad de Cuzco, en el año de 1768, sobre excesos de corregidores y curas," in Sebastián Lorente, *Relaciones de los virreyes y audiencias que han gobernado el Perú* (Lima/Madrid, 1867/72), vol. 3, 212–14. Not only does it criticize the *repartimiento*, but it also proposes a method for obtaining the necessary funds to pay the *corregidor* an adequate salary: pay no more money from the treasury to presbyters (synods), and use this sum to increase what was paid to the *corregidores*.

29 See Carrió de la Vandera, *Reforma*, where he complains of the negative consequences that the abolition of the *repartimiento* would produce.

30 Manuel de Mendiburu, *Diccionario histórico–bibliográfico del Perú*, 2d ed. (Lima, 1931–5), vol. 4, 456–7, provides a list of the maximum amounts allotted for the *repartimiento* in each of the provinces of Peru.

31 See, for example, "Testimonio de los autos seguido por los caciques Hilacatas del pueblo de Calacoto, provincia de Pacages contra el justicia mayor de ella . . . ," *Archivo general de Indias*, Audiencia de Charcas, legajo 592. The case of Manuel Fernández Palazuelos, *corregidor* of Huancavelica, is certainly illustrative, even though it is impossible to establish that it is representative. Palazuelos apportioned more than twice the amount established by the legal tax. This stipulated a maximum of 36,400 pesos for the official's whole term, and the figure actually apportioned was 77,677 pesos 7¼ *reales*. See Moreno Cebrián, op. cit., pp. 440–1, who cites a document of AGI (Lima, 1089); the proceeding was undertaken by the Visitor General Areche himself. The existence of an informal economy or black market, widely alluded to in numerous documents of the epoch, weakens any analysis based on legally authorized *repartimiento* amounts, as in the case of Juergen Golte's book, op. cit. Carrió de la Vandera, in his *Lazarillo de los ciegos caminantes*, 1775 (Barcelona, Labor, 1973), while he thought it was an exaggeration to attribute excesses in all cases of *reparto*, nevertheless believed it was true in the majority of cases: "Foreigners and even many Spaniards would say that the *corregidores* did not follow the rules of the tax and that they exceeded it in quantity and in prices. This opinion, taken as general, is rash

abuses had not existed, the system was conceived to force patterns of demand on a community that resisted it, and also to force on them a stricter and more routine way of life.

The lower rung of the administrative hierarchy in Spanish America was the *cabildo* or town government. From the early days of the conquest, urban communities were the dominant type of political and social organization. Thus genuine municipalities were established from the outset, while the rural population continued to be composed almost exclusively of indigenous people.[32]

The Spanish colonial city was often the result of the growth of a primitive indigenous mission, a frontier fort, or a mine. However, as a general rule there was a deliberate plan for founding cities. The founder was the one who chose the place, indicating the locations of the main square, the church, and the city hall; the streets were laid out, house lots were distributed, and the city was given a name. All present signed the founding papers and swore an oath; the founder then named *magistrados* and a *consejo municipal*, swearing himself in before this body.

In addition to the city proper, the municipality extended its jurisdiction throughout a municipal district, which extended to its neighbors' boundaries. In the early days of colonization, when the cities were separated by large unpopulated zones, these jurisdictions covered immense territories. In the sixteenth century the city limits of Buenos Aires, for example, extended to those of Cordoba.

Mining cities like Oruro generally arose as temporary establishments in the mountains and were located in less hospitable places with steep terrain. Their character did not conform in many respects to the model predominating in Latin America. These cities were sometimes labeled "mining camps," but like other cities, had a city hall and a church on a main square.[33]

This description fit San Felipe de Austria de Oruro. Its town government differed from the other *cabildos* in Peru in that from the time of its founding, the eight appointed *regidores* constituted the nucleus on whom the election of the most important officials rested.

---

because I know that many have reduced the price and have not been able to apportion the entire amount allotted because they did not want to confront tepid resistance. Don Felipe Barba de Cabrera, a person well-known in this city [Lima or Gibón?] has been *corregidor* of the province of Palaz for more than forty years. His success has been as fortunate as his generous principles for having apportioned all his *repartimiento* without violence. We can find a few examples like this, but not many." *Quia apparent rari nantes in gurgite vasto* . . . (Virgil, *Aeneid*, book 1.118): "In this vast sea, rescued from shipwreck, we see some captains who save themselves swimming." But even the reference to Barba de Cabrera may be questioned, as he was Carrió de la Vandera's protector; op. cit., pp. 347–8 and following, edition of Mario Carillo (Barcelona, Labor, 1973).
32 Haring, op. cit., pp. 164–5.
33 Ibid., pp. 165–7.

In general, in all the *cabildos*, authority was represented by two classes of officials: the *regidores*, or town councillors, and the *alcaldes ordinarios*, or magistrates. The number of *regidores* varied according to the importance of the city or its area. In the smallest – those called *villas*, or towns – there were usually four to six. In the larger ones there were usually eight, and only in capital cities like Mexico or Lima were there twelve or more. As for *alcaldes*, there was one in small towns and invariably two in the rest.[34]

The two most coveted positions were, logically, the *alcaldías*. They revolved annually because in theory the position was supposed to rotate widely among the populace. The law required a minimum lapse of three years between successive terms for the same individual.[35]

This regulation was not always strictly observed; there were numerous cases of *cabildos* in which the intervals between terms held by the same individual were shorter. Circumstantial factors often came into play, such as acute conflicts for the job that obliged people to find solutions outside the rules. For instance, the case of Field Marshal Pedro de Eulate considered in Chapter 6; he was elected *alcalde ordinario* of Oruro in 1747 and again in 1749.[36] In general, however, the principle of rotation was adhered to; when it was not, there were conflicts and resentment among the citizens.

Originally this regulation enhanced distribution, among the greatest possible number of individuals, of the honors that went with holding municipal office. It was believed that this would contribute to the growth of civic pride. In addition, by denying successive terms, it prevented the concentration of too much authority and prestige in the hands of a single individual.[37]

Although in theory any resident of the city could be elected to these positions, in fact mestizos, mulattoes, and Indians were excluded. Among the job requirements were not to have any debts with the royal treasury and to be more than twenty-six years old.[38]

The responsibilities of the *alcalde* included the administration of justice in the civil and criminal codes within the urban area.[39] Nevertheless, the

---

34 Ibid., p. 168.
35 J. P. Moore, *Hapsburgs*, p. 85.
36 "Lista de cargos, según pago de media anata," *AGN*, Sala III, Caja Real de Oruro (1700–91). See also Table 7.1.
37 Moore, *Hapsburgs*, p. 85. See also Juan Solorzano's comment on this subject, *Política indiana*, vol. 2, 252.
38 Moore, *Hapsburgs*, p. 83. This prohibition was established by the royal order of July 15, 1620 (*AGI*, Charcas, 55). Nevertheless, on various occasions there were intense debates about what types of debts should prevent persons from voting or being elected to the *cabildo*. In Potosí the miners had successfully argued that debts incurred for mercury and other expenses for the extraction of silver could not be counted inasmuch as they were indispensable for their activities. See Crespo Rodas, *La guerra*, pp. 72–86, for the details regarding the exclusion for debt of some *regidores* in elections for the *cabildo* of Potosí, January 1, 1622.
39 The *alcalde* was the judge of first instance in civil and criminal justice; Ots Capdequi, *Manual de historia*, p. 171. In the *Recopilación* of 1680 it is established that he has jurisdiction in all of a

social prestige enjoyed by this official leads one to believe that those who held it enjoyed – as long as they held office – prerogatives probably not specified by the law but consecrated by custom. According to Cañete and Domínguez,

The *alcaldes* have a lot of authority and spend too much in the year of their term; because in addition to the opulent tables, refreshments, and fiestas they have in their receptions, each one has two, three, or even four pages, dressed in flannel with braid and with the title of Minister, who serve to take prisoners and perform the other duties of justice.[40]

The court presided over by the *alcalde* had to be in session daily, and attend to all the complaints presented before it.[41] The two *alcaldes* had equal judicial authority, and it was even possible for one of them to preside over a case that affected the other. Sometimes they specialized, with one attending to civil and the other to criminal cases.[42]

Other royal officials, like the *corregidor* – who also had judicial attributes – were exempt from performing judicial duties when the case fell within the jurisdiction of the *alcalde*. Nor could they interfere in a case already in the *alcalde*'s charge, except to mediate a flagrant lack of propriety in the administration of justice.

The sentences passed by the *alcaldes* could be appealed to the *corregidor*; if the fine did not exceed a certain sum, they were appealed directly to the *cabildo*.

Colonial practice was very diverse and not always consistent. In places where there was an *audiencia* – not the case in Oruro – the role of the *cabildo* was frequently passed over in the cases just mentioned.[43]

Sometimes the intervention of the viceroy himself altered the normal course of justice. In 1748 the *corregidor* of Oruro, Eugenio Lerdo de Tejada, and the *alcades ordinarios* were prevented by the viceroy from acting in their judicial capacity in the cases pertaining to Melchor de Herrera, his family, and his employees for a period of six months; meanwhile the reasons for this measure were considered by the *audiencia* of the district.[44]

---

corregidor's cases (Law 1, Title 3, Book 5): "[W]e order them (*alcaldes*) to have jurisdiction in the first instance over all matters, cases, and things that the governor or his lieutenant might have, whether civil or criminal." In Mexico and Lima the post of *corregidor* was abolished and its functions in good part assumed by ordinary *alcaldes* (Ots Capdequi, *Manual de historia*, pp. 172–5).

40 Cañete y Domínguez, op. cit., p. 37.
41 See *Recopilación*, op. cit. (Book 5, Title 3, Law 22).
42 See Louis G. Kahle, "The Spanish Colonial Judiciary," *Southwestern Social Science Quarterly*, 32 (1951–2), cited by J. P. Moore, op. cit., 1954.
43 According to Moore, in the middle of the seventeenth century Felipe IV had practically abolished the judicial function of the *cabildo*, establishing that appeals to sentences of *alcaldes* should proceed directly to the *audiencia*.
44 Letter from Eugenio Lerdo de Tejada to the viceroy (Oruro, July 25, 1748); AGN, Buenos Aires, 9-7-6-4, Oruro, leg. 1.

With time, other minor officials, some of them already mentioned, were added to the list in most of the Spanish American towns. The most important of these were: the *alférez real*, standard-bearer of the city; the *alguacil mayor*, chief constable; the *depositario real*, public treasurer, the *fiel ejecutor*, a kind of inspector of weights and measures in charge of the provision of food and the control of prices in the market; and the *receptor de penas*, or collector of judicial fines. At first these jobs were carried out by the *regidores* and *alcaldes* themselves, but later, with the generalization of the sale of the former, the positions proliferated.

There were also other officials who, although they were normally elected by the *regidores* – beginning with the *alcaldes* themselves – did not have a seat in the *cabildo*. These included the *síndico* or *procurador general* (envoy), the *mayordomo* or steward, one or more *alcaldes de la hermandad* (police guards for the rural districts, sometimes called *alcaldes de la mesta*), an *escribano* or clerk, and several *alcaldes de barrio*, or neighborhood officials.

Until 1622, in nearly all the town governments, officials from the royal treasury – *oficiales reales* – were permitted to attend meetings and even to vote as *regidores* of a higher rank. The governor or *corregidor* had the same right if the city was his official residence, in this case presiding over the sessions, but this right was abolished around the time of the period under study here.[45]

As we have seen, the number of municipal officials varied according to the size of the town. In the case of Oruro, in addition to the *alcaldes ordinarios*, the following officials were appointed: *alcalde provincial, alguacil mayor, fiel ejecutor, depositario real, procurador general, alférez real, mayordomo de propios y rentas, jueces diputados de propios, jueces del abasto, amigables componedores, diputados de las fiestas del Corpus*, and *procurador de los pobres de la cárcel*. In some cases, two different functions were performed by the same individual. In 1749, for instance, one of the two *jueces diputados de propios* was also the *alférez real*, and the other was also the *alcalde provincial*, while one of the two *jueces de abasto* was a *regidor* and the other the *fiel ejecutor*.[46] The topic of the election of municipal officers is highly complex; much of the next chapter is devoted to its subtleties.

The ordinances of Charles V in 1523 established that, except for specific provisions to the contrary, the *regidores* must be elected annually by the residents of the city and could not be reelected until one year had intervened. As we have already seen, the *alcaldes* – elected annually, in turn, by the *regidores* on January 1 – could not be reelected until three years had passed.

However, the democratic character of this election, if it ever really existed, did not last long. Early on, in the election of members of the *cabildo*, the

45 Haring, op. cit., pp. 168–9; Crespo Rodas, *La guerra*, pp. 70–1.
46 *Cabildo* held in Oruro, January 1, 1749; AGN, Buenos Aires, 9-7-6-4, Oruro, leg. 1.

influence of the governor or local *corregidor* grew greater, generally through nominations drawn up by the leading *regidores* or those chosen directly by them. There were many cases in which several officials in the most important cities received their appointments directly from the king, or in others, from the viceroy or captain general.[47]

Under Philip II the practice of selling positions to the highest bidder was introduced; the successor of Charles V inherited a virtually bankrupt kingdom and needed to find new sources of income quickly. The sale of public offices was already familiar in Spain and the custom was transferred to America. The preference for abler men and early settlers and their descendants generally was not respected. At first the appointments were for only one generation, but by 1606 all the salable positions were given in perpetuity, with the right to resell or donate during the lifetime of the officeholder, under certain conditions. In this way, the municipal positions became, for all practical purposes, objects of private property.[48] However, this rule admitted exceptions. In some cities – Santiago de Chile, for example – there was a mixed system, with some positions privately owned and others elected. There were cases in which the *cabildo* paid for the privilege of election, officially buying from the crown one or more positions on the city council so as to be able to continue electing his own members. The office, however, had to be connected to the life of one individual so that at his death the crown could charge again for the election of his successor.

There were also cases in which the governor or the *audiencia* leased seats on the city council for an annual fee set by the crown; the town government was permitted to elect the lessee. The position of *alcalde ordinario*, apparently, continued to be elective everywhere, although it was subject to confirmation by the viceroy, the president of the *audiencia* or his delegates, or by the local governor.

It is interesting to note that in Potosí and Quito during the seventeenth century, due to stormy elections the *alcaldes* were ordered to be chosen by lottery.

Notwithstanding this exception, municipal administration remained in the hands of a few influential families in each city, which may explain the backdrop of tensions within the *cabildos*.[49]

In addition to their judicial functions, the *alcaldes* had administrative responsibilities. The governor or *corregidor*, or his delegates, presided over the sessions of the city council; only in his absence was the *alcalde de primer voto* (the highest ranking *alcalde*) in charge of this task.[50] In the absence of

47 See "Actas del cabildo de San Luis," op. cit., pp. 152–65, for cases of the intervention of the *corregidor* or the Captain General of Chile (Amat).
48 Haring, op. cit., pp. 170–2.
49 Ibid., pp. 172–3; see also, Crespo Rodas, *La guerra*.
50 *Recopilación*, op. cit., Book 5, Title 3, Law 12.

the *corregidor* or governor, in some regions the *alcaldes* acted in their place temporarily.[51] The laws likewise established that if the governor or *corregidor* was obliged to leave the city for a time, the *alcaldes* could take over the cases pending under his jurisdiction.[52]

In case of a vacancy in the *alcaldías*, the position was temporarily occupied by the senior *regidor* unless there was a royal standard-bearer, in which case he had preference.

The fifth ordinance of the bylaws of the city of Oruro stipulated this rule with the following wording:

Eight *regidores*, called *veinte y quatros*, shall be elected for the good governance of the republic, preferring in age and vote he who has more. These men will substitute for the *alcalde* whenever he is absent more than five leagues and two days of time. When the *alcalde* notifies the *cabildo* that he needs a substitute, the *alférez real* must take precedence over the *regidores* and in his absence the older will take office of those who have sworn that they will look after the public good and augmentation of the property of the city.[53]

The post of *alcalde* was endowed automatically with other prerogatives such as holding the office of *juez de aguas* (judge of water), *fiel ejecutor*, or *diputado de las fiestas* (deputy of fiestas).

The other officials of the *cabildo* had specific functions assigned to them. The mission of *alcalde provincial* was to assist the *alcaldes ordinarios* in the administration of justice and police duties in the rural zones of the municipal district. In general, the rural area that fell within the municipal jurisdiction was extensive, as we have seen; in the case of Oruro it was enormous.

The responsibilities of the *alcalde provincial* were judicial and administrative, following Spanish tradition. His jurisdiction covered infractions of a criminal nature, and one of his obligations was to impose fines for violations of municipal ordinances, which in part served to remunerate him for the task.[54] The *alcalde provincial* had a crew to help him exercise his authority, and he used them to pursue wrongdoers and delinquents. The composition of the crew was heterogeneous, and it was not easy to recruit members. They were often Indians, blacks, mestizos, and mulattoes; it is said that some were even black slaves purchased for the purpose.[55] The selection of the crew was left to the *alcalde provincial*, although sometimes there were conflicts about it within the *cabildo*. Normally, it was expected that the *alcalde provincial* would arrest the accused and bring charges, leaving

51 Moore, op. cit., p. 82. *Recopilación*, op. cit., Book 4, Title 9, Law 2. In Oruro another procedure was followed with regard to the uprising of 1781, as shown in Chapter 11.
52 *Recopilación*, op. cit., Book 5, Title 2, Law 20.
53 "Representación de los cuatro regidores de Oruro. . . ." (Archivo Nacional de Bolivia, Sucre, 1741, no. 5862, fol. 4).
54 Moore, op. cit., pp. 103–4.
55 This happened in Lima in 1580. See Constantino Bayle, *Los cabildos seculares en América española* (Madrid, Sapientia, 1952), p. 171.

the sentencing to the *alcalde ordinario*; but in practice they often judged, passed sentence, and executed the sentence summarily.[56]

The *alcalde provincial* was originally called the *alcalde de la hermandad*. Subsequently – 1639 in Mexico and 1635 in Peru – he was called *alcalde provincial de la hermandad* or simply *alcalde provincial*. In some cases the custom was preserved of appointing men to both positions, although their duties were the same. In Oruro at the beginning of the eighteenth century there were still *alcaldes de la hermandad*; later only *alcaldes provinciales* were appointed.

This was one of the most desirable jobs in the municipal hierarchy, perhaps because it allowed the incumbent to collect fines – of which the *alcalde provincial* officially received a percentage – as well as to impose more severe penalties. Being one of the positions sold by the crown, its value can be measured by the price the residents were willing to pay for it. Toward the end of the eighteenth century it commanded the highest bids, along with the post of *escribano*.

Another highly coveted job was that of *alférez real*, although in this case its value lay in its prestige, since the incumbent was the one to carry the banner during public festivals. The *alférez real* did not have any collections in his charge nor did he receive any other material recompense.[57]

The importance of material remuneration can be appreciated by looking at the prices commanded by the different positions when they were auctioned off. Table 2.2 shows examples from different localities.[58]

The *alguacil mayor* or chief constable was in charge of the police; his duties were to maintain order and take charge of the prisons, but exclusively within the city limits. He was in charge of the detention of confessed or presumed offenders, and of the enforcement of sentences passed by the *alcaldes* and the *audiencias*.[59] This official received a commission for his duties in addition to his salary.[60]

The *fiel ejecutor* was responsible for controlling the weights and measures utilized by tradesmen as well as the quality of the merchandise sold in the city. He also added a tariff charged on each transaction to his salary.

The *depositario general* held in safekeeping property disputed in litigation; he also charged a fee for each transaction. The *procurador general* was the public defender of the rights of residents of the city, the *cabildo*, and the vicinity, in matters of privileges, honors, and interests. He could act on orders of the *cabildo* or on his own initiative.[61]

56 Ibid.
57 Moore, *Bourbons*, p. 250.
58 Ibid., pp. 251–2.
59 Also, probably, of those promulgated by the *corregidores*.
60 The rights and obligations are expressed in Laws 8, 9, 10, and 16, Book, 5, Title 7, of the *Recopilación*.
61 Bayle, op. cit., pp. 225–51.

Table 2.2. *Prices paid at auction for the positions of* alcalde provincial *(AP) and* alférez real *(AR) by date and location*

Location	Date	Price (pesos)
Cuzco		
AP	1700	18,000
AR	1702	8,000
AP	1745	18,000
AR	1752	3,000
Piura		
AP	1713	2,800
AR	1697	450
AP	1725	2,500
AR	1731	800
Guamanga		
AP	1717	6,000
AR	1724	3,000
Lima		
AP	1738	25,000
AR	1747	20,000

Source: Moore, *Bourbons*, pp. 251–2.

The chapters to follow pose the following questions: were the *cabildo*s in America losing their original features – elective office, relative independence? Was there a progressive loss of interest and support by the populace, thus facilitating the abuses of the governors and *corregidores*?[62] If so, was Oruro the exception that proves the rule? Or, following Haring's line of reasoning, were the confrontations over municipal jobs only about prestige? If this is true, were the elections of city officials as agitated in all the towns and cities as they were in Oruro, where they were habitually stormy?

Wherever some vestige of the electoral process remained in the naming of city officials, these elections were habitually subject to approval by the governor or the viceroy. The latter could fine the electors for not choosing their own candidates, and frequently did so, in spite of the law prohibiting viceroys, presidents, and judges from interfering in the free election of persons to public positions. Thus, to the extent that the cities were deprived gradually of all the initiative and independence they might have possessed originally, the position of *regidor* carried less and less political importance. Nevertheless, it was much coveted by the Creoles. Municipal jobs were nearly the only positions within the political hierarchy to which they could aspire, practically the only sphere of action where they could distinguish themselves above their compatriots. Such positions conveyed little or no political authority, but they conferred great prestige within the colonial society. The *regidores* were considered to be the most distinguished citizens of the untitled aristocracy and the

62 Haring, op. cit., p. 181.

natural leaders of public opinion in the community. In this way, the *cabildo*s continued to represent the interests of the place and, to an extent, to respond to local opinion.

They also retained something of their primitive autonomy, although this was hobbled and restricted in its normal development by the growing centralization of power in the crown. Thus, it is not surprising that it was precisely in the municipalities at the beginning of the 19th century that the first sparks of the revolutionary movements usually ignited.[63]

Jorge Juan and Antonio Ulloa, in their travels through the viceroyalty of Peru, apparently witnessed many confrontations between "bands or factions." The conclusions they drew about the causes are perhaps a little simplistic or incomplete, but there seems to be no doubt that frequently the antagonisms were seen as conflicts between Europeans – or *chapetones* – and Creoles. In reality, the lines of animosity followed more complex paths but frequently they were interpreted in these terms. This direction describes, for example, the clear preference shown by the crown in naming military men born in Spain as *corregidores*. The crown was confident that men selected with these characteristics would be more apt to represent royal interests faithfully and to maintain a more equidistant position vis-à-vis local interests.[64]

It never fails to seem improper, no matter how many examples we see of this kind, that between people of the same nation, the same religion, even the same blood, there could be so much enmity, ill-will and hatred as we observe in Peru, where the cities and large settlements are a theater of discord and constant opposition between Spaniards and Creoles. This is a constant cause of the repeated outbursts here, because the reciprocal hatred each party has for the other is increasingly whipped up and no opportunity is lost for breathing vengeance and unleashing the passions and jealousies that are rooted in their souls.

It is enough to be a European or a *chapetón*, as they are called in Peru, to declare oneself immediately against the Creoles; and it is sufficient to have been born in the Indies to abhor the Europeans. This ill will rises to such a high level that in some respects it exceeds the rage unleashed when two nations in open warfare declare their outrage and vituperation.[65]

In general, according to these chroniclers, in nearly all the settlements there was this schism into two bands or parties, and the *cabildo* was the place "where the most irreconcilable enmities spit out their venom, and the communities where spirits were continuously inflamed with the violent fire of hatred."[66] In their opinion, the mountain cities were most susceptible to this type of scandal and rivalry due to their infrequent contact with the foreign element.

Because the *cabildo*, in practice, was the only political center where these differences could flourish overtly, where they could manifest through an

63 Ibid., p. 181.
64 For figures of relative percentages by profession and birthplace, see Moreno Cebrián, op. cit., p. 165.
65 Juan and Ulloa, op. cit., p. 319.
66 Ibid., p. 320.

act competitive by nature – election – the excesses observed here are not so surprising.

It is true that these elections were increasingly affected in the eighteenth century by the intervention of governors, *corregidores*, and viceroys. Even so, the election of the *alcaldes* held considerable interest in all the towns and cities. Irregularities in these events were common coin, especially in places far from the control of the regional *audiencia* or the governor. One assumes that these officials paid little attention to such conflicts unless there was a scandal. For example, the law of 1573 prescribed that in some cities – those that had a *corregidor* or a governor – the *alcaldes ordinarios* would be excluded from the *cabildo* except when custom dictated the contrary; it is clear that custom seemed to dictate the contrary nearly everywhere, since this law was hardly ever observed. In most cities, in fact, the *alcaldes* met with the *regidores* in the *cabildo* and took an active part in the proceedings.[67]

The governors, *corregidores*, and viceroys gradually acquired the right to confirm appointments; this, in effect, restricted the election to people of their own clique, or at least to those sympathetic to them.

The detrimental effects of this kind of partisanship on municipal autonomy seem to have been common in the most distant parts of the Spanish empire, as was the behavior of the officials themselves. Haring comments, citing Manuel Cervera,

In 1739 the governor of Buenos Aires recommended the abolition of the *alcaldes ordinarios* of Santa Fe, Corrientes, and Montevideo, reasoning that they were unnecessary in small cities and since all the persons were related to each other, and the *alcaldes* were using their staffs of authority simply as instruments of revenge, and they were a cause of disturbances and popular passions. His advice was not heeded, but the abuses he describes are proven by data from other places.[68]

Returning to the hostile cliques and provisionally accepting the interpretation offered by J. Juan and Antonio Ulloa (with the reservations already noted) the enmity between Creoles and Spaniards became accentuated with the passage of time for reasons that are not always clear.

According to these travelers, the "vanity of the Creoles" and the excessive arrogance they showed to Spaniards who arrived from Spain without money irrevocably deepened the antagonism between the two groups. When the Spaniards, backed by the support of other Spaniards and with work contracts, began to strengthen their social and economic position, they finally began to be considered eligible, for instance, as marriage partners

---

67 Haring, op. cit., p. 174.
68 Ibid., p. 175. Haring cites Cervera, *Historia de la ciudad y provincia de Santa Fe* (1907), vol. 1, p. 657. He adds that, for the monopoly of a few families over control of municipal offices in that region, it is useful to consult R. Levillier, *Antecedentes de política económica en el Río de la Plata* (Madrid, 1915), vol. 2, pp. 152–63.

for the daughters of affluent Creole families. Nevertheless, the initial mistrust was never totally overcome, and the slightest thing – generally allusions to the humble working origins of the Spanish native – gave rise to offense generating disputes that divided a multitude of families.[69]

This picture of official jobs in the colonial administration would not be complete without mention of the power some incumbents enjoyed.

A feature common to all was the scant capacity of the formally highest figures in the hierarchy – viceroys or *audiencias* in Peru and later in Rio de la Plata, and the captaincy general in Chile – to impose their decisions upon the ranks beneath them within the territorial areas under their jurisdiction. One of the fundamental reasons for this was that they could not rely on any military or police support to impose their decisions or to repel aggression from other nations.

In 1620, when Dutch naval forces appeared on the Peruvian coast, the viceroy Esquilache was afraid to call out the militia – estimated at potentially eighteen hundred men recruited from among artisans and workers in Lima – because they were undisciplined and possibly more of a threat to the viceroy than to the Dutch.[70]

This situation persisted to the beginning of the eighteenth century, although one may observe a change in policy with the transition from the Habsburg dynasty to the Bourbons, fundamentally with Ferdinand VI (1746–59) and Charles III (1759–88). One of the first consequences of the dynastic change was an increase in the number of viceroys with a military background. Just after the Seven Years' War (1756–63) there was a more drastic change with the decision to create a disciplined and well-trained militia.[71]

The inability of the central government in Lima to lend support to needy zones in the interior can be seen in the case of the uprising of Juan Santos Atahualpa in the region of Tarma and Jauja. This indigenous rebellion lasted for nearly fifteen years and only came to an end with the death of its leader. An expedition sent from Lima in 1745 to suppress it ended in absolute disaster, as the guerrilla tactics developed by the insurgents neutralized all local attempts to quell them.[72]

In the opinion of one official of the times, the Indians who suffered the conquest had considered the soldiers as invincible monsters, almost gods. Those of the eighteenth century, although more accustomed to the Span-

69 Juan and Ulloa, op. cit., p. 322. In this same somewhat schematic but equally illustrative line of argument, Chapter 6 of these travelers' book contains other interesting cases.
70 Leon G. Campbell, *The Military and Society in Colonial Peru (1750–1810)* (Philadelphia, American Philosophical Society, 1978), p. 3.
71 Ibid., pp. 7–9.
72 Ibid., p. 13. See also Francisco A. Loayza, *Juan Santos, el invencible (manuscritos del año 1742 al año 1755)* (Lima, 1942).

iards, continued to think that "the beret, the uniform and the mustache are the companions of immortality."[73] Time tarnished this image, the same observer continues, because the Indians soon became familiar with the weaknesses and vices of the Spanish soldiers. For a while fear continued, because the Indians assumed that there were countless soldiers in the kingdom, ready to destroy them for the slightest disloyalty, "and they lived in submission to this idea that only one infantry battalion in the center of the viceroyalty was enough to ensure peace and prosperity in the whole kingdom."[74]

This optimistic confidence was dashed in 1781 with the massive uprisings of the indigenous peoples. It was thought that the vulnerable point was more due to the faults and inabilities of the crown's forces than to the Indians' capacity to mobilize.

There were many reasons for this weakness. One important explanation was the corruption that existed in the Lima bureaucracy, which, for example, charged a commission to outfit troops for the war.[75] After 1763 and during Amat's entire viceroyalty there was a sustained effort to build up an armed force composed of one regular division and one militia. The latter was divided into urban and provincial sections, but there is no reliable data from which we can assess their strength. They were probably mustered to deal with particular circumstances and financed by *cabildos*, by corporations, or privately by individuals, in the last case independently of whether the sponsor exercised some public function.[76]

This drive swelled the Peruvian army, according to Amat, from 591 regulars and 4,209 militiamen in 1760 to the spectacular numbers of 983 regulars and 49,857 militiamen in 1763.

Although an occasional partial use of these new troops could be considered successful, the reform of the army looked much better on paper than it did in reality. For example, when sent to repress a rebellion in Quito in 1765, the troops reached their destination fourteen months after the rebellion had been defeated using local resources. On the other hand, one might credit them with the dubious merit of a total triumph in the expulsion of the Jesuits.[77]

The figures cited by Amat, and others attributed to him, nevertheless seem excessively optimistic. When Areche made his visit to Peru in 1777, he affirmed that there was nothing remotely like the figures given by the viceroy. The discipline and training of the troops, likewise, was not sufficient to protect against potentially dangerous situations. Furthermore, the Lima civil guard was dedicated to looking after the private interests of the

73 Cañete y Domínguez, op. cit., p. 568.
74 Ibid.
75 Campbell, op. cit., p. 28.
76 Ibid., pp. 17, 39.
77 Ibid., pp. 50–1.

Lima elites, and their duties included collecting debts, pursuing escaped slaves, and practicing various kinds of fraud.[78]

Actually the military's most ambitious intervention operation was a response to the Tupac Amaru uprising of 1780–1. The outcome of this operation demonstrated that the forces of repression were not adequate to confront situations of this kind; furthermore, they were constantly plagued with high rates of desertion.

When the soldiers reached the provinces, military discipline declined even further. Once there, they took mistresses (feeling that marriage would make them effeminate), they frequently fell ill and, most important, they began to establish relations with the local people, which interfered with their military service at critical moments. The same source reports, "They had to risk taking sides with the village on occasions of shortages and crises stemming from trade."[79]

The end of the Tupac Amaru rebellion in January 1782 was more a response to a general pardon offered to the rebels by Viceroy Jáuregui than to any military action by the Spanish army.[80]

The military forces at the viceroy's disposal were no more adequate to impose his direct decisions – or, through him, those of the crown – nor were they capable of enforcing the general laws. The result was that the local authorities could act freely to protect their own private interests, and the extent of this depended solely on their ability to finance, on their own, the imposition by force of their own designs.

The way in which the *corregidores* of Indians were able to accomplish their ends is clear. As explained, their resources were derived fundamentally from *repartimiento*, since their salaries were not sufficient to cover the costs inherent in the exercise of their jobs.[81] Some *corregidores* emphasized in their reports that even the legally allowed *repartos* did not produce a sure profit due to the high costs associated with them.[82]

The job of *corregidor* was, however – with numerous exceptions – highly sought after. The reason is clear: the *corregidores* exceeded the legally imposed limits and prices in their *repartos*. This produced extra profits. They earned more per unit of merchandise distributed, they paid no taxes to the royal treasury (*alcabalas*, or sales taxes) on the excess *repartos*, and on top of this the fixed expenses were diluted on the wholesale level.

The *corregidor's* problem was to cover the costs of collection, which included accounting and the deployment of a force adequate to collect from

78 Ibid., pp. 63, 97.
79 Cañete y Domínguez, op. cit., p. 568.
80 Campbell, op. cit., pp. 143, 145–6.
81 Moreno Cebrián, op. cit., pp. 129–135, 109–110.
82 Ibid., pp. 127–8. Here is examined the situation of the *corregidor* of the province of Arica, concluding that he would lose around 4,000 pesos net in the *reparto*.

recalcitrant debtors. These expenses appear in the account books under the headings "clerks" and "cashiers" for accounting, and "lieutenant general" for the application of force. But the *corregidores* used armed groups who did not appear in their accounts; these groups were paid by the *corregidores* themselves, who behaved like informal entrepreneurs with their own forces of repression.[83] Frequently *audiencias* and viceroys acted in connivance with the *corregidores*; but, as mentioned, they faced difficulties when they really wanted to rectify unfair practices.

Other officials of the crown had various opportunities to take advantage of their public positions to engage in private business. The case of the treasury employees – royal officials – is illustrative, and we will see how negligent they were with the money they were supposed to collect for the Potosí treasury.

This negligence cannot be attributed to personality or temperament, as can be seen in the activities of several royal officials. One case is that of Juan Gelly, proprietor of a mill for ore crushing and silver extraction, who complained against the royal officials Blas Gascón and Salvador Parrilla, to whom in 1776 he had handed over security for mercury removed by a miner.

Gelly had been interim *corregidor* in Oruro, and during his term, according to his own words, "I had seen that a growing sum was collected that was owed to His Majesty and in particular by the Royal Officials. . . . The Royal Officials being angry with me because I had fulfilled my obligation as a faithful servant, they did not want to perform the tasks that I had relinquished," that is, they did not want to return to him the security for the mercury, a debt either already paid or that the royal officials had not bothered to collect.

Gelly had the general inspector Areche, the highest authority in the viceroyalties, write two letters to the royal officials, without success. Because of his actions (according to the plaintiff) they had sent him to prison, availing themselves of accounting and legal trickery. Finally Gelly added, "Because it is very different to bring suit against the powerful arm of the King than against a private person, I humbly beg V. S. to look upon me with justice."[84]

It is interesting to note in Gelly's case how little influence the intervention of the highest official had, and how easy it was for some royal officials to put an individual in jail when they wanted to, even in a case where, as Gelly alleges, he was protected by the mining code.

In 1782, the *intendente general* Fernández, to whom the letter was addressed, sent a message to the new accountant of the Oruro treasurer, Joseph

83 For a detailed description of the possible activities and ruses of the *corregidores*, see Juan and Ulloa, op. cit., second part, pp. 181–207.
84 Letter from Juan Gelly to Intendent General Manuel Ignacio Fernández, La Plata, January 15, 1782, AGN, Buenos Aires, 9-7-6-5 Oruro, legajo 2.

Manuel Bustillo, asking him to clarify the question; when he received no response, he sent another letter in February of the following year.[85] Bustillo had noted, when he took charge of the treasury, that there were fourteen bars of silver there "whose legitimate owners are unknown to this day." This behavior provoked an immediate reaction on the part of the tribunal of accounts in Buenos Aires, which considered that ". . . although it is very strange that the Royal Officials have not made the deposit of this property into the treasury, with all the formalities required by a transaction of such seriousness . . . it is even more reprehensible that they did not advise V. S. immediately of this situation, and their silence implies much malice."[86]

Leaving aside the claims of Juan Gelly, who finally obtained enough documents to validate his position, the news received slightly later about the behavior of the new accountant Bustillo was even more scandalous.

Bustillo kept funds assigned for the payment of soldiers from Cochabamba and, according to a report received by Viceroy Vértiz, "We see him buying gold here, trading in coca there, salvaging silver *piñas* to reduce the bars that have gone to his *espendio* in Potosí." The report also indicated which individuals worked for Bustillo:

Frequently a certain *cabo dragón*-corporal-travels from this town [Oruro] to Cochabamba, with wine, *aguardiente*, and oil. This man lives with Bustillo and consequently is his client and deputy. He has four men under his control to manage the money. Don Fernando Echalecu, principal official of this treasury, the first trustee who as far as we know has in his custody twenty thousand pesos, although there are those who think it is more than thirty. This man buys the *piñas* [crude silver]; they are reduced to bars *en cabeza de* [that is, in the name of] Don Joseph Alvizuri, manservant of the accountant as can be seen in the ledger entries of the Royal Books. This same person takes them to Potosí, and when he is unable to go he sends in his place another man named Don Esteban Maborriaga, and as it is not difficult to be free with other people's money, he also credits certain sums to the official Echalecu, whose expenses do not correspond to the mere 800 pesos he has earned in salary in his just over one year on the job."

Finally, the report adds a few more scandalous items about Bustillo's life:

The [expenses] of the accountant during the time he has been on the job with only the 1900 pesos he has been assigned are incredible, as we see him wearing fancy clothes, valuable gold jewelry and other trappings, it is no less noteworthy that he indulges in the excesses of an illicit and scandalous relationship with a certain woman from Cochabamba, and raising her up from the dust he keeps her in a style that any decent girl would appreciate, what with the trinkets that adorn her room, and he has bought her a slave and fine silk drapery, as is public knowledge.[87]

85 From Intendent General Fernández to Joseph Manuel Bustillo, February 27, 1783. AGN, Buenos Aires, 9-7-6-5 Oruro, legajo 2.
86 From Francisco de Cabrera (*Tribunal de Cuentas*) to the intendent general of Buenos Aires, May 14, 1782. AGN, Buenos Aires, 9-7-6-5, Oruro, legajo 2.
87 From Juan Manuel de Soto (commandant of the militia company of Cochabamba) to Viceroy Vértiz, Oruro, November 17, 1783. AGN, Buenos Aires, 9-7-6-5, Oruro, legajo 2.

Thus can be seen the resources accessible to royal officials, enabling them to combine the powers conferred by their jobs with others financed privately through corrupt manipulation of the assets of the royal treasury.

The case of the *alcaldes* and other municipal officials was different. The *alcaldes* had the same judicial responsibilities as the *corregidores*, but in the lower courts.[88] The strategic advantages of this position were potentially great, and the benefits depended on the interests at play. Once again, power was based on the incumbent's ability to count on adequate force to permit him to impose his decisions or, eventually, to thwart others' decisions. If the *alcaldes* and other officials such as *alguaciles mayors* or *alcaldes provinciales* had sufficient resources at their disposal or were backed by people who did, they could deploy enough armed troops to accomplish their ends.[89]

Frequently the resources available to the *cabildo* were not sufficient, and it was necessary to complement them with private contributions. In places where business was sufficiently brisk, it might be worth the trouble to take on such expenses. Much has been written about the private interests of the members of the *cabildo*, suggesting that these interests frequently guided their public conduct more forcefully than did concerns about the common good. Generally cited to support this view, in particular, is the control of the provisioning of the city and the illicit profits that could be derived from it, forgetting that the functions of a judge – if they were enforced by loyal bailiffs and *alcaldes provinciales* – permitted even greater advantages, in particular the building of a formidable machine to protect private interests.

Here is an illustrative example: in 1608, because of the large amounts owed to the royal treasuries at Potosí, Maldonado de Torres, president of the Charcas *audiencia*, made an inspection visit to the treasury offices. One look revealed that the debts were insufficiently reconciled and that the treasury officials – royal officials – had not tried to collect them for twenty years.[90]

It is true that, when the debts came from miners, the laws protected them from being arrested or imprisoned, or from having their possessions seized, mines or the elements necessary for production such as mercury, tools, and black slaves. Officials could, on the other hand, take the gold or silver pro-

88 Although there were disputes over jurisdictional matters between *alcaldes* and *corregidores* (or, afterward, delegates and subdelegates). See the report of the subdelegate of Oruro, Simón Romano, to Viceroy Pedro Melo de Portugal, Oruro, February 20, 1796. AGN, Buenos Aires, 9-7-6-5, Oruro, legajo 2. The report begins, "The continuous differences that arise each day among the ordinary *alcaldes* and the subdelegates of this town over jurisdiction . . ."

89 See the letter from José Pérez to Viceroy Loreto, October 14, 1788. AGN, Buenos Aires, 9-30-4-1. Pérez was about to be named *alcalde* in 1787, but was arrested and sent to prison by the *alcalde* named in his place.

90 Guillermo Lohmann Villena, "El corregidor de Lima," *Anuario de Estudios Americanos*, 9 (1952), 148.

duced or other collateral property.[91] This lay at the root of many ambiguities in the interpretation of the situations and the judicial decisions and judgments linked to them.[92]

In view of the large debts to the royal treasury, the crown decided to send the senior accountant from the tribunal of accounts in Lima to Charcas. Almost ten years after receiving the corresponding royal order, the viceroy of Lima, prince of Esquilache, appointed the accountant Alonso Martínez Pastrana to undertake an exhaustive study of the subject and draw appropriate conclusions. Martínez Pastrana reached Potosí in August 1618 after passing through La Paz and Oruro. In March 1619 he had the final results: the total debt to the treasury was 2,465,886 assayed pesos – equivalent to 4,084,123 standard pesos of eight *reales*. To get an idea of the significance of this amount, consider that Potosí's annual silver production varied from three to five million standard pesos.[93] Of the total, 1,424,858 standard pesos were owed for mercury, 1,510,981 for Indian *repartimientos*, and 446,064 for offices sold, including those in the *cabildo*.[94]

These figures indicate that neither the *corregidores*, nor the members of the *cabildo*, nor the miners had paid the amounts the law established for the different activities. Furthermore a group of individuals, most of Basque origin, had perpetuated themselves in the *cabildo*, and to all appearances had entered into connivance with *corregidores* and royal officials. Martínez Pastrana, in a letter of 1622, considered that there were no means to collect these debts, affirming that the only way to do it was to prevent those members of the *cabildo* who had debts to the treasury from voting or being elected. That is, given the protective network established by those who ran the *cabildo* – whose resources included judicial powers, corrupt connections, and the direct use of force – the higher officials could not prevail over a power composed of members belonging to the dominant faction in the *cabildo* and their allies.[95]

These were, then, the main characteristics of the power relations of the age. Their contexts and peculiarities, however, differed sharply from place to place and period to period. The case of Oruro, which will unfold in the following chapters, illustrates some of the city's peculiarities without denying the general features described above.

91 Crespo Rodas, *La guerra entre Vicuñas*, pp. 58–9.
92 Ibid., p. 61. Here he mentions the execution of goods against a miner.
93 See the figures for silver in the table in Chapter 3.
94 Crespo Rodas, *La guerra entre Vicuñas*, pp. 58–69.
95 Ibid., pp. 68–87.

3

Oruro in 1741: details of a stormy election

The elections

Between 1741 and 1781 there were a number of confrontations and law-suits of varying importance between inhabitants of Oruro. An analysis of these cases – which are documented in the jumble of judicial papers presented before the authorities – shows a society in conflict, or, at the very least, one that was quite active and prone to disorder.

The lawsuit studied in this chapter arose from the irregularities of an election of town officers in January 1741. The names of the participants in this wrangle reveal, in addition to their position within the local administration, the weight of their participation as members of the mining society of the town.[1]

The conflict centered on the annual elections of the officials of the *cabildo*. At this time – January 1, 1741 – Martín de Espeleta y Villanueva was the *corregidor* who, according to law, presided over the session. He was accompanied in this instance by the *alcalde provincial*, Don Melchor de Herrera, the *alférez real*, Joseph Díaz Ortiz – both outgoing *alcaldes ordinarios* – as well as the *alguacil mayor*, Joseph de Aldave y Salamanca, and the *regidores* (also called *los veinticuatro* [the twenty-four] according to an old denomination) whose names were Agustín Ibáñez de Murzábal, Manuel García de Ayllón, Joseph de Imblusqueta, and Blas Joseph del Barrio.

The description of the solemn opening ceremony, patterned after the strict regulations in force, is interesting:

In the town of San Felipe de Austria de Oruro, on the 8th day of the month of January of one thousand seven hundred and forty one, the *Cabildo Justicia* and *Regimiento* call its officers to join the *Ayuntamiento* at the tolling of the bell as is usual and customary to attend to and confer on the Matters relating to the good and utility of the Republic and being

---

1 In the chapters that follow I will attempt to trace these heads of family genealogically in order to ascertain how long each had been established in the region at the moment of their most active participation in the conflicts. I will also analyze, on the basis of account books and local foundries in Oruro, the course of their respective economic histories. With regard to the first point, it is worth noting that none of the people in the period that concerns us belonged to the founding families of the town (see Chapter 1).

thus together and congregated they attended to and decided on the following and on elections of *alcaldes ordinarios* and other officials.[2]

According to custom, the *escribano* of the *cabildo* – Gaspar Hurtado de Villagómez – reminded those present of the prohibition against voting by anyone who had not settled his debts to the royal treasury pertaining to offices that could be sold and renounced.[3] This prohibition was, in fact, spelled out in the *Compilation of the Laws of the Indies*: "We order and command that no person of any state or condition who is a debtor to our Royal Treasury in small or great amount can be, nor can be elected, *alcalde ordinario* . . . nor have a vote in the elections."[4]

This reminder was probably one of the many formulas recited at the institutional activities of the colony. In fact, it is possible to confirm that in elections in other *cabildos* – and even in the *cabildo* of Oruro itself, on other occasions – it was often omitted.[5]

This time, however, its inclusion was not a mere formality. As reported in the records, the *corregidor* Martín de Espeleta then announced to those present that one of them – the *regidor* Agustín Ibáñez de Murzábal – was one of these debtors, having failed to pay to the royal treasury the costs of his office of *fiel ejecutor*, a statement confirmed by the *escribano*. Accordingly, the *corregidor* ordered Ibáñez to leave the room, as he was legally barred from participating in the election. Although another *regidor*, Blas Joseph del Barrio, offered to cover the amount owed by Ibáñez, this was not accepted by Martín de Espeleta, and Ibáñez had to leave.[6]

Although the acts of the *cabildo* go on to report the results of the election without further commentary on this, the impact of the prohibition against voting by the *regidor* was no small matter. On the contrary, it was

2 Acta del Cabildo de Oruro, January 1, 1741. Archivo Nacional de Bolivia, Real Audiencia de Charcas, Expedientes Coloniales, 1742, no. 5986 ("The *cabildo* of Oruro, on the invalidity of the elections of January 1, 1741").

3 This notarial usage was apparently not followed in other *cabildos* of Spanish America. For example, no such custom existed in Santiago del Estero, even though it was sometimes noted that there was no reason why the *regidores* could not participate in the session; *Actas capitulares de Santiago del Estero* (Buenos Aires, Kraft, 1946), vol. 3.

4 *Recopilación de leyes de los reinos de Indias: Mandados imprimir y publicar por la magestad católica del Rey Don Carlos II*, 5th ed. (Madrid, Boix, 1841), Book 5, Title 3, Law 7. This law covered any kind of debt. There was, however, another law that specified that in the case of miners, the restriction applied only to debts by reason of offices "that were bought and not paid for, if the deadline had passed for satisfying the price or part of it" (ibid., Book 4, Title 20, Law 7). The law had been promulgated in 1635 by Felipe IV for Potosí, but it was also applied in other mining centers.

5 As I have pointed out, in some cases it simply states that there are no obstacles impeding those elected from occupying their offices. In the acts of the elections of council officers of the Cabildo de Sgo. del Estero held January 1, 1777, for example, it is written that "they remained in possession of their offices, since in none of the said cases had there been any obstacle" (*Actas capitulares de Santiago del Estero*, op. cit., vol. 3, p. 8).

6 Actas del Cabildo de Oruro, January 1, 1741, loc. cit., fol. 3.

the beginning of a long and complicated lawsuit whose documentation conveys the profound commotion the event provoked in the vicinity.

Meanwhile, apparently unaware of the prevailing ill winds, the newly elected officials hurried to take charge of their duties. The voting record makes it possible for us to establish the prevailing electoral patterns and discover how each elector voted. One may observe the "peculiarity" of the vote of the *regidor* Manuel García de Ayllón, who voted for himself for the position of *alcalde de primer voto*. Furthermore, the impugned Agustín Ibáñez de Murzábal was nevertheless elected to a minor post: *juez diputado de propios*.[7]

Table 3.1 shows that although votes were cast for different candidates for the positions of *alcaldes* and *procurador general*, the others – considered minor and thus less disputed – were elected unanimously.[8] Another interesting detail is the vote of the *corregidor* Martín de Espeleta: he decided, as president of the session, to vote for García de Ayllón, Alborta, and Tholedo, since for the three principal positions the voting had resulted in a tie. In each of these cases he added his vote to decide the winner.

The complaint

On January 5, 1741, four days after the balloting, four of the officials entered a plea before the *audiencia* of Charcas, alluding to the authoritarian maneuvers of the *corregidor* and the *alcalde*. The signers were Agustín Ibáñez de Murzábal, Joseph de Imblusqueta, Blas Joseph del Barrio – elected to only the lower-ranked posts of *jueces de propios*, *abastos*, and *apelación*, respectively – and the *alférez real* Joseph Díaz de Ortiz.

The terms of the document – syntactical difficulties aside – leave no doubt about the character they attribute to the confrontation:

The need for a remedy compels us to represent before the supreme and just [bench?] of V.A. the clamorous insinuation of the [arrests?] violence and abuses of the Administration of Justice carried out by the *corregidor* of this town and his director the *alcalde provincial* Don Melchor Herrera, in the effects [bewailed by?] his republicans, without freedom to breathe a complaint, to avoid greater suffering to their persons and property. Whose impulse originates on this occasion of the violence perpetrated against us by said *corregidor* and *alcalde provincial*, who aspire to the providence of [justice?] passed by V.A. in order to [remedy?] soon the restoration of our rights [*fueros*] and attention to the treatment due according to your royal laws.[9]

They go on to indicate that in addition, through the previous year of 1740, there had been constant disturbances and scandals provoked by the

7 According to the complaint of the losing side's counsel, voting for oneself was not allowed under the legislation in force; but it is conceivable that they could have done so, and without much embarrassment.

8 Source: Actas del Cabildo de Oruro, January 1, 1741, loc. cit., fols. 3–6.

9 "Escrito de Varios a V. E.," January 18, 1741 (ANB, Real Audiencia de Charcas, Expedientes Coloniales, 1742, no. 5986).

Table 3.1. *Election of authorities of the* Cabildo *of Oruro* 1/1/1741

Voter	Alcalde de primer voto	Alcalde de segundo voto	Procurador General	Mayordomo de la ciudad	Jueces Diputados de Propios	Jueces de Apelación y del Abasto	Diputado de los Propios of the fiestas of Corpus and Santa Rosa	Amigables Componedores
Melchor de Herrera (*Alcalde provincial* and *Ordinario de primer voto*)	Manuel García de Ayllón	Francisco Santos de Alborta	Maestre de Campo Antonio de Tholedo	Diego de la Portilla	Melchor de Herrera Agustín Ibañez[1]	Joseph de Imblusqueta Blas Joseph del Barrio	The *Alcaldes Ordinarios* elected this year	Rev. Padres Prior de Sto. Domingo y Guardián de San Francisco
Joseph Díaz Ortiz (*Alférez real*)	Joseph de Alserreca	Antonio de Oteiza	Francisco de Odría	=	=	=	=	=
Joseph de Aldave y Salamanca (*Alguacil Mayor*)	Manuel García de Ayllón	Francisco Santos de Alborta	Maestre de Campo Antonio de Tholedo	=	=	=	=	=
Manuel García de Ayllón (*Veinticuatro*)	Manuel García de Ayllón	Francisco Santos de Alborta	Mte. de Campo Antonio de Tholedo	=	=	=	=	=
Joseph de Imblusqueta	Joseph de Alserreca	Antonio de Oteiza	Francisco de Odría	=	=	=	=	=
Blas Joseph del Barrio	Mte. de Campo Joseph Francisco de Alserreca	Antonio de Oteiza	Francisco de Odría	=	=		=	=

[1] *Alcaldes* could not be reelected, but other officers could be.

actions of the *corregidor* and the *alcalde provincial*, who furthermore had also been, during this period, *alcalde ordinario*. Thus, the signers said they had felt obligated to stop the progress of these "lamentable events" and to make known the "claims to justice that have operated in this vicinity."

According to the same source, during the days preceding the election there had been rumors about the intentions of the *corregidor* and the *alcalde* to elect new officers from among "the subjects of their faction"; faced with this evidence, the opposition had tried to prevent the naming of anyone belonging to Espeleta and Herrera's side as *alcalde*. When the latter two found out about this, they apparently tried to win Agustín Ibáñez de Murzábal over to their cause, but without success. At this point, they decided to resort to intimidation by means of public force, as related by their accusers:

It so happens, Señor, that on the day of the elections in the morning they made a public display in the town to the admiration and scandal of their neighbors over the novelty of seeing, before entering the meeting, all the leaders and officials wearing military insignias of the companies that are here by order of Your Superior Governor to protect against invasion by the English . . . "By order of said *corregidor* it was conveyed through Commissar Don Diego Hidalgo de Zisneros; ordering that after we enter the chapter room they occupy the anteroom, stairway, and doors of the buildings of said *cabildo* as thus they have done, in sight of the assemblage of all the town. A demonstration so strange that it struck terror in the heart of this unfortunate town, it caused suspicion about to what end this military apparatus was directed, that they intended to rob the senior *veinte y cuatro* Don Augustin Ibáñez of his vote and attendance in said *cabildo*.[10]

It is quite apparent that the four signers of the document tried hard to emphasize the defects of their opponents and that they probably obscured the description of their own conduct at the time, perhaps exaggerating their representation of themselves as impeccable citizens. There is no doubt, however, that their concern about the use of public force to suppress the free expression of the *regidores* was authentic. Their argument that "an *ayuntamiento* that by its nature and statutory laws of your royal person ought to be formed with the greatest liberty necessary in such an important matter as the election of judges," was undoubtedly serious.

This preoccupation had in fact been shared by the crown for a long time, and abundant legislation was directed at preventing governors and *corregidores* from exerting undue pressure or playing favorites in the elections of municipal officers.

In fact, Law VII, Book IV, Title IX of the Code of the Indies establishes

THAT THE VICEROYS, PRESIDENTS AND *OIDORES* [JUDGES] SHALL NOT IMPEDE THE ELECTIONS OF OFFICERS: we order and command that the viceroys, presi-

10 *Ibid.*, fol. 2. The reference to the Englishmen owes to the incursions of Admiral Anson, who threatened the coasts of Peru during these years. In November 1741 he had attacked and sacked the port of Paita in the north of the viceroyalty. In response, militias were organized to repel possible attacks. Arms were difficult to acquire in the viceroyalty, according to Juan and Ulloa (op. cit., p. 146).

dents and *oidores* not impede the free election of officers, nor with their authority, interces-
sion, or exertion of will, nor any other means, shall they intervene through their relatives
nor those of their wives, nor others, since in this justice is offended, and good governance;
and they are warned, that on top of the penalties imposed, we will order further action to
be taken.[11]

Law IX of the same book orders

THAT THE GOVERNORS SHALL LET THE *REGIDORES* USE THEIR DELEGA-
TIONS AND VOTE FREELY: the governors and their lieutenants shall not strip the
regidores of the privileges of their offices, nor disturb them, and shall let them use the dele-
gations and vote in the *cabildos* with complete freedom, as is stipulated.[12]

The case of Manuel de Ayllón voting for himself is another eloquent testimony to the scant respect for custom and legislation during these municipal elections. The signers allude explicitly to this irregular act when they
offer an unfavorable description of the new *alcalde de primer voto*.

And with Don Melchor de Herrera and the *alguacil mayor* electing Don Manuel de Ayllón
as *alcalde mayor de primer voto* since he is their intimate and of the same faction of the said
corregidor as well as his close friend who has accompanied him in all his designs and pertur-
bations in this republic with efficacious foment, which he hopes will continue by wielding the staff of office as said Ayllón has been named by said *corregidor*, and replaced with
his person in the matter of interests, seeing the ambition of Ayllón, the two votes in his
favor applied to himself, and for Don Francisco Santos de Alborda the second vote to which
in reciprocity the said Herrera and *alguacil mayor* continue in this, as he is also a mining
partner of the *corregidor* and interested in his good will.[13]

Also stressed by the signers is the day's tone of extreme intimidation,
which was out of proportion to the small number of individuals present.
The soldiers, in fact, did not content themselves with establishing their
presence in the plaza, but, according to the plaintiffs, stood the entire time
at the door of the meeting room, eavesdropping and spying on what was
happening inside through the cracks in the door.[14] To this offense the
corregidor added another, ordering the participants at the meeting to take
off their swords, "contrary to the custom that has always been practiced in
this *cabildo*."[15]

Melchor de Herrera's opponents apparently suspected by the end of 1740
that the *alcalde* – supported by the *corregidor* – might resort to military force
in order to get his people elected. This was the reason for the inclusion of
Laws VII and IX of the Indies Code in the acts of the *"Cabildo de Dudas y
Conferencias"* held on December 30, 1740.[16]

11 *Recopilación de las leyes de los reinos de Indias*, op. cit., Book 4, Title 9, Law 7.
12 Ibid., Law 9.
13 "Escrito de varios . . . ," loc cit., fol. 3.
14 Ibid., fol. 10.
15 Ibid., fol. 2.
16 Acta capitular del Cabildo de Oruro, December 30, 1740 (ANB, Real Audiencia de Charcas,
Expedientes coloniales, 1742, loc. cit., fols. 19–20).

This *cabildo* was held every year a little before the elections in order to clarify any difficulties or obstacles that might hinder the regular holding of elections. In a memorandum presented by the *procurador* Manuel Montalvo y Luna in mid-January before the *audiencia* of Charcas – in the name of the four injured parties – he complained because at this *cabildo de dudas* no mention had been made of Ibáñez de Murzábal's presumed debt and consequently his inability to vote.

> . . . in the *cabildo de dudas y conferencias* held only one day in advance on December 31 at which my party Ibañez was present, the clerk did not mention it . . . nor did the *corregidor* object to the said debt so that any controversies that might arise during the elections about my party's participation and voting could be resolved; the *corregidor* and the clerk kept silent maliciously.[17]

The confusing progress of the case, which opened with the presentation by the losers in the election, is revealing as long as one can negotiate the overwhelming judicial style of its presentation. Thus, in spite of the meager descriptive agility of court cases of this kind, which at times makes reading them a chore, a step-by-step perusal of them in their original style can cast new light on the judicial mechanisms of the age. In this case some exceptionally interesting and previously unknown curiosities have emerged, along with the context of everyday relationships in which the case developed.

The losers' complaints exposed the whole set of maneuvers carried out by the *corregidor* and the *alcalde provincial* in order to maintain their power over the most important posts in the *cabildo*. Thus it is known, for example, that two *regidores* preferred to resign their posts rather than confront the existing tension and find themselves obliged to take sides. They were Martín de Mier y Terán and Juan de Albarracín, attached to the anti-Herrera faction, according to the plaintiffs' brief.[18]

The progress of court cases was notoriously cumbersome. For better or for worse, delays were used politically in all lawsuits of the epoch, and they became a crucial factor influencing the outcome of a case.

In the case in question, one can see that the matter of the "transfer" (*traslado*) played an essential role in the delay and final dropping of the plea. Within the broad framework of the judicial mechanisms of the age, we can see that this – generally mentioned in historical texts only in passing – had decisive consequences that went to the heart of the matter. Here, the time the plaintiffs had to win their case was very short, for there was less than a year until the next elections would be held.

17 "Memorial presentado por Manuel de Montalvo y Luna ante la Audiencia de Charcas," January 18, 1741 (ANB, R.A., Charcas, Expedientes coloniales, loc. cit.).
18 Traslado de la audiencia de La Plata al cabildo de Oruro de los cargos del apoderado Montalvo y Luna. La Plata, January 30, 1741, in "El cabildo de Oruro," ANB, Sucre, Expedientes coloniales, 1742, no. 5986, fol. 45v.

Thus, the judicial process continued all year without the *audiencia* coming to any decision, in spite of the exhortations of the litigants' lawyer and later requests by the *audiencia*'s own *fiscal*, who in his first consideration found in favor of the plaintiffs.[19]

The suit clearly fell within the category of what was called a *caso de corte*, meaning that it had to be heard before the *audiencia* because it was a complaint against a *corregidor*.[20] However, the plaintiffs clearly believed that they were obviating an *instancia anterior* (a lower court hearing) – that of the *cabildo* itself – and they justified this in the following manner: "we omit appearing in the *ayuntamiento* named, as is our right, in order to avoid greater outrages.[21]

In spite of this, their first action was directed at the viceroy himself, to whom they wrote a letter on January 3, recounting their version of the events. The letter was formally received in Lima on February 22 and from there it was passed on to the *fiscal*. He, realizing that the letter contained the same information as the statement already presented to the *audiencia* of La Plata, advised them to wait for the results of that case. On April 6 the viceroy ordered the *audiencia* to report to him on the state of the matter, and that was the end of his participation in the case.[22]

The litigants began their presentations before the *real audiencia* of Charcas – or La Plata – on January 5, 1741, two days after writing to the viceroy.[23]

The *procurador* for the group, Manuel de Montalvo y Luna, gathered together all the probatory evidence that might have helped his cause. The most important documents were certified copies of the three sessions in the *cabildo* where direct allusions were made to the events in question.[24] In addition he presented a certificate from the royal officials of the treasury of Oruro testifying that Ibáñez de Murzábal – one of the four litigants who had been prevented from participating in the election – owed nothing to the treasury for the office of *fiel ejecutor*.[25]

---

19 Dictamen del Fiscal sobre el Memorial presentado por Ibáñez de Murzábal y otros. La Plata, January 22, 1741 ("El cabildo de Oruro sobre nulidad...," ANB, Sucre, Expedientes coloniales, loc. cit.).

20 Ricardo Levene, *Historia del derecho argentino* (Buenos Aires, Kraft, 1946), vol. 2, p. 98 (dealt with in the *Recopilación de leyes de Indias*, Book 2, Title 15, Law 72).

21 "Traslado de la audiencia de La Plata al cabildo de Oruro...," loc. cit.

22 Petición del Alférez Real Don Joseph Díaz Ortiz y otros ante el Virrey del Perú Marqués de Villa García, Oruro, January 3, 1741 ("El cabildo de Oruro...," loc. cit., fols. 65–66).

23 The *audiencia* received the presentation on the 12th of the same month, with a hearing before the *fiscal* on the same day. Montalvo y Luna's petition was received on January 18.

24 These were: that of December 30, 1740, entitled "On Doubts and Conferences"; that on elections, January 1, 1741; and that of "Ordinances," January 9, 1741.

25 "Memorial presentado por Manuel Montalvo y Luna en nombre del Alférez Real Don Joseph Díaz de Ortiz y de los veinticuatro Don Agustín Ibáñez de Murzábal, Don Joseph de Imblusqueta y Don Blas Joseph del Barrio, ante la Audiencia de Charcas," in "El cabildo de Oruro...," loc. cit.

The simultaneous presentation before the viceroy and the *audiencia* seemed redundant from a procedural point of view because, as we have seen, the *audiencia* was the superior court under whose jurisdiction the case belonged, but apparently this was not an unusual procedure in the judicial system of the times.

The letter to the viceroy probably had only one objective: to make the highest colonial authority in Peru party to the current state of affairs and its possible consequences. One assumes that the plaintiffs knew in advance what course the viceroy would follow with their petition, that is, send it to the *audiencia*. In this way, however, they made sure that the viceroy was aware of the behavior of the *corregidor* of Oruro.

As for the *alcalde* Melchor de Herrera, it was known in Oruro that the viceroy was keeping an eye on his leadership because of a significant disturbance in the town two years earlier. The Marqués de Villa García mentions it explicitly in his memorandum relating to the conspiracy by Juan Velez de Córdoba of 1739 and the adjudication of sales taxes the following year:

Don Melchor de Herrera and Don Pedro Villar y Zubiabur were made to appear in court in this city, they being those who most noticeably promoted the rivalries and discord; a means which has served me very subtly several times to calm them down, which resulted in containing the others and restoring peace and quiet.[26]

In spite of the marqués's efforts, the letter from the four plaintiffs reminded him of the precarious situation in the town of Oruro, which to its accelerating economic decline added the symptoms of increasing latent violence.

The *alférez real* Don Joseph Diaz Ortiz and *los veinticuatro* say that considering it is his obligation to prevent the inconveniences that can result in harm to the public peace, the good administration of justice and respect for those who govern it, without making the populace eager to violate the check of the superior and respect with which it must venerate them . . . they proceed to make known to V.E. the scandalous and unheard of manner in which the *corregidor* acted.[27]

There was another motive for sending the letter to the viceroy: the proceedings of the city elections of January 1 had been signed by everyone, losers and winners. The signatures of the defeated parties was, consequently, an implicit validation of the results.

The plaintiffs feared that this argument would be used against them, and that it was already too late to demand that the elections be annulled. As a result, they hurried to explain to the viceroy that their conduct dur-

---

26 "Relación que escribe Don J. A. Mendoza, Marqués de Villa García," in *Memorias de los virreyes que han gobernado el Perú durante el coloniaje español* (Lima, Bailly, 1859), vol. 4, pp. 379–80.
27 "Memorial presentado por Manuel de Montalvo y Luna . . . ," loc. cit., fol. 65.

ing the elections was a response to their fear of the violence that might be used against them: ". . . without having dared to expressly ask for annulment, fearing some attack on our persons or the return of the soldiers, with the idea of coming with the testimony of all to allege it before the *audiencia* of La Plata."[28]

The case continued in Charcas before the *audiencia*. As in similar suits, the cumbersome bureaucratic machinery ground along at its usual snail's pace.

First, the *audiencia* showed the *fiscal* all the documents presented by the plaintiffs. He responded with two briefs, first to the presentation that the four signed on their own behalf and then to the one their *procurador* made in their name.[29] After receiving them on the 25th or 26th of January, the *audiencia* resolved on the 30th to transfer the court record to "the party of the Court of Justice of the *Cabildo* and *Regimiento* of Oruro." In this way, the "transfer" made its appearance in the case, initiating the familiar sluggish cycle of delays and halts in the course of events.

At this time the recently elected *procurador* of the *cabildo* of Oruro, Antonio de Toledo, was in La Plata. The clerk of the *audiencia*, Sebastián de Toro, notified him personally on January 31 about the case being brought. But Toledo, not very elegantly, excused himself from receiving the transfer of the suit in a note that the *Sala de Relaciones de la Audiencia* received on February 8. He said, "I must declare to V.A. that I have no part in this matter, nor am I obliged to respond to the said transfer." The reason he gave for this was that

if said transfer is meant for the *procurador* of that town, it was not me last year, and this year, although I am elected *procurador*, first of all, I am not confirmed in the position because the election has been challenged, and thus I should not have to take part in this matter, and second, because I have no information whatever about the matter.[30]

This initiated the dilatory maneuvers of the victorious group, although behind Toledo's petition we cannot rule out a certain hope to avoid the struggle between the factions.

Meanwhile, time was on the side of the elected officials: on February 16, 1741, the *audiencia* ordered the case transferred directly to the *cabildo* in Oruro; but the notification arrived a month later, on March 21.

The format of the transfer was standard for royal acts of the *audiencia*. The brief opened with the familiar formula "Don Felipe by the Grace of God King of Castile," and then transcribed the records of the proceedings, fixing in this case a peremptory time limit of twenty-five days for a response. The text ordered the following:

28 Ibid., fol. 65v.
29 Ibid., fols. 1v–2v, 25–26.
30 Ibid., fol. 27.

We command that within 25 days beginning on the day after the notification that we make from our letter and royal provision in advance that you in person or your *procurador* appear in our royal *audiencia* . . . otherwise if the said period passes with your absence and contempt the part of the said [parties] will be heard by Don Joseph Díaz Ortiz . . . and all that they wish to say and allege and determine the cause for all degrees and instances for which and for all that which you must by law be cited . . . and we serve you and will take as served the subpoenas of our said royal *audiencia* where all the decrees, *autos* and sentences will be made and announced which in said case shall be given and promulgated . . . and they will be as valid as if they were speaking with yourselves.[31]

On March 21, the notification was received in the *cabildo* of Oruro. In response, all the new members were called to attend a session, including the four plaintiffs – who although elected only to minor posts nevertheless had to attend meetings. Predictably, they offered a variety of excuses for failing to attend the ceremony.

The *alférez real* Don Joseph Díaz Ortiz and the *veinticuatro* Don Agustín Ibáñez de Murzábal and Don Blas Joseph del Barrio did not attend, even though they were informed by the *cabildo* porter Gabriel who said that the *alférez real* pleaded illness and at the house of Don Blas Joseph del Barrio they told him he had gone by mule to the mine and Don Agustín Ibáñez, who was walking down Cruz Verde street when he was informed by the porter that he had to attend, answered, tell them that I am sick.[32]

Those who did attend, following the established procedural rules of the *cabildo*, complied with the ritual of receiving the brief:

. . . having heard and understood they recognized said royal decree . . . standing up one by one they kissed and placed upon their heads obeying it with due respect and reverence as a royal decree of our King and Natural Lord, may the Divine Majesty protect him, and conserve in the increase of greater kingdoms and dominion as Christianity needs. And as for his compliance they order that it be kept, complied with, and executed completely and altogether according as his Highness commands. And in the execution they say that they are ready to act by themselves or by their agents to the *real audiencia*.[33]

After the traditional emphatic expression of obedience, they acted according to what was probably sacred custom: they discreetly allowed the twenty-five days to pass without making the slightest move.

One day after the deadline, April 16, 1741, the attorney for the four plaintiffs appeared in La Plata to request that from then on the case proceed in that court and that all the notifications and transfers be made there and not in any other place. In his brief, Montalvo y Luna argued, since the time limit by which they or their attorneys had to appear in court has expired, and they have not done nor said anything . . . accuse them of con-

31 "El cabildo de Oruro sobre nulidad de las elecciones del 1ro. de Enero de 1741. Traslado de la causa a la parte del cabildo," La Plata, February 16, 1741. ANB, Sucre, Expedientes coloniales, 1742, no. 5986, fol. 29v.
32 "Notificación de los autos al cabildo de Oruro," loc. cit., fol. 49v.
33 Ibid., fols. 49v–50.

tempt on account of which V.A. should subpoena them for the continuation of this case.[34]

On April 29 the high court accepted Montalvo y Luna's petition and announced the resolution to the other party.[35]

Days later, the *cabildo*'s lawyer, Ambrosio Cabrera, asked that the records be sent "by the usual route" so he could prepare his defense, and this was allowed by the *audiencia* on April 29. On May 4, Montalvo y Luna petitioned again:

since they have not appeared in court in the time allotted and since the deadline has passed, I accuse them of contempt and so it serves V.A. to decide and command what I have asked to be done.[36]

A few days later, the same attorney informed the *audiencia* that Cabrera had returned the records "without any response"; he therefore asked the court to expedite the matters contained in them.[37]

Montalvo y Luna's position was formally very strong. The time allowed had expired and the defendants in the *cabildo*, through their attorney, had returned the records of the case without comment.

However, the *real audiencia* did not seem to be very committed to its own resolutions. The procedure of the new "transfer" diluted the time constraints established, weakening the position of the plaintiffs.

On May 10 Cabrera appeared again before the *audiencia* to explain the return of the *autos* without response: the lawyer for the *cabildo*, Dr. Eugenio Calvimonte, had to leave Oruro suddenly, without preparing the brief. Cabrera explained that "for this reason, acting in a hurry, I returned the *autos* fearing imprisonment. [Furthermore, the deputy lawyer,] needing said *autos* in order to study them and begin said defense [it behooves] V.A. to command that they hand them over for the usual period of time."[38]

The *audiencia* passed this petition on to Montalvo y Luna, and he responded on May 12 as follows: "I say that these are all malicious delaying tactics with which they are trying to keep this case from coming to sentencing, and by the time a year has passed any sentence favorable to my side will be laughable and useless. It behooves V.A. to deny the contrary presentation."[39]

In spite of this request, the *audiencia* gave Cabrera two more days so the *cabildo* could respond, handing over the *autos* once more on May 16. When the two days were up, Montalvo y Luna lost no time, appearing again be-

34 "Petición de Montalvo y Luna," La Plata, April 16, 1741, loc. cit., fols. 28–29.
35 Ibid., fols. 28–29.
36 "Peticiones de Antonio Cabrera y de Montalvo y Luna," loc. cit., fols. 51–52.
37 Ibid., fol. 53.
38 Ibid., fol. 53.
39 Ibid., fols. 54–55v.

fore the court with a brief requesting that the *cabildo* be declared in contempt, the *autos* removed without delay, and that justice proceed.

The *audiencia*, however, did not seem to have very strict intentions concerning its own time limits. On April 20 Cabrera replied, arguing in his brief that there had been a fundamental procedural error: they had neglected to present the *autos* to the *alguacil mayor* Don Joseph de Aldabe y Salamanca.

In the opinion of the *cabildo*'s attorney, the declaration of the *alguacil mayor* was very important

because since said *alguacil mayor* is one of the principals whose welfare directly or indirectly is affected by the exclusion from the vote that elected the *alcaldes* and *procurador* ratified, by cohesion [or coercion?] that they assume there was to make it happen; in consequence not having been informed of the transfer that was so justly ordered by V.A. so that this case could be legitimately substantiated without at any time could any nullity be argued, we must before anything else practice this diligence.[40]

Again the *audiencia*, parsimoniously, ordered the transfer to the other party. Montalvo y Luna, when he received the brief, responded without delay, complaining about the dilatory tactics of the authorities of the *cabildo* and asking the *audiencia* to oblige them to "respond directly" to the substance of the matter.

It was clear enough what lay behind the maneuvers of the *cabildantes*, and this was not lost on the plaintiffs' attorney: simply put, they were trying to delay the sentencing until the year was finished. He wrote:

[N]ot only would the elected officials have enjoyed the use and privilege of their offices, but also the *alcaldes ordinarios* would have a voice in the elections of the coming year and . . . in this way the claims of my parties will be illusory. So you can see that the malice of this *cabildo* has diverted the course of this lawsuit through mere pretexts for nearly six months without anything having been accomplished of more consequence than this.[41]

As for the objection about the failure to notify the *alguacil mayor*, Montalvo y Luna responded that

[in order for] these citations to be sent to *cabildos universidades*, or *comunidades*, it is enough to present them to the head of those individuals who form the body of the *cabildo universidad* or *comunidad* in the act of the citation and that they be present in their *ayuntamiento* or chapter room . . . [as for the participants of the *cabildo*] they were called thus by the ringing of the bell by the porter of that *cabildo* . . . so that any individual who did not attend because of illness, pretext, or absence lost the right to take action.[42]

The agent's brief concluded by asking that it be shown to the *fiscal*. The *audiencia* provided this on June 6, 1741. Half a year had passed; in six months the plaintiffs would have to drop their case.

40 Ibid., fols. 57–57v.
41 Ibid., fol. 58.
42 Ibid., fols. 58–58v.

For most of that time the parties exchanged briefs, defending their respective positions. The *fiscal* finally leaned decidedly in favor of the plaintiffs and agreed with them that the authorities were acting with "studied evasiveness, with which they were trying to retard the case which[,] being summary[,] they hoped to make . . . go on forever as the very process manifested: so that thus what the law might disallow would be approved by virtue of this tangle."[43]

At this point the viceroy's decree reached La Plata; it requested that the *audiencia* inform him of the status of the case. Montalvo y Luna asked that this be shown formally to the *fiscal*. The latter pronounced on August 1: "[I did not find] objection that V.A. [the *real audiencia*] thus command, even though the case is not settled after seven months; whether because this *real audiencia* is closed, or for the same reason that the *autos* were furnished. . . ."[44]

The different courses of conduct followed by the *fiscal* and the *audiencia* are revealing, first because they illustrate the relative independence of the colonial powers in that epoch. Second, one can appreciate that the two warring factions each had their own support in high judicial circles, and that the viceroy himself expressed his concern over the development of this conflict.

Nevertheless, neither the latter's query about the case, nor the repeated statements by Montalvo y Luna and the *fiscal* pointing out the dilatory tactics of the accused, caused the *audiencia* to proceed more rapidly.

On August 29, 1741, Montalvo y Luna appeared again before the tribunal, asking them, since they had the records in the courtroom, to make "the decision they felt was most appropriate."[45]

The *audiencia*, however, did not respond to any of these demands. Once again they transferred all the records to the agent Cabrera, who answered on November 11, that is, practically at the end of the terms of the challenged authorities.

In his response, Cabrera alluded to one of the themes touched on by Montalvo y Luna, who had challenged the appointment of Melchor de Herrera because of the debts of *azogue* he had with the *caja* of Oruro. Cabrera asked to see a copy of the royal decree of October 15, 1635, "in which it is prohibited for *azogueros* [silver processors] to be provided with *corregimientos* and other public offices." On the 27th of the same month the *cabildo*'s agent argued in another brief on the validity of the election, asking in turn to expedite the case and show it to the *fiscal*. The latter answered on December 14, saying that the court clerk did not agree to deliver the testimony solicited:

---

43 Ibid., fol. 63v. The court's resolution of this question is lacking, but one can infer from the further course of the case that the position of the *fiscal* was approved.
44 Ibid., fols. 67–67v.
45 Ibid., fol. 68.

The *fiscal* says that in short it will be a year since the testimonies have been requested of the *autos* about various recourses that have been pursued for the residents of the town of Oruro . . . he has not been able to have the testimonies in question nor others delivered from the *real* [*haber*] for them to look at.[46]

The *audiencia* responded to this on December 17, ordering the court clerk Sebastián de Toro to deliver "within eight days under pain of two hundred pesos and suspension from office for six months all the testimony that you have been ordered to give to said *Señor Fiscal*.[47]

Conclusion

By this time it made no sense to continue with the lawsuit and in effect the case ended there. Only a few days remained until the next election and it was ridiculous to think of annulling the previous one. The apparent objective of the accused was accomplished.

Once control of the offices was achieved in the colonial *cabildo*, then, it was possible for the incumbents to manage the situation indefinitely from positions of power through succeeding elections.

This was, in fact, what happened in subsequent years in the *ayuntamiento* of Oruro. A short respite occurred during the intermediate term of the *corregidor* Landaeta, who managed for a time to soften the confrontation between the two warring bands. At the end of his term and with the assumption of power by the Rodríguez family, however, the friction was renewed.

The lawsuit of 1741 illustrates several points. On the one hand it confirms the commonly held notion about the slow pace of colonial administration; on the other it indicates that this procedural slowness did not always form part of an accepted style. In this case, it seems clear that the slowness was voluntarily imposed, not only by the defendants, but by the *audiencia* itself.

Of course, although one understands the political advantage the defendants drew from this situation, doubt remains about the attitude of the *oidores* of the high court.

One cannot discount the possibility that, for various (unprovable) reasons, the officers of the *audiencia* chose to support the faction of the *corregidor* Espeleta and the *alcalde* Melchor de Herrera; but other interpretations are equally possible. Even if the *audiencia* did not want to address the situation created by the irregular elections, this does not necessarily lead to the conclusion that it endorsed the defendants' behavior.

Hostility between conflicting factions of neighbors, whether veiled or overt, was nothing new in Oruro; nor was such behavior alien to other Span-

46 "Petición de Montalvo y Luna," op. cit.
47 Ibid.

ish cities and towns in America. Insults, affronts to individual or family honor, and various accusations among members of small settlements copiously fill the documents relating to the lawsuits of the era. In the case of Oruro, the economic decline of its mining industry did not contribute to tranquility among its inhabitants. The dilatory attitude of the *audiencia*, then, might have evidenced a desire to avoid adding more difficulties to those already in existence. It is obvious that a finding against the *corregidor* and the *alcaldes* in office would have fanned their anger to unpredictable levels. The delays in reaching a decision, therefore, ought not necessarily to be seen as a position adopted in favor of one side. Indeed, given the annual change of *alcaldes* and other municipal offices, opportunities to compensate for the irregularities of 1741 would likely arise later on.

For the time being, one thing can be perceived with clarity, namely that the fiction of the "colonial siesta," so often used to simplify the social reality of the colony, is not an accurate description of the prevailing climate – at least not in Oruro.

4

The people

Who were the litigants in this confrontation? An approximate reconstruction of their biographies on the basis of various references and scattered fragments of documentation indicates that they were important individuals in the town because of their prestige and influence as well as their economic resources.

Melchor de Herrera, faction leader and a favorite target for the wrath of the opposing coalition, appears to have been a man of considerable resources. In the petition made before the *audiencia* in La Plata by his attorney Ambrosio Cabrera, he is described as an affluent, enterprising, and responsible man:

[H]e is *alcalde provincial* of this town [Oruro] and of the provinces of Paria and Carangas and owns his house and has the largest family in the vicinity and he has twice been *alcalde ordinario* and *alcalde de la hermandad* and a *corregidor* of the province of Carangas; . . . he has discovered several minerals and going into the land in the year thirteen he registered a patent on the gold mine called Choquetanca and today he is the largest quicksilver miner in that town where he is working two mines in Poopó, one in Oruro, three in La Joya whose mine he has just equipped at his own considerable expense, and he produces more metals and silver marks in a single month than all the others as is obvious from the accounts.[1]

Later he adds, "He is a son of the place where his grandfathers and his relatives were all occupied . . . in the first employments and in the exercise of their own work."[2]

Melchor de Herrera had been, in fact, *justicia mayor (corregidor)* of Carangas in 1721, and later, in 1732, *alcalde provincial* of Oruro, Paria, and Carangas. In addition, he was twice *alcalde ordinario* of Oruro, first in 1735 and then in 1740.[3] In the decade of 1710 one Joseph de Herrera, possibly his father, had been *teniente de corregidor*.

The petition contains a description of Herrera as "the largest miner and *azoguero* in this town"; this, however, is not confirmed by the figures re-

---

1 "Respuesta y alegato de Ambrosio Cabrera" presented before the audiencia of La Plata, November 27, 1741, in "El cabildo de Oruro," ANB, loc. cit., fols. 74 and following.
2 Ibid., fol. 77v.
3 "Cargo de medias anatas," AGN, Buenos Aires, 13-18-2-7 to 13-18-4-5.

corded during the period, as he was always behind several members of the *cabildo*.[4] Nor did the others who belonged to his faction figure among the top producers of the period.

Everyone was, in any case, connected to mining production. Manuel García de Ayllón owned a mill for grinding and separating silver in Socotiña and was one of the moderate contributors to the Oruro treasury. In the fiscal period 1736–7 he paid a little more than 586 pesos (of eight *reales*) by way of tithe (*décimos*), while Juan de Otalora, the largest taxpayer of the year, paid more than 13,000 pesos. Another member of the defendant group of 1741, the *alguacil mayor* Joseph de Aldave y Salamanca, only sporadically paid his *décimos* to the treasury.[5]

The members of the plaintiff group in the suit of 1741, on the other hand, were economically more important. At least two of them – Blas del Barrio and Joseph de Imblusqueta – appear in the documents as the leading taxpayers of the 1740s, the former from 1745 to 1746 and the latter from 1748 to 1750.[6]

If one includes as part of this group the two *regidores* who tendered their resignations before the lawsuit, this characteristic is even more pronounced. Juan de Mier y Terán was among the largest silver smelters who paid taxes to the treasury for many years. By 1718 he was one of the three most important, and he held this position nearly every year until the end of the 1730s.[7] Juan de Albarracín also figures in the Oruro treasury as a buyer of quicksilver and a silver *piña* smelter. Although the size of his operation was much smaller than that of Mier y Terán, the volume of his smelting was larger that of Melchor de Herrera from 1735 to 1745.

A comparison of the total amount paid by each of the two groups reveals another interesting fact: between 1735 and 1745 the total *décimos* paid by Herrera's faction was a little more than 10,375 pesos, while their rivals paid 27,598 pesos, or nearly three times as much. These figures do not include Mier y Terán and Albarracín, the *regidores* who resigned; if they are added to the group of anti-Herrerists, the difference becomes immensely greater. The total of *décimos* then rises to about 97,500 pesos, or more than nine times the amount paid by the incumbent Herrerist group.[8]

Another interesting point emerges from an analysis of the public jobs held before the dispute of 1741. Counting both voters and candidates, the five members of the Herrerist group investigated here had formerly held positions in the *cabildo* or as *corregidores* on thirteen different occasions.

4 See the table "*Décimo* payments by tithes of miners and mercury processors in the *caja* of Oruro," at the end of this chapter.
5 "Libro real manual de décimos de esta real caja de Oruro, 1737–38," AGN, Sala XIII, C. VIII, n. 3 Book 11.
6 See the table "Payments by tithes."
7 Ibid.
8 Taxes for 1740–1 are lacking in this series of figures.

Another member of the Herrerist party, Antonio de Toledo, had been appointed administrator of a mine by the *cabildo* in 1717, the owner of which – whose name was Torresgolpes – brought a lawsuit for debts that produced a serious incident between the two men. This led to an armed confrontation, although no blood was shed. Joseph de Aldave y Salamanca, from the same party, was *teniente de correos* during this period, and apparently lived exclusively on the salary from his position.[9]

In the anti-Herrerist group, only three people had held positions, and on only four occasions.[10] Antonio de Oteiza, *teniente de corregidor* in Sica-Sica,[11] was still on a relatively low rung of the ladder in the institutional hierarchy.

Similar situations have occurred on other occasions. An example that is like Oruro with respect to the relative positions of the two main political forces – although admittedly in a more significant national context – was that of the elites of the Radical Party (UCR) and the Conservative Party (which had several names) in Argentina at the beginning of the twentieth century. In fact, among the radicals one can find cases of greater wealth, yet fewer occupancies of public office, than among the conservatives.[12]

In the case of Oruro, it is reasonable to assume that the richest individuals in the city wanted to match their economic situation with correspondingly high positions in the *cabildo*, and that, by the same logic, those who already held those positions and were able to profit from them resisted giving them up.

The following paragraphs cast some light on the difficult-to-discern relationship between economic position and politics. It is symptomatic that, in the lawsuit of 1741, the losers implicitly accused their rivals of an interest in public affairs that included objectives of a monetary nature. In one paragraph they state that "we resolve to keep an eye on persons . . . who do not need to wield the staff of authority for their support and propriety."[13]

Some details are also added about the supposed relations of interest among the members of each group. For example, it says that García de Ayllón was

9 "Demanda de Antonio de Tolego contra Sebastián de Torresgolpes," Oruro, February 17, 1717, in "Escrituras notariales," Archivo de la Corte Suprema, Oruro.
10 See the table "Payments by tithes."
11 "Memorial presentado por Ibáñez de Murzábal y otros," La Plata, January 5, 1741, in "El Cabildo de Oruro," loc. cit., ANB, Sucre, fol. 3.
12 See Ezequiel Gallo and Silvia Sigal, "La formación de los partidos políticos contemporáneos: La UCR (1890–1916)," in J. Graciarena, T. Di Tella, and G. Germani (eds.), *Argentina, sociedad de masas* (Buenos Aires, Eudeba, 1965), p. 124. Social scientists have proposed generalizations regarding these situations in terms like "subordinate groups with high aspiration levels," "status crystallization," or "status incongruence." See, in this regard, Everett Hagen, *On the Theory of Social Change* (Homewood, Ill., Dorsey, 1962); Gerhard Lenski, "Status Crystallization: A Non-Vertical Dimension of Social Status," *American Sociological Review*, 19, no. 4 (1954), 405–13; Torcuato di Tella, *Sociología de los procesos políticos* (Buenos Aires, Grupo Editor Latinoamericano, 1985), pp. 28, 246, 403, 412.
13 "Memorial presentado por Ibáñez de Murzábal," loc. cit., fols. 3 and 10.

in debt to the *corregidor* – in addition to being a straw man for Aldave y Salamanca – and that the latter was, in turn, a partner of the *corregidor* in the exploitation of a mine, a situation inconsistent with his low salary.

It is reported that Francisco Santos de Alborta was in debt to the *corregidor* because the latter financed his mining activities.[14]

As we can see, the relevance of *cabildo* positions in supporting economic interests is not easy to discern. Although the claims of the plaintiff group may be true, they do not explain why it would be in the *corregidor*'s interest to give political power to some of his debtors when, in principle, he would have more resources for collecting the debts if his debtors had no political connections or positions. On the other hand, if positions in the *cabildo* offered business opportunities, it would benefit the *corregidor* if his debtors could improve their financial condition.

All this raises an interesting point: as in similar societies, the political, human, and economic links among the inhabitants of Oruro become more complex the more closely one delves into their details. When we attempt an interpretation of power relations between the political and socioeconomic fields, then, it may be precarious to generalize about Latin America as a whole.

For the moment – taking a more microscopic view of this small society – we can say that Oruro had two groups that were difficult to dismantle. Both apparently built their networks over a long time; thus, in the period under study, each network already included several members of the administration and many officials.

The characteristics of their disputes contribute perspective to the analysis. During the lawsuit of 1741, both parties argued several themes that either supported or weakened their positions. One of the controversies had as its protagonist the *veinticuatro* (*regidor*) Agustín Ibáñez de Murzábal. As we saw earlier, his right to vote in the *cabildo* had been disputed since January 1. The Herrerist faction claimed that he could not vote because he had not paid "the emoluments connected to the powers of *fiel ejecutor*." These might have been due for the purchase of the office or related to the annual tax of *media anata* (a half or a third of the annual salary).

In his defense, Agustín admitted not having paid the charges in question, but argued that he had not obtained the staff of office (*vara*) through his own efforts; rather, he said, it had been passed on to him after the death of the previous incumbent, as he was the oldest *regidor*.

. . . and I say that having vested in me as *Regidor Decano* of this worthy Council, the staff of *fiel ejecutor* due to the death of Don Pedro de Rivera Galves, who held this office in his own right, with no duty nor obligation to contribute anything to His Majesty as you are well aware, thus during the many years that I have held this office, I have not paid to the

14 Ibid.

Royal Treasury anything for this reason and because the emoluments of this *vara* are very small, and belong to it and because the *corregidores* cash them as they are at present, and this is evident to you.[15]

Ibañez requested the royal officials to inform him whether or not he owed the royal treasury anything for any reason, and they replied: "The royal officials of the Royal Treasury of His Majesty and the Treasuries of this Town ... certify that having examined the Royal Books in our charge, we find in them nothing to indicate that the *veinticuatro* Don Agustín Ibáñez de Murzábal owes any quantity to the Royal Treasury of His Majesty for any account."[16]

In spite of this reply, the treasurer expressed certain reservations of his own about Ibáñez's conduct in the matter:

[A]lthough it is true that I the Treasurer, looking out for the best interests of the Royal Estate in accordance with my duty, having received the *vara* of *fiel ejecutor* of this Town on the said *veinte y cuatro* through the *vía de depósito*, on account of the privilege held by the senior *veinte y cuatro* because of the death of Don Pedro Ribera Galbes, seeing that in more than three years since it came to an end with Don Andrés de Otalora, that it was annulled by the superior *gobierno de pedimento* of Don Pedro Durán, and he again made a public proclamation and that until the present there has been no right to said *vara*, I commanded the *escribano* Gaspar Hurtado de Villa Gómez to notify said *veinte y cuatro* that with respect to his having benefited from all the emoluments connected to said *vara* from the time he obtained it that he paid his Majesty some quantity in each year with the provision that he would not use said office, and that he would lease it.[17]

In consequence – according to the treasurer of the *caja* – Ibáñez did not owe this amount but, for some reason, had to pay a portion of what he received for his activities as *fiel ejecutor*. On the other hand, the *vara* was leased until completion of the complicated paperwork hindering the adjudication of the sale of the position to Pedro Durán, who seemed to have the best qualifications for the position.

In light of all this, Ibáñez's argument was that, although it was true that he had debts as *fiel ejecutor*, he did not have any as *regidor*; and it was as *regidor* that he had a right to vote in the *cabildo*. Notably, this would be the same argument presented by Herrera, his opponent, in defending his own right to vote.

Another important consideration was the offer made by *regidor* Del Barrio to take charge of Ibáñez's presumed debt, an offer rejected by the *corregidor*. The petitioners brought as evidence an earlier resolution by the viceroy Marqués de Castel Fuerte, who in a similar conflict in Cuzco had decided to accept the lifting of the debt on the same day as the elec-

15 "Pedido de certificación de no ser deudor a la real hacienda presentado por Agustín Ibáñez de Murzábal," Oruro, January 14, 1741, in "El cabildo de Oruro," ANB. Sucre, loc. cit., fol. 16.
16 "Respuesta de los oficiales reales al pedido de certificación de A. I. de Murzábal," loc. cit., fol. 16v.
17 Ibid., fol. 17.

tion, and in addition had resolved that "in the future the *regidores* for this reason must be reconvened fifteen days before election day to settle this matter of debts to your royal exchequer and not on the same day as the voting."[18]

Another question, perhaps the most interesting one, relates to the vote of Melchor de Herrera himself. In their suit against him, the plaintiffs adduced that if the *corregidor* had prevented Ibáñez from voting because of a supposed debt relating to his post as *fiel ejecutor*, there was even more reason to prevent the hated *alcalde provincial* from voting. This was argued by the lawyer Montalvo y Luna, who said that the zeal of the treasurer for public funds did not seem as legitimate as he pretended:

Why have you not collected the growing amounts Don Melchor Herrera owes to the present day in taxes from the time when he was *corregidor* of the province of Carangas? Why has he not been charged either for what he owes on account of *azogues*, and you tolerate him from one Armada to the next, as is well known?[19]

These accusations may or may not be simply pretexts, depending on the source of the debt. Against the charge of delinquent taxes Herrera advanced, making the *escribano* read an earlier decision reached by the *ayuntamiento* in its session on February 9, 1741: "At this town council meeting I the *escribano* read the decision in the *cabildo* that took place on January 18 of the previous year of 1735 concerning the privileges that miners and *azogueros* may enjoy and that they may not be personally harassed about any debt."[20]

In the course of the suit, Herrera's lawyer amplified this argument with a transcript of the royal document of October 15, 1635, which contained the following:

Document of October 15, 1635. In order that the residents and *azogueros* of the town of Potosí may hold office in *corregimientos* and other public offices and *consejiles* [councils] even though they owe money to the royal treasury from loans or mercury they have incurred, as long as the debt does not have to do with the office they intend to fill or the one they have. The King. Whereby the King my lord and father (may he be blessed with glory) by his decree on the fifteenth of July of last year declared that no person who owes money to my royal treasury for anything in small or large quantity may be, nor be elected as *alcalde ordinario* of any of the cities, towns and places of the Indies, nor vote in such elections . . . ; which is practiced and executed in those parts. The *cabildo* and miners of the imperial town of Potosí having informed me of the inconveniences that would follow in carrying out this decree there; by another of my decrees of February 25, 1624, I declared that in spite of what is said above, persons who are in debt to my royal treasury may have active and passive vote in the election of public officers, except when they want to vote by virtue of an office they have bought and not paid for, the time having passed during which that should have been done, as in more detail is described in said decrees.[21]

18 Ibid., fol. 3v.
19 "Petición de Montalvo y Luna," loc. cit., fol. 10.
20 "Petición presentada por Antonio Cabrera," loc. cit., fol. 21.
21 Ibid., fols. 71v–73.

The same royal decree goes on to cite several cases in which the Potosí *tribunal de cuentas* opposed the appointment of miners as *corregidores* because they were in debt to the royal treasury. These debts were connected to the purchase of mercury for the extraction of silver.

> ... whereby all those who have profits from mines, being most of those who are involved in them, persons of high quality and well qualified to occupy such positions, were prevented from holding honorable jobs or office, and they are not deserving of this and ought to have better rewards for it depends on their work and the risking of their lives and property, to make secure my royal taxes.[22]

In fact, Melchor's rivals claimed that the impropriety of his vote was not due solely to the debts he had acquired purchasing mercury for his mining business. They also accused him of not having paid the tributes levied during the time when he was *corregidor* of Carangas. In addition, they said his *vara* as *alcalde provincial* was defective, because Pedro de Villar had filed a motion with the *audiencia* of Charcas claiming to have better rights to the job.[23]

Thus, debts originating from mining activities did not appear to be an obstacle to holding any office in the *cabildo*. The other imputations, if true, would indeed have constituted an impediment.

Another topic that carried genuine weight – whether businessmen could or could not be members of the *cabildo* – sharply divided the members of the different factions. This was reflected in the session of January 9, 1741 when, by order of the new authorities led by the Herrerist side, a city ordinance was read concerning the election of *alcaldes ordinarios*. This indicated that "subjects of low class who have public stores shall not be elected to these offices."[24]

This ordinance had a counterpart in Law 12, Title 10, Book 4 of the *Recopilación de Indias*, which among other things stated, "Councilmen must not deal or contract in cities, towns or any places, in merchandise or other things, nor keep stores ... nor must they be retailers, or engage in low occupations, and those who wish to do so must first resign from their office."[25]

The reading of the ordinance was promoted by Herrera who, according to the record of the session, "said ... the contents of this ordinance are to be observed fully." His intention was clear: some of his opponents owned stores that sold to the public, while none of his allies did.

In these movements of the Oruro *cabildo* one can read several signs of a more general process that developed more markedly in Latin America in the last third of the eighteenth century. This was a period of particular

22 Ibid.
23 Ibid., fol. 10. Also, in the already cited memoirs of the Marqués de Villa García, pp. 379–80.
24 "El cabildo de Oruro: Acta de la sesión del 9 de enero de 1741," ANB (Sucre), Expedientes coloniales, loc. cit., fol 21v.
25 *Recopilación*, p. 115.

attraction for peninsular Spaniards, because even as America experienced prosperity, the economic recovery in Spain was less vigorous due, among other things, to population growth.[26]

As a result, the massive impact of new Spanish immigration was seen as a threat by the locals because the new arrivals advanced easily into the most important positions, both civilian and ecclesiastical.

It is clear from a reading of the names on the available lists that many who participated in the internal quarrels of Oruro came from this new migratory current, which originated in the north of Spain – the Cantabrian coast and Galicia. Other names belonged to Spanish Americans whose origins could be traced through four or five generations to those Andalusian or Extremaduran ancestors who arrived during the epoch of the conquest.[27] Thus, the traditional opposition between central-southern and northern Spaniards was transplanted to America.

Among Melchor de Herrera's opponents, as we have seen, there were traders and shopkeepers. As in the rest of Latin America, recently arrived Gallegos and Basques probably predominated in these occupations. They were, furthermore, already accustomed to a more efficient management of commercial and financial activities than were their local rivals.

Given this picture, it is not surprising that the losing side was opposed to Herrera's demand during the session, "Let us hold to the custom that has been in force on the matter."[28] Later, his lawyer – in the petition directed to the *audiencia* of Charcas on January 18 of the same year – pointed out that the ordinance forbidding merchants to participate in the *cabildo* was "an old ordinance contrary to the practice in all the cities, towns, and places."[29]

Naturally, the prevailing regulations and ordinances were ambiguous about the type of commercial activity considered incompatible with the office of *alcalde* or *corregidor*. Law 12, Title 10, Book 4 of the *Recopilación* mentions those who trade in merchandise in general as well as those who engage in retail trade (*regatones*); this could be interpreted broadly as covering all business, or narrowly as concerning only retail trade.

During the session, Ibáñez de Murzábal defended the possibility of electing *alcaldes* who were businessmen, making it clear that "in 40 years in these parts he has known many *alcaldes ordinarios* who have shops and businesses

26 M. Hernández Sánchez Barba, "La sociedad colonial americana en el siglo XVIII," in V. Vives (ed.), *Historia de España y América, social y económica* (Barcelona, V. Vives, 1971), vol. 4, pp. 261–5.

27 Thus for example, among the first: Oteiza, Murzábal, Otalora, Uriquela, Imblusqueta, Urquieta, Ruvín de Celis, etc. Among the second: Herrera, Tholedo, Ortíz, Cisneros, Uriarte, Navarro, Tejada, Rodríguez, etc.

28 "Cabildo de Ururo: Acta de sesión del 9 de enero de 1741," loc. cit., fol. 21v.

29 Petición presentada por el apoderado Montalvo y Luna ante la Audiencia de La Plata, el 18 de enero de 1741," ANB (Sucre), loc. cit., fol. 18.

Table 4.1. Décimo *payments by miners and mercury processors in the* Caja *of Oruro (in pesos and reales)*

Name	1735–6	1736–7	1737–8	1738–9	1739–40	1740–1	1741–2	1742–3	1743–4	1744–5
Melchor de Herrera							1,263p, 2r 212p, 2r			
Joseph de Aldave y Salamanca								72p, 2r		
Manuel García de Ayllón	618p, 2r	586p, 1r					1,032p, 4r			
Ibíñez de Murzábal										
Joseph Díaz Ortiz										
Joseph de Imblusqueta					2,145p		509p, 2r	1,201p	2,994p	1,517p, 2r
Blas Joseph del Barrio	3,769p, 6r	2,408p	891p, 2r		1,250p, 4r					3,378p, 3r
Manuel de Herrera			1,992p, 6r					2,234p		2,366p, 4r
Antonio de Oteiza					991p, 4r	4,060p, 3r	2,093p, 4r			
Francisco Santos de Alborta								392p, 3r 221p, 1r		

Source: "Oruro, Manual de Décimos 1735–50," *AGN,* Buenos Aires.

and who have administered justice at the same time that they have engaged in trade."

Nevertheless, the argument did not convince Herrera, who insisted in the same session, "I say once again that none of the members of this worthy *cabildo* had the right to vote against the ordinances and [therefore] by no means would they elect a tradesman as *alcalde*."[30]

In expressing his opinion, the *fiscal* of the *audiencia* agreed with Ibáñez, giving an opinion favorable to the idea that merchants could hold office as *alcaldes* or *regidores*:

[The *fiscal*] says that although it is found in the rules of common and municipal law of these kingdoms that it is prohibited for merchants to perform the duties of the republics being in these kingdoms considered as not indecent people, it is informally assented that this should not be an obstacle to obtain the honor of their principal employments and the administration of justice according to the way it is authorized in most of the cities in these dominions. And [do it thus], custom having so much vigor and force over the law."

In spite of these affirmations, the *fiscal* did not seem to be convinced of the practical authority of his opinion; he added that, in any case, it was not appropriate for the *audiencia*

to go on to resolve on its own authority certain points that could produce a disturbance . . . and because of all this your *fiscal* feels that as far as the *cabildo* is concerned on the question of determining whether merchants cannot be elected as *alcaldes ordinarios* you must wait for your viceroy to resolve it.[31]

The *audiencia* thus avoided endorsing the refutations – just as they had done in the case of the complaint analyzed in the preceding chapter – so as not to exacerbate the existing conflicts in the town. In addition, this type of problem was probably disappearing, especially with the reign of Carlos III (1759–88), under whose mandate the commercial rejuvenation of the colonies took place.

---

30 "Cabildo de Oruro: Acta de la sesión del 9 de enero de 1741," fols. 23 and 23v.
31 "Repuesta del fiscal a la petición de Montalvo y Luna, 25 de enero de 1741, El Cabildo de Oruro," ANB (Sucre), loc. cit., fols. 25 and 25v.

5

"Madmen, comedians, and hypocrites"

The years following the agitated elections of 1741 passed, apparently, without significant trouble. Judging by what followed, however, it appears that the animosity between the opposing factions continued unabated. In the period 1745–7 things reached another boiling point.

In 1745 there was a change of viceroy: the Marqués de Villa García (1735–45) was succeeded by José Antonio Manso de Velazco, count of Superunda (1745–61). At least concerning Oruro, the new administration showed itself to be more energetic and disposed to put a definitive end to internal discord.

By the middle of 1745 the familiar symptoms had already begun to make their appearance again. Letters to the viceroy from one side or the other, containing various ploys and manipulations, indicate that the recurrent theme of every year's end was beginning to gleam on the horizon: the question of who controlled the votes for the *alcaldías*.

By October 1745, the Herrerist acolytes began their campaign, sending the viceroy a paper on the topic. In it, they recalled with nostalgia the good old times when the *corregimiento* was in the hands of Martín de Espeleta, and they revived an interesting point of view:

Since the time when Don Martín de Espeleta was *corregidor* of the town, on account of the punishment he gave to Juan Vélez de Córdoba and his supporters, because of the plot whereby they tried to revolt against these provinces to the detriment of these kingdoms, there have been several enemy disputes that continue in this area with no small disruption.[1]

That is, they attributed the origins of the division in the city to the revolt of 1739 and the subsequent severe repression by the *corregidor* against its leader, Vélez de Córdoba.

The outgoing viceroy, the Marqués de Villa García, shared this interpretation. In his memoirs he observed that the conspiracy, put down by

---

1 "Carta de los regidores Melchor de Herrera, Manuel García de Ayllón, Lorenzo Rodríguez y Manuel de Herrera, del cabildo de Oruro, al Virrey," Oruro, October 5, 1745. Archivo General de la Nación (AGN), Buenos Aires, Oruro 9-7-6-4, legajo 1.

Espeleta, had been an attempt to stir up the Indians, "so they would unite (with the rebels) and shake off the yoke of obedience."[2]

This implies that the group led by Espeleta and Herrera hoped to continue to repress the process begun by Vélez de Córdoba, which was cut short by his sentencing. It also indicates that for a variety of reasons, part of the mining community in Oruro felt more confident about its relations with the indigenous masses than did its rivals in the same business. It was this group – in which Creole families predominated, whereas recently arrived Spaniards made up the ranks of their opponents – that in 1781 nearly brought the town to ruin precisely because of the trust they initially placed in their alliance with the indigenous people.

As for the repression suffered after the revolt of 1739, Villa García recalled with relief in his memoirs that the *corregidor*'s response was swift and definite. Espeleta's action was, presumably, approved by the viceroy with his royal decree. In any case, the viceroy himself recognized that Espeleta's response led to serious consequences and discord, not only in Oruro but also in La Plata:

This noisy event provoked several rivalries in the town of Oruro and the sentiments of the residents and the *regidores capitulares* were sharply divided . . . and led to complicated lawsuits pitting some against the *corregidor* and others in his defense of his actions, and this led to internal conflict among the few ministers still remaining in the *real audiencia* of La Plata.[3]

The violence aroused by annual elections in the *cabildo*, described earlier, may be at least partially explained by these circumstances.

It seems clear that even during the years of apparent calm, the district remained divided and tense. This became evident, for example, during the provisional "peace" imposed in 1741 by the successful machinations of Herrera's group after the elections mentioned above; it happened again in subsequent years, when the unstable balance between formal and actual power alternated between the warring factions.

The year 1745 had not been propitious for the soothing of spirits, although the previous election seemed to reflect an attempt at harmony. Manuel de Jáuregui and Joseph de Imblusqueta had been elected *alcaldes* with second-highest and highest seniority, respectively. The former had managed to retain a certain amount of independence from the two factions, but the latter, it will be recalled, had been one of the losing challengers to the Herrerist group in the turbulent election of 1741.

Melchor de Herrera and the others who signed the above-mentioned letter to the viceroy united in praise of Jáuregui, "a subject in whom all the quali-

2 "Relación de Don José Antonio de Mendoza Camaño y Sotomayor, marqués de Villagarcía," in *Memorias de los Virreyes* . . . , op. cit., p. 378.
3 Ibid., p. 379.

ties of Christianity and zeal for royal service and total commitment to public good are present." They were, however, far from making similar statements about Imblusqueta, "who has only made use of his own personal and inappropriate interests in the administration of justice, with the object of revenge."[4]

They also referred to their knowledge of Imblusqueta's maneuvering to place candidates from his faction in office in the next elections. Because of this, they asked the viceroy to name the new *alcaldes* himself, meanwhile enthusiastically suggesting that Jáuregui continue in office. To replace the detested Imblusqueta they proposed three names: Juan Joseph de Helguera, Pedro de Eulate, and Diego Hidalgo de Cisneros.[5]

This request by the *regidores* from Herrera's group was extraordinary. By law, *alcaldes* were elected by the members of the *cabildo*, and the viceroy preferred to leave this matter to local forces. Only on occasions of great unrest did he opt to make appointments directly, and this is precisely what happened in 1746. By the end of 1745 it was known that the viceroy would replace Imblusqueta with a candidate from the list suggested by the Herrerists. Although the viceroy thus satisfied the desires of Herrera's group, he was a long way – as we will see later – from validating the policies of this faction.

As might be expected, the news alarmed the anti-Herrerists, who immediately wrote to the viceroy in an attempt to counteract the influence of their rivals. They claimed that the Herrerists had given a false and biased description of the situation in the town:

Having read the letters of Your Excellency in this *cabildo* sent to inform us that your higher judgment will prevail over the elections of *alcaldes ordinarios* and other officials of this republic with the objective of establishing peace and calm in the vicinity, it appears that your assumptions are distorted by the report presented to Your Excellency . . . it is necessary for us to say . . . that for three years here there has been no unrest that has caused any problem . . ." Signed: Martín Mier y Terán (*corregidor*), Joseph de Imblusqueta (senior *alcalde*), Joseph de Aldave y Salamanca (*alguacil mayor*), and *regidor* Blas del Barrio.[6]

They added that furthermore it was unjust to accuse them of abuse of power, given that they had never curtailed their opponents in the pending judicial cases nor had they posed any difficulties during the *cabildo* "when (their opponents) have had the advantage."[7] On the contrary, they stated that the Herrerists – convinced they could count on the viceroy's support in appointing *alcaldes* from their party in the next year's elections – had begun to commit excesses and irregularities:

4 "Carta de los regidores Melchor de Herrera *et alii*," October 5, 1745, loc. cit.
5 Ibid.
6 "Carta del corregidor Martín de Mier y Terán, del alcalde ord. Joseph de Imblusqueta, del alguacil mayor Joseph de Aldave y Salamanca y del regidor Blas Joseph del Barrio, al virrey Manso de Velazco," Oruro, December 18, 1745. AGN, Buenos Aires, Oruro 9-7-6-4, legajo 1.
7 Ibid.

What is happening now, Sir, is that abusing the higher decision of Your Excellency . . . and boasting about having had subjects favorable to their side named as *alcaldes*, the authors of that letter constantly make all kinds of threats against those who do not side with their ill temper, and because of that they treat us as enemies . . . and in the end we find ourselves insulted, disregarded, and possibly ruined by their spiteful behavior, which will lead to our having to leave our houses, jobs, and businesses, which as is well known augment His Majesty's income by a large amount.[8]

The letter did not move the spirit of Viceroy Manso de Velazco, who wrote in the space reserved for replies the word "nada." No doubt his attitude was influenced by other information from Oruro that cast a definitely unfavorable light on Joseph de Imblusqueta.

A letter from Pedro Coro, for example, head *cacique* of the Indians of Oruro and its jurisdiction, accused the *alcalde* of several damaging and high-handed actions. Coro had been appointed *cacique* by the previous *alcalde*, with the approval of the *audiencia* of La Plata. He had several complaints against Imblusqueta. He accused him of exploiting and penalizing Indians and "poor people" for his own profit. To this end, the letter reported, the *alcalde* utilized the services of two of his own acolytes,

who assist him like ministers, called Luis Hidalgo, a free half-breed [*pardo libre*], and Domingo Basado [or Dorado], alias Conchero, of low birth and perverse nature, followers and favorites of this *alcalde* who do all the dirty work they can, both to the miserable Indians as well as the rest of the poor people, taking their animals and the burden they are carrying; and when they cannot steal from someone because they defend themselves, they pursue them and accuse them of imaginary crimes with the most incredible cruelty; and Luis Hidalgo finds witnesses who after promises and threats say what they are told to say and in the way they are told to say it.

In particular, Coro's denunciation continues, the *alcalde* had two soap factories whose raw material was obtained from his subjects, "taking for it the tallow brought by the miserable Indians and the rest of the people at ridiculously low prices so his profits would be large; and he sends Luis Hidalgo, the half-breed, and Domingo Dorado to round up everyone who enters the town."

According to the *cacique*, these henchmen kept track of people entering the city and, finding out who was carrying tallow, went to find them in their houses, threatening to place an embargo on their goods and put them in jail, "and in this way they take all the tallow there is, paying much less than the asking price and sometimes they don't pay anything at all."[9]

Coro had still more complaints to add, among them that the *alcalde* and his followers obstructed the collection of tributes that he, as *cacique*, was supposed to collect. Coro, furthermore, had the right to imprison Indians who did not pay tribute. Hidalgo, one of Imblusqueta's henchmen, had been

8 Ibid.
9 "Carta del cacique Pedro Coro al virrey Manso de Velazco," Oruro, December 19, 1745, loc. cit.

cacique before Coro, who had replaced him by authority of the *audiencia* of Charcas. Hidalgo had not forgiven this displacement; his revenge consisted of a simple recourse, endorsed by the *alcalde*: he set free the Indians whom Coro imprisoned for nonpayment of taxes. He also recorded them as mestizos, and thus they no longer had to pay the indigenous tax.[10] Coro, like all *caciques*, had pledged his own property as a guarantee to the royal treasury for the collection of tribute. If the tribute did not reach the stipulated amount, *caciques* were obliged to cover the difference with their own funds; otherwise they would default with the consequent loss of their position.

Coro relates that on one occasion he imprisoned one of his taxpayers, Bernardo de Almansa, "who owed me two hundred pesos; when he found out about this the above-mentioned Luis, continuing his persecution of me, went to the house of the above-mentioned *alcalde* who immediately freed the taxpayer."[11]

Finally, another of the *alcalde*'s tactics – which also contributed to the bankruptcy of the beleaguered *cacique* – was to pass many of his Indians "*a reserva.*" In effect, when Indians reached the age of fifty, they entered a category called "reserved," and no longer had to pay taxes. It so happened that, given the imprecise records of their ages, there was considerable arbitrariness about the moment when this status was actually conferred.[12]

According to a large number of the existing testimonies, Imblusqueta did not practice his duties as *alcalde* with moderation. Nevertheless, we must remember that his main accusers were those who, led by Herrera's group, seemed to maintain fluid links with the indigenous sector or at least with some of its leaders, such as Coro himself. In any case, other negative factors about Imblusqueta may have carried even more weight at the time of the viceroy's decision.

In September 1744 a judicial case was brought by a certain Alonso Ramírez. Captain of the *yanaconas* (a class of domestic servants excluded for the most part from the *mita* obligation), he was the natural son of the late Domingo Ramírez, whose executor and trustee was the polemical Imblusqueta. Alonso, displeased with the manner in which the *alcalde* was managing his father's affairs, had brought a complaint against him in the *audiencia* of Charcas, appointing as his attorney Diego Hidalgo de Cisneros.

The *audiencia* decided in favor of Ramírez, demanding that Imblusqueta justify his behavior. When he received this notification, Imblusqueta apparently uttered coarse epithets against the *audiencia*, saying that "the gentlemen sitting at Chuquisaca are a bunch of rogues." This gave rise to another suit in Oruro, which was heard before the senior *alcalde* Alzerreca.[13]

10 Ibid.
11 Ibid.
12 Ibid.
13 "Autos contra Joseph de Imblusqueta," 1744. Archivo de la Corte Superior de Justicia, Oruro.

In spite of Hidalgo de Cisneros's efforts, it was not possible to obtain any direct testimony about Imblusqueta's rebuff: all the witnesses repeated that they heard the same version told by Fray Silvestre Peláez, Augustin prior of the convent of Challacollo, who in turn based his account on the declaration of the *cabildo's escribano*. The latter, predictably, denied in writing having said anything against Imblusqueta. In the end, *alcalde* Alserreca considered the case closed.[14]

In spite of the scant legal value of the declarations of Hidalgo de Cisneros and his witnesses, the *audiencia* must have been left with the impression that in fact Imblusqueta had insulted them. Representatives from the clergy added their voices against him, as well. The chaplain of Oruro, Francisco Xavier Alvear – who on account of this was obliged to leave the town – summarized his own opinion in a letter to the viceroy:

Although I consider that Your Excellency's patience has been sorely tried already by repeated complaints, which I know have been sent to you by several clergymen unjustly calumniated in the judgments of Mr. Joseph de Imblusqueta; nevertheless I cannot fail to present my own view for your excellency's mercy, occasioned by the ease with which the above-mentioned gentleman attacked me before my curates, a practice he is accustomed to perform against everyone, and the result of his grave insinuations and indecent reports has damaged the good reputation and credibility that a religious person must maintain.[15]

Faced with such an overwhelming number of complaints and negative opinions against Imblusqueta, the viceroy sought a way out of the vicious circle of reciprocal hatred, accusations, rumors, and lies. Although he probably did not need any more information to complete his picture of the chaotic situation in Oruro, the following reflections by the curate and vicar of the town, Father Aldunate y Rada, constituted a pointed synthesis:

Finding myself in this town of Oruro in the post of Curate and Vicar, my conscience pricks me to provide your excellency with the best explanation of the miserable state in which this town finds itself, motivated by its most important inhabitants, since they have resolved themselves into two bands or parties, one against the other, from which one fears some great calamity, and for its remedy I appeal to the higher justice of V.E. that you impose the quickest and most effective remedy as this matter requires, since the *Regidores* and *Capitulares* of this town are disunited and in confrontation; thus do I hope, for the peace of all the residents of this town.[16]

If any doubts remained in the viceroy's mind after this overwhelming bombardment of letters, he finally confirmed that he would personally appoint the *alcaldes*, disregarding the protests of Imblusqueta's supporters, who kept insisting that peace reigned in the city.

14 "Declaración de Gaspar Hurtado de Villagómez," Oruro, September 28, 1744, loc. cit. "Pedimento de Diego Hidalgo de Cisneros," Oruro, October 9, 1744, loc. cit.
15 "Carta del capellán Francisco Xavier de Alvear al virrey," Oruro, January 25, 1746. AGN, Buenos Aires, Oruro 9-7-6-4, legajo 1.
16 "Carta del cura y vicario de Oruro, Dr. Juan Ascencio de Aldunate y Rada, al virrey," Oruro, November 6, 1745, loc. cit.

At this point Father Pedro Ignacio Romero, rector of the Society of Jesus in Oruro, entered the picture. The viceroy decided to use his good offices, trusting in his position as a neutral observer, and probably in his moderation and good judgment.

At the beginning of 1746, when the day came to renew oaths of office, Romero kept his word and wrote as follows to the viceroy:

Respected Sir:

I address Your Excellency on the first day of January of this year and at the same hour in which the electors of this town of Oruro gathered to elect the council officers, as is usual. I went to the *cabildo* and in the presence of the *corregidor*, *justicia*, and *regidor*, I handed over the letter Your Excellency sent me by mail earlier which I then kept myself in utmost secrecy as you entrusted me to do and punctually in obedience to your desire.

It was received with universal rejoicing by all and read by the secretary . . . and I promise that coming from your excellency's hand and the persons being so well qualified [this refers to the new *alcaldes* designated by the viceroy, Joseph de Helguera and Diego Hidalgo de Cisneros] it has to be the remedy for this town, both in the timely administration of justice and in the necessary reestablishment of peace.[17]

With this decision, the viceroy acted to bring events in line with the demands of the Herrerists. As we will see later in this chapter, Manso de Velazco did end by endorsing the policies of this faction by naming Manuel de Herrera interim *corregidor*; but it must be noted that at the beginning of 1746 the program of its adherents seemed more sensible than that of its adversaries. On the one hand, it had also been suggested that the *alcaldes* be appointed directly from Lima; on the other, the names that had been proposed for the *alcaldías* – accepted by the viceroy – did not seem objectionable. Joseph de Helguera, certainly, presented no problems. Hidalgo de Cisneros, however, had a sharp confrontation with Imblusqueta in the abovementioned court case against the *audiencia* of Charcas, so perhaps the *oidores* had taken sides in favor of his candidacy after this incident.

The biographies and experiences of the two *alcaldes* appointed by the viceroy reveal that they were very dissimilar in social extraction, way of life, and probably in character.

Joseph de Helguera y Palacios was a wealthy businessman who acted mainly as a financier, although on his death it became apparent that he also owned several mines.[18] In the fiscal year 1745–6 that coincided with his term as *alcalde*, for example, he paid taxes to the treasury of nearly ten thousand pesos for silver smelted. Nevertheless, he does not appear in this year – or in any prior years – as a buyer of mercury, which indicates that, at least around 1750, he was primarily financing other miners' silver production, often collecting his fees in the form of ingots.[19]

17 "Carta del Padre Pedro Ignacio Romero, rector del colegio de la Compañía de Jesús, al virrey," Oruro, January 28, 1746, loc. cit.
18 In Chapter 8 I present a detailed analysis of these economic modalities of mining in Oruro.
19 "Oruro, manual de Décimos, 1737–1750," AGN, Buenos Aires.

The same impression emerges from the will he drew up in 1763: the document reveals that he was an important lender to several members of the Herrerist faction. His principal debtor, in fact, was Manuel de Herrera, son of Don Melchor, who on the date of the making of the will owed him the considerable sum of 80,000 pesos. He also loaned money, albeit much smaller sums, to Lorenzo Rodríguez and Martín de Espeleta, the ex-*alcalde*. The latter had moved to Chuquisaca, leaving behind several hard-to-collect debts, one of them owed to Melchor Rodríguez.[20] Relations between Helguera and Imblusqueta do not seem to have been bad, given that the latter had deposited with him 4,000 pesos for the dowry of a nun.[21]

In sum, Helguera seems to have had a solid position and numerous connections in town. The absence of documents involving him in judgments, complaints, or lawsuits reveals a personality of moderate habits not too inclined toward political posturing.

The other *alcalde* appointed, Diego Hidalgo de Cisneros, was a man of much more modest means. His father, Antonio Hidalgo de Cisneros, was a captain of the Spanish Guard, and had been governor and superintendent of the royal factories in Cantabria. When his son was appointed *alcalde*, Don Antonio was still a governor in Galicia, having earlier been a *corregidor* in the province of Moquegua and inspector of the Carangas treasury.[22] Don Diego's income came from a bakery that his wife had brought into the marriage; "I live at my wife's expense, from a bakery," he reported.[23]

The viceroy soon understood that Hidalgo de Cisneros lacked the right personality for the job. Soon after assuming his post and promising that he would exercise his power "to try to reestablish peace and quiet and good relations among his neighbors,"[24] he urged the viceroy to restrict the activities of Francisco de Ugalde, who had been named *corregidor* of Carangas. The viceroy sent back an angry reply, after which he decided that the appointed *alcaldes* would not serve his goal of creating order in the town, and hurried to intervene directly in Oruro's turbulent affairs. Probably his experience with the inhabitants led him to agree with the expert colonial

---

20 "Testamento del Gral. Don Joseph de Helguera y Palacio," 1763. Archivo de la Corte Suprema, Oruro, escrituras notariales. The paragraph of Helguera's will that refers to the ex-*corregidor* Espeleta reads as follows: "Likewise, I declare that I was the executor and heir of the lieutenant colonel of cavalry Don Martín de Espeleta y Villanueva, whom I begged to restore to Chuquisaca a thousand pesos in a *barretón*; he did not pay me it and I was also obliged to pay the *veinticuatro* Don Melchor Rodríguez, more than seven thousand pesos for him, which the said Espeleta owed him and had not satisfied. I order that it be paid from the mines that the said colonel left in the mining town of Antequera and that these satisfy the said creditor.
21 Ibid., fol. 168.
22 "Diego Hidalgo de Cisneros al Virrey Manso de Velazco," Oruro, April 30, 1746. AGN, Buenos Aires, Oruro 9-7-6-4, legajo 1.
23 Ibid.
24 "Carta de Diego Hidalgo de Cisneros al Virrey Manso de Velazco," Oruro, 1746. AGN, Buenos Aires, Oruro 9-7-6-4, legajo 1.

official who supposedly enlightened Alonso Carrió de la Vandera about the nature of the men in the region as mentioned in the *Lazarillo*:

What does the change in these men consist of, that converts them from a mild and peaceable manner to gruffness and arrogance? There is no such change, replied the visitor. Most of these men are a troop of crazies. Some are madmen, and one flees from them. Others are comedians, and one is amused by them. And the rest are hypocrites.[25]

25 Alonso Carrió de la Vandera ("Concolorcorvo"), *El lazarillo de ciegos caminantes* (Barcelona, Labor, 1973), pp. 302–3.

6

Captains of shipwreck

After the death of the *corregidor* Martín de Mier y Terán at the beginning of 1746, the *audiencia* at Charcas – in another demonstration of sympathy toward the Herrera family – named as interim *corregidor* the son of Don Melchor, Manuel de Herrera.[1]

In spite of the personal intervention of the viceroy in the election of *alcaldes* that year, there was still an angry mood in the town. The naming of Herrera's son as interim *corregidor* probably added to the defeat felt by his opponents, again raising the temperature of the confrontation in the city to intolerable levels. Although copies of all the letters that each faction sent to the viceroy have not been preserved – letters endorsing their own side and denigrating their opponents – Manso de Velazco's replies indicate that he was wavering, by this time, between boredom and indignation. Persuaded that the time had come to act harshly, the viceroy decided to stop listening to arguments from the two sides – and probably also to the advice of the *audiencia* in Charcas – and make independent decisions.

He began by sending a letter of admonition to the members of the *cabildo*, in which he said, "I cannot find words adequate to express the extreme extent to which my just displeasure extends." Considering that "this hotheaded disorder ignited by your hateful rivalries has lasted a long time" he added that he was considering using all the means at his disposal to placate the high-handed behavior ruling the town. If persuasion were fruitless, he would give orders to tear out "by the roots the seed of these ancient outrages even at the cost of exterminating that place without any other form of justice than that of its execution."[2]

Curiously unanimous, the members of the *cabildo* replied with a swift and prudent mea culpa.

Having read in this *cabildo* Your Excellency's letter of March 11 in the presence of all its members . . . we are advised of your answer and with particular pain for having been the

1 "Carta de Manuel de Herrera al Virrey Manso de Velazco," Oruro, March 19, 1746. Archivo General de la Nación, Buenos Aires, Oruro 9-7-6-4, legajo 1.
2 "Carta del cabildo de Oruro al Virrey Manso de Velazco," Oruro, April 23, 1746 (in which they mention warnings that he had sent them in a previous letter, not preserved), loc. cit.

reason for the unpleasantness and just disturbance our constant quarreling has caused in the upright and just spirit of Your Excellency, by now having reached the utmost limit of universal discord. We confess our guilt and we deserve severe castigation and [we understand] that Your Highness's accustomed pity has looked upon us with the mercy corresponding to your magnanimity . . . in the future we will not give cause to induce the displeasure that we have provoked up to now. Signed: Manuel de Alserreca, Joseph de Helguera, Diego Hidalgo de Cisneros, Melchor de Herrera, Pedro Durán Valencia de Salazar, Lorenzo Rodríguez, and Manuel de Ayllón.[3]

The viceroy was pleased at this demonstration of submission, but believed that the attitude of retreat might not be lasting. Thus, he replied that only time would tell if their promises would bear fruit. Meanwhile, he said, he would wait with a vigilant eye on Oruro.[4]

Although of short duration, the viceroy's master stroke during this phase was his appointment of the new titular *corregidor* Juan de Landaeta. The discord prevailing in the town was exorcised, at least momentarily, through the joint action of these two men and that of their "secret messenger," Father Romero.

Only a few times in the documented history of Oruro do the differences in character, style, and background of the colonial personalities appear with such clarity as they do in this period. The viceroy, the *corregidor*, and the messenger showed deep knowledge of the brutal and intractable nature of the contenders, and appealed as much to dissuasion as to threats and punishment, with brilliant results.

It is interesting to compare the relatively brief exchange of missives and arguments that bring out two diametrically opposed human types, sometimes discernible even in their syntax and concepts or in that of their scribes. In the long run, however, the stormy nature of the miners predominated, and after a brief incursion by the century of enlightenment, everything returned – to the relief of the majority – to its natural disorder. As we will see in the next chapter, the man who succeeded Landaeta as *corregidor* – Eugenio Lerdo de Tejada – also tried to act in a strictly subordinate fashion to the viceroy's directives, in an attempt to maintain order. In spite of this prudence, however, he seems to have had neither Landaeta's broad vision nor his authority.

By the first months of 1746 the promises of moderation made by the *cabildantes* were already hollow. Landaeta had not yet been installed as the new *corregidor* when one of the *regidores*, Joseph de Alserreca, again initiated the familiar routine: complaints in writing to the viceroy about the behavior of the other *cabildantes*. Manso de Velazco adopted drastic measures, sending the following acerbic response: "I have received your letter of April 3

3 "El cabildo de Oruro al Virrey Manso de Velazco," Oruro, April 30, 1746, loc. cit.
4 "El Virrey Manso de Velazco al cabildo de Oruro," Lima, no date (but immediately after the letter just cited), loc. cit.

... whose measures have been suspended until now with reserved motives that it is not important for you to know, until the effects of what it communicates show you the care with which you must keep the peace among those who live under your jurisdiction."[5]

In the letter quoted, Alserreca describes his quarrel with Manuel de Herrera and claims that the latter, on becoming interim *corregidor* in 1744 on the death of the incumbent, had been roundly repudiated by the majority of the council members because of their antipathy to his father, Don Melchor, who was, according to the Alserreca, a well-known agitator of passions in the town. Apparently, Manuel de Herrera had insulted him in writing; as a result, Alserreca had appeared before one of the current *alcaldes*, Manuel de Jáuregui, who after several vain attempts at reconciliation sent the case to the viceroy. However, Alserreca's suspicion also fell on the *alcalde* himself because, as he belonged to the Herrerist faction, Alserreca felt he had probably hindered the investigation, "damaging his honor and reputation." He also accused the *alcalde* Cisneros and the assistant clerks of distorting the reports and misrepresenting the facts.[6] It should be noted that Manuel de Herrera had begun the offensive against Alserreca at the end of 1744, when he related his own version of the events in a long letter to the viceroy. According to him, Alserreca had used every means to turn the people against him. The letter reveals the violent and impassioned nature of Don Melchor's son: in chaotic and frequently incomprehensible handwriting and syntax, one sentence after another describes the opponent as "declared and well-known cardinal enemy of me and my father," "hateful and suspect," and so on.[7]

After rejecting Alserreca's demand, the viceroy sent his letter to Landaeta to inform him of the history of the situation but also probably to enlighten him about the prevailing climate in the town and the kind of problems he would face in office.

The viceroy's instructions to Landaeta were clear: not to make any judgments about anything that happened among the inhabitants without the concurrence of Father Romero and himself.[8] Furthermore, he should first appeal to persuasion, since "not so much desiring the punishment of public conflict as its solution, I would be most pleased if you could achieve it without needing to cost me other methods of achieving it."[9]

A short time after assuming his post, Landaeta wrote to the viceroy with optimistic news: the *alcaldes ordinarios*, and in general all the *capitulares*, had promised in his presence to suspend the suits they had pending before

5 "El Virrey Manso de Velazco a Joseph de Alserreca," Lima, June 6, 1746, loc. cit.
6 "Carta de Joseph de Alserreca al Virrey Manso de Velazco," Oruro, April 1746, loc. cit.
7 "Carta de Manuel de Herrera al Virrey Manso de Velazco," Oruro, December 9, 1744, loc. cit.
8 "El Virrey Manso de Velazco a Juan de Landaeta," Lima, no date, loc. cit.
9 "El Virrey Manso de Velazco a Manuel de Herrera," Lima, June 6, 1746, loc. cit.

the *audiencia*. Gratefully, he acknowledged that "no small thanks is due to the respect and zeal of the Rev. Rector of the Company of Jesus" and to the intelligent and pacifist attitude of the viceroy himself.[10]

One of the first problems the new *corregidor* had to confront was, inevitably, a suit over the right to a job: the irreconcilable Joseph de Imblusqueta and Manuel de Herrera had carried on an abrasive struggle for the possession of the *vara* of *alférez real* (royal standard-bearer), which was nevertheless essentially an honorific post. In this matter, Landaeta wrote to the viceroy that he had decided to concede the title to the neutral Pedro de Eulate, whom he praised as "a person of known good sense."[11]

The next paragraph of the same letter illustrates the conduct – unheard of in this town – of the new *corregidor*:

I also made sure, with the greatest tact possible, to personally solicit the opinions of the inhabitants belonging to either faction, who were both impassioned and independent, taking quite a lot of time to visit them in their houses in order to inform myself quite thoroughly about the controversies and lawsuits that have perpetuated the disagreements.[12]

Landaeta applied himself tirelessly to a difficult task, with a notable capacity for discrimination. Soon he knew the inhabitants by their tendencies, friendships, and even personal characteristics. He wrote the viceroy that

I have figured out who is fomenting the discord with the most tenacity and stubbornness, and the origin of everything can be traced to the *alcalde provincial* Don Melchor de Herrera, on one side, and on the other the *regidor* Don Joseph de Imblusqueta, the latter deeply immersed in the false presumption that he has conceived about the truth of his opinions, his prudence not being the most adequate for the good conduct and management of the government.[13]

His persuasive manner was nevertheless allied with strictness: he imposed a fine of 2,000 pesos on anyone who violated the agreement to keep the peace because, in his own words, "It is my understanding that whereas integrity oftentimes fails to guarantee honorable behavior, the fear of punishment often succeeds."[14]

By July 1746, the solemn promises of compliance by the residents of Oruro were apparently only remembered by the *corregidor*, the viceroy, and Father Romero. The litigious and intractable character of the Orurans cropped up again the moment the *corregidor* relaxed his control or tired momentarily of taking a position of extreme strictness.

10 "El Corregidor Juan de Landaeta al Virrey Manso de Velazco," Oruro, no date, loc. cit.
11 Ibid.
12 Ibid.
13 Ibid.
14 Ibid.

On July 28, 1746, Landaeta wrote to the viceroy after learning that Pedro de Orosco, a resident of the town, had appealed directly to the *audiencia* of Charcas to accuse the *alcalde* Diego Hidalgo de Cisneros. According to the plaintiff, Cisneros had demanded payment of 500 pesos that Orosco owed to an official of silversmiths.[15] Landaeta quickly took control of the situation and succeeded in bringing about an agreement between them; "I myself personally attended to the reconciliation," he noted.[16]

In spite of the *corregidor*'s efforts, however, the lawsuits began to accumulate again and Landaeta grew tired of the situation. In the same letter in which he refers to the above-mentioned arbitration, he reaffirms his loyalty to the viceroy and his commitment to the work proposed. Nevertheless, he also requests that in case of disorder the viceroy

dissolve this *ayuntamiento* completely, or make sure that the *varas* pass to other residents or to those who have not before been *regidores* . . . because the damage that has been done to the Republic in these past upsets is owing to the fact that those who hold these jobs imagine themselves to be sovereign.[17]

The *corregidor*, seeing that he could not prevent the returning hostilities, tried to cut things short to avoid more serious consequences.

The same day, July 28, Landaeta wrote to the viceroy about the already mentioned complaint brought by Joseph Francisco de Alserreca because he had not acquired the post of *justicia mayor*, which had been granted to Manuel de Herrera for the interim term mentioned earlier. Landaeta dismissed the most rhetorical aspects of Alserreca's demand – which overflowed with pages of baroque language asking for justice to wash clean the besmirched honor of his family – but considered others that in his judgment were important. For example, there was the violent plundering that Don Melchor, father of the accused, had perpetrated at a mine belonging to Alserreca in the district of Poopó.[18]

This was not the only complaint against the Herreras, however; their brief period of contrition before the viceroy had come to an end and the mining family once again began to show who held the real power in the town.

Nicolás Lezcano Bernal had also brought suit against Manuel de Herrera, because the latter had said in writing that Lezcano's wife had married "a subject of low station."[19] Landaeta understood that this type of suit did not merit a hearing, but he was unable to convince Lezcano Bernal, who returned with another complaint, this time against the patriarch of the

15 This example illustrates the relative position of the *alcaldes* in commercial suits and, therefore, the importance of that position for the achievement of their particular goals.
16 "El Corregidor Juan de Landaeta al Virrey Manso de Velazco," Oruro, July 28, 1746, loc. cit.
17 Ibid.
18 Ibid.
19 Ibid.

Herreras, Don Melchor, because he too had said insulting things about him when opposing his appointment as *regidor*.

Landaeta observed to the viceroy that this was another typical case of "interminable mutual accusations" and that, knowing the miners, neither would give in. Therefore, he was in favor of interrupting this type of law-suit of calumnies, believing that if no such action was taken, "there will never be any peace in this town, because [as] there is no one who does not think he has been injured in past disagreements, the offended parties have to use this method to promote their rancor."[20]

The opinion of Father Romero about the level of disorder in the town was no less carefully thought out. In a letter of beautiful handwriting and refined language – which in itself indicates the education and bearing of this diplomatic individual – the rector of the Jesuit college presents the viceroy with a synthesis of his impressions. Although the letter is rather long, I quote it at length because it conveys an accurate view of his intelligence as an observer:

Your Excellency:

I have not taken up pen earlier to inform Your Excellency of the part I played in the establishment of peace in this town of Oruro because it seemed to me that it was only my duty to execute Your Excellency's orders and to tell others that I had done so. . . . I can tell you, Sir, that in the three and a half years that I have lived in Oruro as Rector of my College, I have not had to do anything more often than to pacify angry feelings, mending private disputes and trying to solve public ones, although with more success in the case of the former than in the latter . . . in obedience to Your Excellency's request I will tell you my observations on the subject.

After the careful consideration with which I have observed events, I fear that this serenity is not very stable, because although everyone protests to be sincere in his accord, nevertheless one can see outbreaks of the previous conflicts that continue to cause harm. A convincing proof of this is that the town council did not respond as you proposed to the letter Your Excellency sent to them asking for an end to the upheaval with a single joint letter, humble and submissive, signed by all of them, but rather each faction wrote individually and signed separately. The motive for this is not difficult to discern in the context. To this I may add that some of them, in order to conceal the lack of sincerity with which they had been reconciled, are presenting all kinds of papers, requesting with cunning intent that credit that had been taken away from them be restored, without heeding the fact that the judgment itself states the contrary. . . .

Thus I would argue that in order to prevent worse trouble, it would be opportune to eliminate the great ease with which the residents of this town can appeal to the Higher Government for everything, as if there were no judges in Oruro or as if they did not have more immediate recourse to the Royal *audiencia* in Charcas. . . .

As for the question of which subjects are likely to disrupt the peace established, I confess that I cannot say for sure. I can only say, and I believe with some basis, that those who keep on filing briefs, alleging vain pretexts, do not want peace, because behind the causes they pretend they are arguing, it is easy to discover their inflamed passions.

You can be better informed on this matter by the *Justicia Mayor* of this town [Juan de

20 Ibid.

Landaeta] a person whose good judgment, moderation, indifference [that is, objectivity], disinterest, healthy intentions, and Christianity all contribute to the worthy execution of his post.[21]

Father Romero's observations were precise, which can be verified in the letters that the participants in the two suits continued to send to the viceroy. Their contents demonstrate that the campaign of "pacification by force" undertaken by the viceroy and the *corregidor* had accomplished only one objective: now the pleas brought in the pending lawsuits contained, interspersed in picturesque and incongruent juxtaposition to the usual insults and accusations, phrases of compromise in which the litigants maintained, with innocent assurances, that in spite of everything they shared the goal of pacification.

Thus, for example, the intractable Alserreca affirmed to the viceroy that, at the insistence of Father Romero and the *alcaldes*, he had made peace with Manuel de Herrera "so you can see that for my part I am ready to do that . . . even though it goes against my honor and my interests, which are both damaged by Don Melchor and his son." Further on he again enumerates, with a wealth of details, all the charges already presented against these two in his previous letter, bringing up the robbery of his mine, the offenses they committed against his family "with such false slander, the child of their rancorous and vengeful natures," and insisting on his petition for restitution on the part of the Herreras. After these words of undisguised ill will, he finishes his letter by saying that in spite of all the offenses against him, "when all these arguments are counterbalanced on Your Excellency's accurate scales of justice, my only wish is to abide by your highest mandates, to which I resign myself with blind obedience."[22]

The same attitude can be seen in the letters of Lezcano Bernal, who had decided not to forgive the insult about his wife's "low station" made by Manuel de Herrera. Apparently, Herrera had been Bernal's wife's guardian before she and Bernal were married, and Herrera's remark was quoted in a brief presented at the *audiencia* of Charcas in the context of another lawsuit concerning the custody of Lezcano's younger brothers. Bernal's fear was that, because this statement of character had been introduced as evidence, in the future his descendants might be hurt by distrust in their "purity of blood."[23] Thus, in spite of his demand for "just vindication of my damaged reputation," Bernal finished by stating that for some time he had held back his complaint, "seeing at the ill will of the times and not wishing to ignite the fire again, having practiced the same in regard to the goods and accounts that [I] ought to have collected [from Manuel de Herrera] from the time

21 "Carta del Padre Pedro Igancio Romero, rector del colegio de la Compañía de Jesús, al Virrey Manso de Velazco," Oruro, July 27, 1746, loc. cit.
22 "Carta de Joseph de Alserreca al Virrey Manso de Velazco," Oruro, April 30, 1746, loc. cit.
23 He does not use this expression but we can suppose he is alluding to it.

when he was the guardian [of my wife] since always my blind obedience has no other guiding star than the commands suggested by Your Excellency."[24]

Some time later, the viceroy responded with a brief note, drily telling Bernal that he found his decision to postpone his confrontation with Herrera very correct.

By this time, however, none of the three crusaders for peace harbored even a hope of finishing their mission in Oruro successfully. Father Romero, in the letter of July 27, informed the viceroy that in a few more days he would be leaving for La Paz to take charge of another college. There is no way to confirm whether this move originated from higher orders or was his own decision.

As for the viceroy, in September 1746 he decided to hold another chapter meeting to have a brief he had written read before the members of the *cabildo*. In it he expressed some not-very-favorable opinions: "I have private, true, and certain news that the amicable relations that have occurred have been superficial and my orders and communications have been complied with on the surface [but that] everyone still holds within his breast the motives of discord and revenge."[25]

He then ordered them to publicly burn the briefs presented in the cases between Manuel de Herrera and Joseph de Alserreca, as well as those between Herrera and Lezcano Bernal, "these being the cases that burden a secure and eager amity."

In fact, Manso de Velazco was not so naive as to believe in the earlier affirmations. Probably he had already accepted that the causes of the "Oruro malady" were endemic and perhaps ineradicable. He was nevertheless determined to trap the miners in their own rhetoric and arguments. He went on to say,

In which knowledge I must warn the *Cabildo Justicia*, and *Regimiento* that now no motive nor even appearance remains not to comply with what I have ordered . . . [and that] I will have individual news of the procedures of each one and all those who foment discord and rivalries [who, persevering in this] must not hope for any other fate than to journey to this city [Lima] to put themselves very distant, which will serve not only as punishment and example, but also as medicine and remedy for the corruption that is found in such perturbed and unhappy souls.[26]

Again going through the ritual of obedience, the *cabildantes* met on September 6 and in solemn assembly burned the book of the acts of the *cabildo* from January 5 of that year until then.[27]

24 Ibid.
25 "El Virrey Manso de Velazco al cabildo de Oruro," Lima, September 3, 1746, loc. cit.
26 Ibid.
27 "Certificación de los escribanos del cabildo [alluding to the meeting of the members of the *cabildo* on September 6, 1746]," Oruro, March 3, 1747, loc. cit.

In this way Manso de Velazco managed to pacify people's spirits somewhat in the months prior to the new elections. The candidates for the *alcaldías* – suggested by Juan de Landaeta and the vicar of the town, Juan Asencio de Aldunate – were Pedro García de Eulate and Manuel Cayetano Jáuregui, who received the *varas* in January 1747, after apparently peaceful elections.

Nevertheless, Landaeta had decided, like Father Romero, to put distance between himself and the town. Manso de Velazco accepted his resignation and replaced him with Don Eugenio Lerdo de Tejada. This did not turn out to be a poor choice, but hostilities in the town made their appearance once more, first timidly and then with their usual rhythm.

The reformist vigor and the efforts of the only three clear heads had become compromised. We may suppose that Father Romero, in his new college in La Paz, and Juan de Landaeta, returned to civilized Lima, where Viceroy Manso de Velazco was waiting for him, meditated at length on the vicissitudes of this impossible enterprise.

7

Returning to the known

Although an analysis of the years between the events related in the previous chapter and the uprising of 1781 does not form part of this study,[1] a summary of the period extending until just past the first half of the century is helpful to prepare for what follows.

The term of the *corregidor* Juan de Landaeta went against the grain of Oruro's high-strung society, and the town endured it with scarcely concealed impatience. When the next *corregidor*, Eugenio Lerdo de Tejada, took office, the town reverted to its interminable quarrels, mutual accusations, and factional hostility.

Melchor de Herrera – unshakable in his post as *alcalde provincial*[2] – reappeared on the scene with no need for discretion. His office was strategic in that its holder gave orders to the rural police. As noted in the preceding chapter, the possibilities for wielding effective power depended in this case, as in that of *alcalde ordinario* or *corregidor*, on the private resources of the individual who had the job. In some cases it was also possible to arbitrarily make use of the resources of the royal exchequer.[3] The opposition to Herrera's group seemed more disorganized in this period, his main enemies being the *corregidores* and people sent from Lima. But the weak authority of the latter – compared to the firm discipline of Juan de Landaeta – caused the

---

1 This intermediate period forms part of another work in progress, in which I am studying violence, political coercion, and daily life in the society of Alto Peru.

2 See "Lista de cargos, según pago de media anata," AGN, Sala III, Caja Real de Oruro (1700–91). Melchor de Herrera appeared for the first time exercising this office in 1732. He remained in it during this entire period, except for 1740 and 1751, when he occupied the office of *alcalde ordinario*. In 1755, the post of provincial *alcalde* was occupied by his relative and successor, Manuel Rodríguez de Herrera.

3 It is possible to find examples of these different situations. A case of the use of a *corregidor's* private, or allegedly private, funds is found in Arequipa in 1780, on the occasion of disturbances against the customs house. The *corregidor* was Semanat and a certain Cosio financed and directed a company to support his tenure. See "Relación de lo acaecido en la ciudad de Arequipa con el levantamiento de los Indios e individuos mal contentos," in Melchor de Paz, "Diálogo sobre los sucesos varios acaecidos en este reyno del Perú, los cuales pueden servir de instrucción y de entretenimiento al curioso lector, Año de 1786," in Luis Antonio Eguiguren, *Guerra separatista* (Lima, 1952), pp. 87–9. For abuses by members of the *cabildo*, see ibid., p. 119; for the defense of the *corregidor's* interests at the cost of the royal treasury, see p. 126.

viceroy to adopt a somewhat tolerant position toward the Herrerists and their followers. Not finding any way to eradicate this leadership, Manso de Velazco seems to have reasoned that it was better to inaugurate the new epoch with benevolence and to accept as inevitable the lawsuits and confrontations as long as they could be contained within reasonable limits. It is also true that an aptitude for conflict and a lack of tact in the management of public and private affairs was not the exclusive territory of Herrera's group.

It is interesting to note that sometime later the viceroy reappointed his trusted *corregidor* to office in an attempt to cope with what had become an extreme situation in the town. Nevertheless, Juan de Landaeta did not stay long during this second attempt – only one year, from 1754 to 1755 – which implies that he may have agreed to return to the Oruran inferno only to rescue part of the family honor. In fact, his two sons, who held important positions in the city, were far from repeating their father's performance in their own public positions, one as *corregidor* and the other as an official of the royal treasury.

On January 1, 1748, elections were held in the *cabildo*, presided over by the new *corregidor*, Juan de Landaeta's successor, Don Eugenio Lerdo de Tejada. On this occasion the viceroy decided to allow the free play of municipal regulations without apparently intervening in the naming of *alcaldes*. Nevertheless, he probably had some indirect influence in support of the new victors in the election.

On the day of the election, the *corregidor*, following instructions from Lima, urged the *capitulares* to

concur in compliance with your obligation and vote without introducing items irrelevant to the matter, conversations or other alien speech in this act, each one speaking in the place that belongs to him due to his office, observing the politics, modesty, and respect due to such a respected place and he who acts to the contrary shall have a fine imposed of 1000 pesos of eight *reales* by the *escribano* present.[4]

The *alcaldes* elected were Francisco Navarro and Mathías de Uriarte, about whom too little is known to identify their political allegiances at that moment.

In this manner, with a formally irreproachable act, the new political year began. However, it soon became apparent that things were not as civilized and harmonious as the proceedings in the *cabildo* seemed to indicate.

In fact, in February of 1748 the *corregidor* wrote to the viceroy informing him that although for two months he had tried to maintain harmony and put a stop to "the remnants of partisan activity that remained hidden [in the town]," he had not achieved his aim. Above all, he complained about having to accept that "I have not been able to tame the obstinate spirit of

4 "Actas del cabildo de Oruro, presidido por El Corregidor Eugenio Lerdo de Tejada," Oruro, January 1, 1748. Archivo General de la Nación, Buenos Aires, Oruro 9-7-6-4, legajo 1.

Don Melchor de Herrera, *alcalde provincial*, who more than anyone in the town (which with unheard-of docility has calmed and suppressed its hostilities) has given me cause to find some way to correct him."[5]

The old *caudillo* was not disposed to give up his power over the town again; he probably made this eloquently known to the new *corregidor* from the very moment of the municipal elections, judging by Lerdo de Tejada's complaints to the viceroy.

But Manso de Velazco did not seem to trust excessively in the ability of this official to outmaneuver the Orurans. Although, judging by the later *juicio de residencia*, Lerdo de Tejada was thought of as a moderate and honest *corregidor*, he never appeared to exercise authority over the intractable miners of the town.

In March he again sent the viceroy a long litany of his difficulties in which he revealed that he had also made enemies in other quarters. In this case, Thomás, the son of the respected Juan de Landaeta, felt he had been offended by the *corregidor* during a public ceremony.

Thomás de Landaeta was at that time an official of the royal treasury, and judging by the tone of his letter to the viceroy, he was far from sharing his father's style. In fact, the reason for his extreme anger was, in his own words, that "on Good Friday [the *corregidor* tried] to insult my person because I had taken the standard in his procession, carried by ancient custom by my ancestors, saying that I could not carry said standard [and that I must not] go in front."

This change of protocol apparently provoked a scandal in the middle of the procession, and the *corregidor* had to retreat from his apparent attempt to humiliate Don Thomás. However, that was not the end of it: once the ceremony was over, neither the *corregidor* nor the *alcaldes* accompanied the royal official and his companion, the accountant for the royal treasury, to their homes, again breaking with custom.[6]

After the *corregidor* tried to justify his attitude toward Landaeta to the viceroy, Manso de Velazco responded with a brief and sharp reply. It is not possible to establish if he really thought Lerdo de Tejada's attitude was so deplorable, or if his respect for Thomás's father, Juan de Landaeta, was more important. Nevertheless, his words leave no doubts about which side he took:

In your letter of April 23 you say, *Señor*, that you find no means to maintain peace and tranquillity in this Neighborhood . . . I cannot but say to you that I am very sure that you

5 "Carta del Corregidor Eugenio Lerdo de Tejada, al Virrey Manso de Velazco," Oruro, February 16, 1748, loc. cit.
6 "Carta de Thomás de Landaeta al Virrey Manso de Velazco," Oruro, April 23, 1748, loc. cit. According to Cañete y Domínguez (op. cit., p. 361), a royal order dated March 19, 1777, took into account the dignity of the work of royal officials, stating that they should be seated after the ordinary *alcaldes* in *cabildo* sessions and wear the uniforms of war commissioners.

are not behaving as you want to persuade me you are and that private enmities are being fomented, one of them being the one you pointed out during Holy Week with Don Thomás de Landaeta, official of the royal treasury.[7]

He went so far as to threaten the *corregidor* with a transfer to Lima if he failed to apologize to Landaeta.

Although there is no evidence of it, Lerdo de Tejada probably yielded to viceregal pressure, given his insecure position. Although his personal conflict with Don Thomás did not reoccur, neither did any others with that endemic motive of local dissention: the movements of Don Melchor and his group.

In July, an unsigned letter attributed to "a group of neighbors" (probably followers of Herrera) informed the viceroy about "the evils of the town." In the letter, Manso de Velazco heard yet again that "the origin of this abominable outrage arises from the [conflicting] bands," and that the faction in conflict with the authors of the letter was that which, in their opinion, "unwisely has been reviving the old bitterness, which is easily taking hold in the hearts of those who take it up."[8] The letter does not mention names, skirting the context of the accusations; it can be attributed to the Herrerists, if only because of a mention of who had won the municipal elections "in which they kept their pledges, and all the winners distributed all the favors and the power among their chosen partisans, and the losers [that is, those who lost the election] had a year of bitterness, and their families suffered repeated insults, forsaking their work in the mines and consuming their wealth in lawsuits."[9]

The viceroy, again at the end of his patience, tried to place himself equidistant from both parties. Although the *corregidor* and the anti-Herrerists did not seem to have his sympathies originally, he began to suspect that Herrera's band would not postpone reviving their old methods. In a letter to Thomás de Landaeta and Joachím de Careaga, he asked them to act as intermediaries, communicating his profound anger at the inhabitants and threatening with punishment anyone who promulgated disorder at the next elections.[10]

Apparently relations between the forces continued in this manner until the end of Lerdo de Tejada's term as *corregidor*. At the beginning of 1749, Francisco Navarro was again elected *alcalde*, accompanied this time by Pedro de Eulate, a neutral figure who was always relied upon during difficult times.[11]

As in a story that repeats itself without end – and probably to simulate a position of power that did not really exist – again Lerdo de Tejada as-

7 "Carta del Virrey Manso de Velazco al Corregidor Lerdo de Tejada," Lima, June 4, 1748, AGN, loc. cit.
8 "Carta s/f al Virrey Manso de Velazco," Oruro, July 20, 1748, loc. cit.
9 Ibid.
10 "Carta del Virrey Manso de Velazco a los oficiales reales de Oruro," Lima, no date, loc. cit.
11 "Acta del cabildo de Oruro," Oruro, January 26, 1749, loc. cit.

sured the viceroy, as he had at the beginning of the previous year, that all the inhabitants were in a perfect state of peace and harmony, thanks to his efforts.[12] Although there is no documentation on what happened that year, it is not difficult to conjecture how the game of alliances and confrontations played itself out until the end of the *corregidor*'s term.

Lerdo de Tejada left the job at the beginning of 1750, possibly after definitively losing the support of the viceroyalty, or perhaps making the decision himself after the wear and tear of daily conflict. On March 15, 1750, the viceroy received the report about Tejada's residency. According to the testimonials, "not only has no one complained about this gentleman for any injury or injustice [but] of all the acts and public voice there is evidence only that he has been so beneficial to the republic that it has never been seen to be so peaceful or well governed as in his time."[13]

It went on to say that by virtue of all this, Lerdo de Tejada had been elected *alcalde de primer voto* "by general acclamation," in the municipal elections of 1750.

After what happened during his term, in particular after his stormy relations with the viceroy and the Herrerist band, there remain serious doubts about the objectivity of the evaluation of his tenure already mentioned. Probably, like many other institutions of the epoch, it merely fulfilled a formal role and did not reflect the actual term of government, as it had done to some extent in the early years of Spanish American colonial history. There may also have been some agreement between the conflicting parties now that the new *corregidor* – perhaps a temporary one, as in 1743 – was the controversial Manuel de Herrera. There is no documentation on this period, unfortunately; but the appearance of the other son of Juan de Landaeta, Miguel, at the head of the *corregimiento* in 1752 speaks of an equally agitated state of affairs. With the appointment of someone belonging to such a prestigious family, the viceroy again had confidence in following the erratic path of events in Oruro. It was nevertheless another unrealistic project: like his brother Thomás, Miguel de Landaeta had little in common, politically speaking, with his illustrious father.

The first problem mentioned in Miguel de Landaeta's correspondence with the viceroy is his conflict with Sebastián de Acero. The latter was a legal resident of Lima who had been living in Oruro for many years, and had already had a problem with the preceding interim *corregidor*, Manuel de Herrera, in 1750, on the same subject, that is, the exemption from serving in the town militia because he was not a legal resident.[14]

---

12 "Carta del Corregidor Lerdo de Tejada al Virrey Manso de Velazco," Oruro, January 27, 1749, loc. cit.
13 "Carta de Joseph Infanzón al Virrey Manso de Velazco," Oruro, March 15, 1750, loc. cit.
14 "Escrito presentado por Sebastián de Acero al Virrey Manso de Velazco," Oruro, August 1750, loc. cit.

By municipal law, residents of Oruro who refused to participate in public processions, marching in the corps corresponding to their membership in the city militia, were fined twenty-five pesos and served eight days in jail. This was the penalty Manuel de Herrera meant to impose on Acero in 1750, when the latter declared his right to be exempt. According to his own words, however, his refusal to participate in the public parades of Oruro was based on other issues as well:

> [These marches are] not only arduous, but they defame the men of the city [because] the *corregidor* makes them go out in only one company . . . one composed of mestizos, and Indians, silversmiths, tailors, blacksmiths, and other manual trades among which individuals they require the businessmen march and not only those of the town, but those who have their domicile in Lima . . . doing obvious harm to those who are not from the same social class as men of the country . . . and making them suffer the disgrace of going in the company of base men.[15]

This complaint clearly shows, in addition to the usual pretensions of superiority by a businessman from the capital city, the survival of the professional and social "castes." In addition, the letter expresses concern about racial mixing, due to the inexorable advance of the mestizo population. One can also establish some relation with the already mentioned distance kept between "old Spaniards" – early settlers – and peninsular businessmen who had arrived more recently.

The *corregidor* Manuel de Herrera, when questioned by the viceroy about the incident, answered indignantly that Acero was lying, since the guilds marched separately and the Spaniards were not mixed with the "base" elements. In his opinion, the businessman from Lima only wanted to "make trouble in the town and upset the tranquil peace in which its residents lived."[16] The case went on for months with profuse exchanges of letters between Oruro and Lima after which, apparently, Acero felt fortified in his demand to be exempt.

With the advent of the new *corregidor* Miguel de Landaeta in 1752, however, the topic came up again in the context of a religious procession in honor of Santa Rosa. Miguel de Landaeta organized the event for the whole city, including the time-honored march of the residents, with strict orders for attendance. Sebastián de Acero, as might be predicted, again saw an opportunity to insist on his privileges, and this time two others joined him – perhaps businessmen from the same place – Isidoro Ocaño and Andrés Lianos.

This time the conflict acquired major proportions because, in the middle of the solemn procession, Acero and the *corregidor* had angry words, to the shock of those present.

15 Ibid.
16 "Carta del Corregidor Manuel de Herrera al Virrey Manso de Velazco," Oruro, February 7, 1750, loc. cit.

In a letter to the viceroy, Miguel de Landaeta gave a description of the event according to which Acero, in step with the image of the saint, rebuked him out loud for having ordered him to attend the march on pain of fine and imprisonment. Landaeta reported to the viceroy that, in spite of considering the incident as an unpardonable offense, he decided not to argue with Acero in public because the latter was a protégé of Don Juan Joseph de Helguera, a powerful resident of Oruro. According to his version, they were both conspiring against him with "infamous methods" and he refrained from acting in defense of his honor in order to avoid being accused of "proceeding with passion." Nevertheless, he thought it necessary to begin proceedings against the rebellious businessman, asking the viceroy to support his cause.[17]

Subsequent letters from the *corregidor* to the viceroy with complaints about other conflicts similar to the one started by Acero reveal that his position in the town was weak. Judging by the style of his letters, furthermore, the son of Don Juan lacked his father's diplomatic talent, and seemed susceptible to bellicosity. This lost him the opportunity to capitalize on the internal dissention between the residents, and by the end of his term the opinions of both Herrerists and anti-Herrerists – until that time irreconcilable – were united against him.

After exhausting the viceroy with accusations about his enemies' "sinister reports," intended to "blemish my careful procedures," he concentrated his ire against Joseph de Helguera, "one of the principals who urge on the gangs of disgruntled thugs," who, he said, constantly insulted him and behaved disrespectfully.[18]

Helguera had offended the *corregidor* in full public view, in the presence of the *alcalde ordinario* Joseph de Herrera, the *alférez real* Pedro de Eulate, and the *regidor* Joseph de Imblusqueta. Meeting these men and their families on the main street of Oruro, he had effusively greeted all except Landaeta, before whom he ostentatiously put his hat back on his head, walking slowly past him without saying a word.[19]

The motive for Helguera's anger had an apparently banal basis, although it might have formed part of a long series of reciprocal insults: on a certain occasion, while visiting the *corregidor* at his home at night, the latter received him in his pajamas. Landaeta adduced in his defense that Helguera's visit had been unexpected, and that he had already retired to his bedroom.

On account of the public snub, Landaeta brought suit against Helguera, for which he began to collect testimony from those who had accompanied

---

17 "Carta del Corregidor Miguel de Landaeta al Virrey Manso Velazco," Oruro, September 4, 1752, loc. cit.
18 Ibid., September 9, 1752, loc. cit.
19 Ibid., August 31, 1752, loc. cit.

him that day. Pedro de Eulate and Martín de Espeleta y Villanueva – although the latter was not mentioned earlier as being a member of the party – did not find it improper to support the *corregidor*'s complaint, but the same was not true of Imblusqueta. He stated that he did not want to testify against a man who was one of the wealthiest merchants in town. In response, the *corregidor* fined him 2,000 pesos for contempt, and in this way obtained his reluctant testimony, although the *regidor* nevertheless insisted that the way in which he had been obliged to testify be included in the court record. As for the *alcalde* Juan Joseph de Herrera – son of Don Melchor and brother of the previous *corregidor* – although he signed his name at the bottom of the brief endorsing the testimonies, he also seems to have been pressured by the circumstances into doing so.[20]

The viceroy lost his patience again; his attempt to revive, in the figure of Juan de Landaeta's son, the role of the moderating intermediary played by his father years before, had failed. Now the viceroy found himself obliged to appeal to the services of another official from outside the town, the *oidor* Joseph López Lisperguer, of the Charcas *audiencia*, who went to Oruro around October 1752. At once he assumed the role of arbitrator (*amigable componedor*) in the case Landaeta was trying to bring against Helguera y Palacio. The *oidor* felt that the offenses alleged by the *corregidor* were very difficult to prove; the question of discourtesy was resolved by having Joseph de Helguera make a personal apology to Landaeta.[21]

In spite of this, there was no way to avoid another conflict, in this case between the *corregidor* and the *alcalde* Juan Joseph de Herrera, in the *cabildo* itself. There is no explanation for the motive – perhaps it had to do with the latter's testimony, which Landaeta had extracted practically by force – but there is one for the consequences: Landaeta, in a rage over the turn the discussion had taken, threatened to hit the *alcalde* with his baton. Imblusqueta came between them to prevent bloodshed. The other *alcalde*, Don Manuel de Plantarrosa, informed the *oidor* about the incident so that he would act as arbitrator again; but Landaeta had already appealed to the *audiencia*, modifying his usual routine of informing the viceroy first. Lisperguer achieved a formal reconciliation after arduous negotiations, with the good offices of the Jesuit priest Juan Joseph Ordoñez.[22]

López Lisperguer's letters to the viceroy also became frequent. Their style recalls the relationship between Juan de Landaeta, Father Romero, and the viceroy; like the ideas exchanged in the earlier letters, those of Lisperguer

20 "Autos sobre el desacato cometido por D. Joseph de Helguera contra el corregidor Miguel de Landaeta," Oruro, August 31 and September 1, 1752, loc. cit.
21 "Carta del Oidor Joseph López Lisperguer al Virrey Manso de Velazco," Oruro, December 14, 1752, loc cit.
22 "Carta del Corregidor Miguel de Landaeta al Virrey Manso de Velazco," Oruro, December 28, 1752, loc. cit.

seem prudent and to the point, unlike the subjectivity and blind partiality of the participants in the quarrels. But like Juan de Landaeta and Father Romero, he soon became weary of so much daily struggle and asked to be relieved of his post. This was not granted, however, until the end of 1753.

At the end of 1752, the viceroy began to see that he would again have to have his own choice of men installed at the next election. The *corregidor* Miguel de Landaeta, finding out about this, supported the initiative warmly; but he warned the viceroy about the maneuvering of Herrera's group. According to Landaeta, the old *caudillo* had also found out about the viceroy's intentions – perhaps through leaks from officials of the *audiencia*, among whom he had friends – and this news made him extremely nervous. The Herrerists were known to have a majority in the *cabildo* on this occasion; logically, the decision made in Lima would leave them out of power again since the viceroy would, predictably, choose men uncommitted to either faction.

Following the viceroy's instructions, Pedro García de Eulate[23] and Francisco Santos de Alborta were elected. López Lisperguer informed the viceroy that total tranquility reigned in the town after the elections, although the *corregidor* Landaeta and the merchant Helguera continued at loggerheads over their old argument. Patiently, he had them meet again at his house to order them – this time severely – to forget their hostilities and make up, which they agreed to do.[24]

The year 1753 was punctuated by various complaints and conflicts. The state of relations between the *corregidor* and the residents was no longer amenable to palliatives. The *corregidor* had been prohibited from making his inspection of the mines at Poopó on account of the increasing antagonism of the Herrera family. The *corregidor* finally put Manuel de Herrera in prison, seizing his property and the mills of his father, Don Melchor, which Don Manuel managed. The Herreras appealed to the Charcas *audiencia*, apparently with the consent of the viceroy.[25]

Nevertheless, the situation had come to a head months before, prompted by a noisy confrontation between the *corregidor* and an official of the royal treasury of Oruro, Manuel de Plantarrosa, who had been *alcalde* the previous year. Plantarrosa, who was weighmaster and assayer of the *caja*, had a

---

23 Pedro de Eulate appears for the first time in the office of ordinary *alcalde* in 1739, along with Joseph de Alserreca, and then in 1743 with the son of Don Melchor, Manuel de Herrera. In both instances the *corregidor* was Martín de Espeleta y Villanueva. Therefore, his participation up to that moment had been favorable to Herrera's group. Nevertheless, he is not mentioned in writs and letters as having participated actively in any confrontation, so he should be considered a neutral figure.

24 "Carta del Oidor Joseph L. Lisperguer al Virrey Manso de Velazco," Oruro, March 22, 1753, loc. cit.

25 Ibid., October 8, 1753. Here we observe the higher judicial status of the *corregidor* with respect to the *alcalde*. The latter could imprison a judge in the first instance.

complicated situation at home because his wife's sister – an 18-year-old minor – had run away from home. For reasons that are not clear, in the subsequent judgment brought before the royal *audiencia*,[26] the girl ended up lodging in Miguel de Landaeta's house without the consent of her brother-in-law and guardian. When her return was arranged, Landaeta appeared the next day at Plantarrosa's house, accused him of physically abusing the girl, sentenced him to prison, seized the royal official's property, and arrested other members of his family. Plantarrosa fled to Charcas, deciding to place his defense directly in the hands of the royal *audiencia*, upon which Landaeta pursued him with armed men.[27]

The incident had the mark of scandal; the viceroy entrusted López Lisperguer with the corresponding judgment, after which the *corregidor* was obliged to return Plantarrosa's property to him and was severely reprimanded under pain of immediate removal from office if he again became involved in any more conflicts of this kind.[28] This marked the end of his troubled and unhappy term of office in Oruro.

In October, Miguel de Landaeta sent the viceroy a long letter filled with baroque and in some places confused and incomprehensible passages. He was worried about the rumor circulating in town that if it had not been for the mediation of López Lisperguer, there would have been bloodshed. According to Landaeta, the *oidor*'s sympathies had been swayed by the influence of Don Melchor and his people, whom he had protected in every way. Landaeta finished his letter by asking the viceroy to relieve him of his job in the town, adding that, in his judgment, to struggle against Melchor de Herrera was an impossible undertaking.[29] The viceroy replied caustically, defending the position of the *oidor* who, he said, was only carrying out his orders; he added that he did not need Landaeta's opinions on Oruro, whose situation he understood perfectly.[30]

Undoubtedly, Landaeta's conduct in office is reason enough to avoid taking his opinions too seriously; but one cannot entirely rule out a certain amount of tolerance in López Lisperguer's attitude toward the Herreras, keeping in mind the history of the *real audiencia*'s attitude toward them. In any case, nothing in the *oidor*'s letters reveal any such partiality.

López Lisperguer also asked to be relieved of his duties, but not without first expressing his opinion to the viceroy about his decision to summon old Juan de Landaeta to again take charge, as *corregidor*, of keeping order in

26 *Plantarrosa* v. *Landaeta*, trial of 1753, Archivo Nacional de Bolivia, Sucre, exp. 1753, no. 46.
27 From the papers of the trial it is not clear what funds were used to pay for their services.
28 *Plantarrosa* v. *Landaeta*, loc. cit.
29 "Carta del Corregidor Miguel de Landaeta al Virrey Manso de Velazco," Oruro, October 2, 1753, loc. cit.
30 "Carta del Virrey Manso de Velazco al Corregidor Miguel de Landaeta," Lima, November 28, 1953, loc. cit.

the city. According to the *oidor*, in spite of the irreproachable image the senior Landaeta commanded in all circles, his position would become compromised and awkward; as the father of Don Miguel, he would find it impossible to avoid becoming involved in the consequences of his offspring's disastrous term in office.[31] Nevertheless, the senior Landaeta accepted.

There are, however, no documents relating to his second term, in 1754.[32] Probably he considered this duty a necessary one, more in consideration of his family's honor than in expectation of a normalization of the city.

---

31 "Carta del Oidor Joseph L. Lisperguer al Virrey Manso de Velazco," Oruro, October 8, 1753, loc. cit.

32 See "Lista de cargos, según pago de media anata," loc. cit. (The complete list of offices taxed with the *media anata* were taken between 1730 and 1784).

8

"The fruits of the earth"

The litigious tradition of the residents of Oruro and the notable disorder of their daily lives cannot be comprehended without establishing a few links to their basic economic activity: mining. The social and economic development of mining towns in Spanish America showed peculiarities that distinguished them from other kinds of settlements. In the opinion of two authors,

Characteristic of every mining center . . . is rapid growth after the discovery of the mines, an epoch of splendor and then the slow decline and abandonment of the city when the natural riches that gave rise to its establishment are exhausted. Sometimes the city continues to exist, changing its economic base, and survives through time with a different physiognomy.[1]

Such economic vicissitudes give rise, predictably, to conflicts and irreconcilable confrontations like those described in the preceding chapters, as well as to peculiar strategies of alliance among different groups, some of which will be analyzed in the last part of this book.

In keeping with the local economic activity, one of the most frequently mentioned places in the documents of this period in Oruro – after the *cabildo* and the church – is the *caja real*, or royal treasury. Its importance is easily understood: it was the legally mandatory destination of miners who needed to have their silver cast into ingots.

In fact, not only miners used the services of the *caja*. It was also used by the "*mercaderes de plata*," or silver dealers; in general, anyone who possessed minerals or pieces of silver was eligible to use the *caja*.[2]

This was, however, the final step in an arduous process, the costs of which were not always proportional to the effort required. One part of the process was "amalgamation"; this technique was discovered in Mexico by Bartolomé de Medina in 1555,[3] and was very useful in processing silver from mines with ores containing little silver.

1 Mesa and Guisbert, op. cit., p. 57.
2 "Oruro, manual de décimos," AGN, loc. cit.
3 See Modesto Bargalló, *La amalgamación de los minerales de plata* (Mexico City, Fundidora de Fierro y Acero de Monterrey, 1969), pp. 51, 55.

The *beneficio* by amalgamation – that is, the obtaining of purified metal – required that the mineral first be ground up and then pulverized. Local water mills, locally called *ingenios*, were employed for this purpose, although more primitive methods were frequently used, consisting of simply striking the mineral with a mallet to break it up and pulverize it. Such fine division of the material permitted the more effective action of mercury on the particles while diminishing the amount of silver lost.

The process was long and complicated; after the amalgam was obtained, the remaining mercury was extracted from it by pressing the mixture with a coarse sheet of linen or a leather hide.[4] The silver thus obtained was called *piña*; this was then distilled by heating to eliminate the residual mercury. The silver was cast into ingots.

After this last step, the crown took its share. On the silver pieces a royal tax was imposed called *diezmos* – which was 10 percent of the value of the ingot – followed by another tax called *cobos*, 1.5 percent of the value of the silver after the *diezmo* was deducted. The tax was charged directly to the individual who brought the silver, usually a *piña*, to the royal treasury, where the silver was cast into ingots, a process for which the building was equipped.

The ingots were then assayed; that is, their *ley*, or pure silver content, was established. This determined their value in pesos and thus the tax to be paid. Once the tax was paid, the ingots were stamped to indicate their *ley* officially.

Legislation established that the ingots must be exchanged for money at the *casas de moneda* (money exchanges) in Potosí or Lima, or in the same *cajas reales* where the bars were stamped, since theoretically they had enough currency to affect the exchange – or else exported to Spain within six months of being stamped.[5]

It is easy to see why these regulations were not observed with much enthusiasm. As one who should know, Cañete y Domínguez, the *intendente* of Potosí, remarked, "A taxed and stamped bar is marketable all over the kingdom and is the equivalent of money."[6]

Every individual was obliged to bring any silver that had come into his possession by whatever means to the *cajas reales* in order to pay the corresponding tax. Obviously, part of the silver produced never reached them, and the tax was avoided. A good part of the metal sent to Europe as contraband originated from this untaxed silver.

It is difficult to determine the magnitude of the illegal production of silver, but to some extent it was limited by the royal officials' ability to

4 Bernabé Cobo, *Historia del Nuevo Mundo*, Book 3, chapters 39–40, transcribed by M. Bargalló, op. cit., p. 295.
5 *Recopilación de leyes de Indias*, op. cit., Law 4, Title 13.
6 Cañete y Domínguez, op. cit., p. 148.

calculate the approximate production of silver based on the mercury consumed.[7] This was because mercury – or *azogue* – was controlled by the crown; the government reserved an exclusive monopoly on its trade and allowed it to be purchased only by miners and mill owners. Resale of mercury to private parties was prohibited.[8]

Estimates of the silver obtained per 100 pounds of mercury consumed varied according to the silver content of the ore. Although the calculations were not precise, in Potosí a yield of fifty pounds of silver per 100 pounds of mercury was acceptable, on average. In Oruro, the yield was a little less.[9]

Given the economic importance of the subject, it is understandable that the authorities would try to establish this ratio as accurately as possible. In 1780 a detailed and exhaustive investigation was begun by Jorge Escobedo, one of the new officials who had come from Alto Peru for the administrative reorganization started in the preceding decade.

Cañete y Domínguez, an official with long experience in Potosí, considered it necessary to intensify studies on the question:

This matter, judging by what we have seen, is one of the most uncertain matters in the metallurgy of Potosí. It leads to so much variation in the computation of the ratio and it is not adequate for making an accurate judgment based on what the authors say, nor is it absolutely certain what they add, about getting 150 marks[10] for each *quintal* of *azogue*, which is 100 pounds.

As the assistance of mercury is distributed in the Bank according to the correspondence of the silver that has been exchanged . . . supposing that its only object is to prevent the loss of untaxed silver (*plata sin quintar*) at the source[11]; but it being true that the government economy must take care of the advancement of mining, as a branch of business and an object of its ministry of finance, all these precautions are very just, in order to prevent as much loss as possible, so that this silver will circulate mostly within the State in order to stimulate trade and industry.[12]

---

7 Assessment of the magnitude of activities such as illegal trade or unregistered production of silver is always influenced by the subjectivity of the historian, inasmuch as there is no way to obtain precise measures. For trade, see Sergio Villalobos, *Comercio y contrabando en el Río de la Plata y Chile, 1700–1811* (Buenos Aires, Eudeba, 1965), who stakes out an extreme position in asserting that contraband of all kinds was so intense that the decree of free trade of 1778 had practically no effect on the real volume of goods traded.

   Some functionaries of the period came to believe that the greater proportion of the silver production of Potosí in the decade of the 1780s was exported to foreign markets, where the mark brought up to fourteen pesos instead of the eight paid in Potosí; see John Lynch, *Administración colonial Española* (Buenos Aires, Eudeba, 1962), p. 116.

8 Haring, op. cit., pp. 274 and following.

9 Cañete y Domínguez, op. cit., p. 70.

10 Two marks was the equivalent of one pound.

11 *Quintar* meant "to tax." The usage dates to 1736, when the tax on silver was one-fifth of its value rather than one-tenth, as it later became.

12 Cañete y Domínguez, op. cit., p. 71. In Mexico, the proportions were similar; the average was the same even though in Guanajuato 125 marks of silver were obtained for each *quintal* of mercury. See D. A. Brading, *Miners and Merchants in Bourbon Mexico, 1763–1810* (Cambridge University Press, 1971), p. 141; and Whitaker, op. cit., p. 5. On the other hand, the ore was richer in Mexico; see Tandeter, op. cit., p. 100.

Another way to illegally obtain mercury could have been by theft during its transport. Aware of this, the crown imposed stiff fines on shippers for shortages.

Again, the two sources of mercury for silver production in America were Huancavelica in Peru and Almadén in Spain. Until the middle of the eighteenth century, production in Huancavelica had been sufficient to provide all the mercury necessary for the viceroyalty of Peru. But after this – when production there began a pronounced decline – it became necessary to rely on Spanish mercury.[13]

For the crown, the sale of mercury ensured silver production; in this way, its price was fixed politically, even taking into consideration direct profits from such sales. Between 1774 and 1779, for example, the crown paid 72 pesos per *quintal* of mercury from Huancavelica and sold it for 99 pesos 1 *real* in Potosí. Taking into account that transport between the two cities cost 17 pesos, the total cost per *quintal* was only 89 pesos, leaving a gross profit of 10 pesos 1 *real* – or more than 11 percent.

Considering the costs of administration, control, credit, and so on, it is doubtful that the operation showed a net profit. The following incident illustrates that the government had no particular intent to profit from the sale of mercury: when the *visitador* Areche reached an agreement with a miner of Huancavelica for a monopoly concession on the total production of mercury of that area – under the condition that the product be delivered for 45 pesos per *quintal* – the price of mercury to private buyers was immediately reduced from 70 to 55 pesos.[14] In Potosí, in turn, the price was reduced to 73 pesos 3 *reales*.

The price of mercury varied widely throughout the eighteenth century. From 1774 to 1779, as we have just seen, mercury from Huancavelica was officially sold in Potosí at 99 pesos 1 *real* per *quintal* – at 8 *reales* to the peso.

In 1779 the price was slashed drastically to 73 pesos 3 *reales*. This reduction lasted until January 1783, when it began to rise again, this time to 99 pesos 6 *reales*. This new price lasted until April 1784, when it was reduced to 60 pesos; in June 1787 it was increased slightly to 71 pesos, where it remained stable.[15] In Oruro prices were a little lower: in 1779, for example, the price of a *quintal* of mercury from Huancavelica sold for 97 pesos 10.5 *reales*.[16]

The price of mercury from Almadén differed from that of Huancavelica; sometimes it was higher and sometimes lower. That year it was decided to

---

13 Almadén mercury was partly from the place of the same name, but in part was imported from Idria, Austria.
14 Whitaker, op. cit., p. 60.
15 Cañete y Domínguez, op. cit., pp. 78–80.
16 "Libro real común de la caja de Oruro – 1781," AGN, Buenos Aires, Oruro, Sala XIII-VIII-A6.

standardize the two prices; in 1786 a higher price was assigned to mercury from Idria, Austria, whereas the price of mercury from the other two sources apparently remained stable.[17]

It is helpful to understand the importance of the circulation of mercury in such a mining society. Its acquisition was indispensable for local production; shortages or high cost gave rise to tensions that were difficult to resolve.

Mercury was sold on credit by the *cajas reales* themselves, under terms that varied from six months to a year. It was common practice for the miners to pay when they brought their *piñas* to be cast into bars.

The royal officials, however, tried to shorten the length of the credit arrangements; this was due not only to financial economy, but also to their goal of preventing as far as possible the resale of the mercury, which in principle could be sold only to miners and mill owners.

This obligation was explicitly incorporated in the ordinances of the *Banco de Rescates* in Potosí.[18] Commenting on this regulation, Cañete says:

> If this precaution were not observed, and mercury were sold to anyone, without examining how it would be used, it would ensue that buying it from the *caja* for 60 pesos per *quintal* . . . it would then be sold in the marketplace on credit[19] to miners from elsewhere for at least 50 percent more and not infrequently for 100 percent more, contravening the laws that prohibit trading in government monopoly products and furthermore hurting the miner by doubling the price of this material, since he would have to pay to another person money he might otherwise have used to extract and process more silver.[20]

Mercury was sold solely to miners and mill owners in Oruro, as well.[21] Credit was extended for a maximum of one year. An examination of the mercury books reveals that the majority of buyers paid their loans back within ten or eleven months. Before 1770 – when the fiscal year went from May 1 to April 30 – purchases made at the beginning of the period were usually paid in March or April of the following year.[22] After 1770 the dates of purchase and payment were transferred respectively to January and November or December. One more proof of the difficulties of mining after this date, when unfavorable conditions totally altered the conditions of payment, is the list from 1781: it shows that many individuals owed the *caja* of Oruro sums that in some cases went back four years.[23] This situ-

17 Cañete y Domínguez, op. cit., p. 108. See also Chapter 4, note 5.
18 Ibid., p. 146.
19 In Spanish: en calidad de avíos.
20 Cañete y Domínguez, op. cit., p. 146.
21 Mercury purchase transactions by miners and mercury dealers were recorded in the account book titled *Manual de azogues*, where credit sales (wholesale) were distinguished from cash (retail) sales. This is highly useful data, for these books contain the names of the principle miners in their capacity as mercury users.
22 See for example the *Manual de azogues* for the fiscal year 1767–8, AGN, Buenos Aires, Sala XIII-VIII-6-3.
23 AGI (Seville), Audiencia de Charcas, legajo 64.

ation affected more than a few miners; in the report corresponding to that year, the treasurer and the accountant of the *caja real* established that of the 120,000 pesos that should have been collected for mercury sales, only 25,000 had been paid.[24]

These arrears might be explained in part by the rebellions that took place early in the year. Nevertheless, sorting the debts by age, it becomes immediately apparent that more than 80 percent – approximately 78,000 pesos – were for purchases made at least two years before, which obviates any link with the uprising.

Silver production in Oruro shows pronounced differences from that in Potosí. The first and most important of these was the lack of forced labor – that is, *mita* – in Oruro.

The *mita*, which revived an ancient form of labor practiced in the time of the Incas, provided Indian labor at low prices for the mines at Potosí.

The royal code obliged every Indian who lived in a specified region to do his *mita* service in Potosí once every seven years. The geographic area covered for this service was very large, extending from Cuzco in the north to Tarija in the south. Indians from regions adjacent to Cuzco had to travel more than a thousand kilometers to comply with the obligation.[25]

Some writers have concluded that, from a technological point of view, the *mita* was pernicious. It inhibited the emergence of labor-saving procedures, perpetuating the existence of production alternatives that artificially depressed labor costs. As a result, mining entrepreneurs did not adapt to their real costs, as represented by the cost of labor on the free market.[26]

In Oruro, by contrast, labor was paid on the basis of a free market. Of course, mining entrepreneurs in the area tried to bring the benefits of the *mita* to their province – as noted in Chapter 1 – but in vain. Their main obstacle was the opposition of the Potosí miners, who feared that this would increase their own costs because they would have had fewer *mita* workers. Later, however, they centered their complaints around the higher salaries offered in Oruro, arguing that this enticed their workers to move there.[27]

The difference in labor costs did not, however, translate into an interest in new labor-saving techniques. This is revealed in a 1791 study by Zacharias

24 In round figures, without *reales*. See "Libro real común de la caja de Oruro," AGN, loc. cit.

25 Manuel de Amat y Junyent, *Memoria de gobierno* (Seville, Escuela de Estudios Hispanoamericanos), p. 264. See also Tandeter, op. cit., and Ann Zulawski, "Wages, Ore Sharing and Peasant Agriculture: Labor in Oruro's Silver Mines, 1607–1720," *Hispanic American Historical Review*, 67, no. 3 (1987), 405–30. Tandeter holds, on the basis of his detailed study, that the Postosí mining industry depended mainly on the *mita*. Zulawski cites divergent opinions.

26 D. A. Brading, "Las minas de plata en el Perú y México colonial: un estudio comparativo," *Desarrollo Económico*, 2, no. 41 (April–June 1970), 101–12.

27 See Marcos Bertrán Avila, *Capítulos de la historia colonial de Oruro* (La Paz, 1925), p. 35. Remuneration of workers in Oruro was higher than in Potosí. A pick miner earned between eight and twelve pesos weekly in Oruro, but in Potosí around seven pesos (in the case of free workers; *mita* workers earned only three pesos weekly). See also Tandeter, op. cit.

Helms, a German specialist sent by the Spanish crown to improve production technology in the principal mining centers of Peru and Alto Peru. Helms concluded that the Oruro mines were richer than those of Potosí, which perhaps explains their capacity to produce silver without the help of the *mita*. Nevertheless, that year, in spite of its potential, Oruro not only failed to exhibit outstanding production efficiency, but had fallen into an irreversible downward slide.[28]

Another feature that merits analysis is the marked difference in the trend of silver production between Potosí and Oruro during the eighteenth century.[29]

The comparative trend of silver production in both cities is shown in Figure and Table 8.1.[30] Until the mid-1740s, production in both centers was maintained at constant levels. In Potosí, during the first part of the century production never exceeded two million pesos annually. In the mid-forties, however, the trend took an upward curve, and each year surpassed the previous one, beginning in 1750.

The rise in production did not stop there, but passed the three-million-peso mark in 1776. After this date, the figures reached a plateau on a slightly higher average: between 1776 and 1800 it stayed at approximately 3,164,552 standard pesos of eight *reales*.

After the middle of the century, Potosí showed clear signs of sustained vigor; while it was not restored to its former splendor, it was able to double its production between the first and second halves of the century.

Oruro also experienced renewed vigor during the same periods; but the recovery of production was neither as spectacular nor as sustained as in Potosí.

In Oruro, production from 1700 to 1746 averaged 660,000 pesos annually. From 1746 to 1778 it increased to an average of about 970,000 pesos a year, an improvement of about 50 percent.

Oruro's higher average in the second half of the century indicates a more important difference, however: whereas Potosí continued to grow uninterrupted until the end of the 1770s, then maintained the high levels it had reached, Oruro reversed its trend in 1761, beginning a moderate and oscillatory slide that became steeper in 1779 and 1780, then dropped abruptly

28 Anton Zacharias Helms, *Tagebuch einer Reise durch Peru* (Dresden, 1789), p. 126. On production techniques, see Rose Marie Buchler, "Technical Aid to Upper Peru: The Nordenflicht Expedition," *Journal of Latin American Studies*, 5, no. 1 (1953), 37–77.

29 See the comparative listing, pp. 285–6.

30 The following sources were used for the compilation of these series: Brading, "Las minas," 101–11; Brading and Harry Cross, "Colonial Silver Mining: Mexico and Peru," *Hispanic American Historical Review*, 52 (1972), 568–9; "Libro real manual de décimos de esta real caja de Oruro," AGN, Buenos Aires, Sala XIII, c. VIII, no. 3; Peter Bakewell, "Registered Silver Production in the Potosí District, 1550–1735," *Jahrbuch fuer Geschichte von Staat, Wirtschaft und Gesellschaft Lateinamerikas*, 12 (1975), 67–103.

Table 8.1. *Potosí and Oruro: Comparative silver production from 1700 to 1800 (in regular pesos of eight reales)*

Year	Oruro	Potosí	Year	Oruro	Potosí
1700	593,633	1,912,698	1742	767,736	1,427,101
1701	484,332	1,597,037	1743	679,418	1,463,709
1702	586,372	1,756,825	1744	698,502	1,373,797
1703	658,567	1,698,650	1745	794,176	1,437,356
1704	644,099	1,574,066	1746	880,053	1,568,896
1705	NA	1,505,962	1747	872,608	1,622,519
1706	745,332	1,672,641	1748	1,019,533	1,735,876
1707	628,712	1,718,938	1749	1,009,339	1,896,766
1708	NA	1,765,014	1750	1,090,564	2,058,828
1709	963,335	1,575,849	1751	NA	2,101.365
1710	823,243	1,457,584	1752	847,691	2,001,171
1711	709,842	1,161,070	1753	754,431	2,157,603
1712	620,898	966,655	1754	811,215	2,151,083
1713	541,247	1,320,344	1755	971,242	1,954,819
1714	408,997	1,250,410	1756	901,621	2,198,352
1715	406,375	1,076,528	1757	1,020,405	2,156,475
1716	181,243	1,128,712	1758	1,105,559	2,315,726
1717	858,903	1,683,037	1759	1,056,801	2,323,356
1718	1,303,002	1,520,051	1760	884,881	2,396,995
1719	1,004,748	1,337,702	1761	1,230,105	2,304,669
1720	442,846	1,515,358	1762	1,056,537	2,266,088
1721	470,395	1,080,198	1763	1,011,770	2,463,788
1722	815,395	1,076,452	1764	869,524	2,317,991
1723	505,219	1,012,924	1765	858,678	2,484,449
1724	585,034	1,159,400	1766	808,801	2,488,149
1725	608,297	1,052,278	1767	889,903	2,675,330
1726	653,446	1,294,415	1768	1,011,277	2,701,973
1727	731,261	1,350,603	1769	895,268	2,564,537
1728	665,518	1,041,028	1770	1,022,149	2,574,475
1729	612,718	1,700,080	1771	1,034,317	2,711,585
1730	589,610	1,430,948	1772	1,061,559	2,634,211
1731	541,908	1,384,419	1773	979,806	2,704,185
1732	461,735	1,453,476	1774	906,167	2,799,145
1733	NA	1,437,537	1775	1,051,806	2,928,008
1734	545,745	3,646,622	1776	886,581	3,051,268
1735	588,476	1,281,183	1777	959,788	3,442,079
1736	330,085	705,504	1778	1,005,118	3,101,268
1737	702,300	1,618,537	1779	811,031	3,066,387
1738	806,009	1,403,101	1780	763,093	3,524,775
1739	955,471	1,614,933	1781	231,428	2,846,775
1740	NA	1,499,814	1782	300,758	3,085,453
1741	937,163	1,582,140	1783	314,440	3,526,325

Table 8.1. (cont.)

Year	Oruro	Potosí	Year	Oruro	Potosí
1784	227,568	3,271,911	1793	NA	3,270,881
1785	228,079	3,099,356	1794	567,225	3,322,731
1786	356,402	2,929,577	1795	513,727	2,916,378
1787	401,013	3,443,488	1796	554,899	3,262,519
1788	649,383	3,353,303	1797	514,194	3,147,268
1789	415,797	2,955,665	1798	NA	2,411,233
1790	476,255	3,170,044	1799	NA	3,164,132
1791	605,110	3,255,189	1800	NA	3,161,515
1792	725,322	3,334,290			

in 1781, the year of the Indian uprisings. Given the desolation and destruction, the meager numbers should come as no surprise.

They do, however, call attention to the area's feeble capacity for recuperation throughout the rest of the century. This suggests that silver production in Oruro had been sustained on such a flimsy base that war presented an insurmountable obstacle to subsequent production growth, even long after peace had returned to the vicinity.

Another interesting difference between Oruro and Potosí concerned financing arrangements.

In Potosí there was a cooperative mining bank for quite a long time, the *Banco de Rescates de Platas* (Silver Exchange Bank), that, after a succession of owners, became the property of the crown. In Oruro, on the other hand, the financing of mineral production was mostly handled by the so-called *mercaderes de plata* – private financiers – as shown in more detail in this section.

The history of the Potosí *Banco de Rescates* is long and full of vicissitudes. It dates to 1747, when it was founded by the league of miners, who wanted to eliminate at least part of the financial role of the *mercaderes de plata*.[31]

According to the official account of its founding,

In his role as official inspector of the *caxas reales*, Don Joseph Hervoso, Minister of the *tribunal de cuentas* in Lima, promoted the formation of a company between the *azogueros* or individuals who were then working the mines and mills of that celebrated source, and all meeting together on January 12 of 1747, they executed a contract obliging themselves, in order to collect funds, to deposit two *reales* and three *quartillos* per mark of the price paid to them in silver *piñas* by the *mercaderes* who engaged in this negotiation.

The purpose was to supply mercury, iron, wood, and other materials necessary to the work and subsistence of mines and mills, at reasonable prices.[32]

31 *Real cédula de incorporación del Banco de Potosí a la real hacienda* (Madrid, Benito Cano, 1795), pp. 1, 6.
32 Ibid., p. 1.

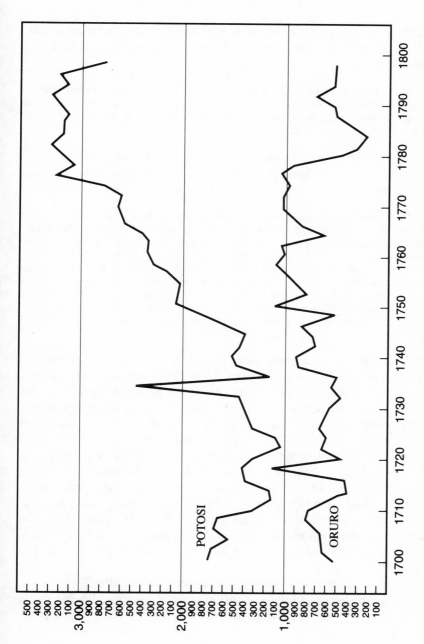

Figure 8.1. Comparative silver production in Potosí and Oruro, 1700–1800 (in thousands; standard pesos of 8 *reales*)

Others writing near the end of the eighteenth century were more categorical about eliminating private financiers. According to Cañete y Domínguez,

The miners of this riverbank, thinking about the convenience of profiting themselves from the services provided by the silver financiers, tried to establish a company with whose funds they could foment mining and support the necessary supply of mercury, copper, iron, leather, wood and tallow for running the mines and mills.[33]

Four years after opening, the bank declared bankruptcy. The governor of Potosí, Ventura de Santelices, attempted to reestablish it with similar objectives:

Since by this time the private financiers in the negotiation and purchase of silver *piñas* had also ceased operating, that zealous Minister [Santelices] proposed that the guild itself organize and form a bank in which it would continue the discount of two *reales* and three *quartillos* in currency in order to amass and deposit funds that, later divided into shares, would make equal participants of all those interested in the great services and earnings that would necessarily result . . . and this proposal approved by all on January 8 1752, it was later confirmed by the royal decree of June 12 of the same year; and in the ten years until 1762, its gains and good management were well accredited, as according to the inventory taken in January of said year, Santelices passed on to his successor in capital and other liquid assets 704,342 pesos and 2 *reales*.[34]

This reveals two interesting facts: first, that in four years the bank had made the private financiers disappear from the marketplace; and second, that the new institution was able to restructure in its previous form, that is, as a cooperative composed of the mine owners themselves. It is nevertheless worth noting that the management operations of the bank always fell under the jurisdiction of the governor of Potosí.

After this second attempt, the enterprise was successful, and its first ten years ended with an abundant surplus. However, this promising new beginning could not be sustained; the shift of the city government from Santelices to San Just brought on the bank's second bankruptcy in 1767. Because of this and similar incompetence, San Just was replaced by Pedro de Tagle, who with enthusiasm and diligence managed to put the bank into operation again around 1770, at the same time establishing a formal code of operations in writing.

The governors who succeeded Tagle in Potosí were as effective as he was in running the bank, and the institution's capital grew steadily from then on. In 1773, for example, it had capital of 778,272 pesos 4.5 *reales*; four years later, when Escobedo took charge of the city government, this had grown to 915,461 pesos 5 *reales*.

33 Cañete y Domínguez, op. cit., p. 137.
34 *Real cédula de incorporación*, p. 1.

In 1779, at Escobedo's initiative, the miners' guild ceded ownership of the bank to the crown, and it became part of the *real hacienda* known as the Royal Bank of San Carlos.[35]

The effective functioning of the bank was extremely important to the mining industry in Potosí from several points of view.

First, it allowed a variety of sizes of mining operations to exist. The large mine owner and the small independent miner obtained the same price at the bank when they brought their silver, as price did not depend on quantity. The officially regulated price was 7 pesos 4 *reales* per silver mark of 11 *dineros* 22 grains of silver content, or *ley*.

This situation was possible only because the bank assayed the silver content of the *piña* by sight. When the assay was made by casting the *piña*, the quantity had to be sufficient to produce a bar of about 180 marks in weight, equivalent to 1,550 pesos 4 *reales* at standard pesos of 8 *reales*. This meant that in the *cajas*, where the assay was done only by casting the silver (as in Oruro), small producers who brought silver in lower quantities – sometimes less than one mark in weight – were excluded.

The Bank of San Carlos of Potosí also took charge of the royal tax – 10 percent plus 1.5 percent – and the costs of casting the *piñas* into silver ingots.

Comparing the prices received by a large producer weighing the alternative of cashing in his silver at the bank or bringing it directly to the *caja real*, the advantage of the latter option was less than 1.5 percent. In addition, doing business with the bank gave him the right to obtain credit, both for fixed capital and for labor.[36] The banking code limited the quantity of a loan to 50,000 pesos, which had to be paid off in cash or in materials such as iron.

As for the financing of mercury, there was no difference from other places where it was used. Real guarantees such as mortgages were required for credit. The associations of miners did this frequently with individuals able to put up the necessary collateral.

The terms of payment for mercury were also similar to those of the other banks: one year, in weekly payments beginning 180 days after the initial date of the loan. In the case of the Potosí bank, Ordinance Number 13 spelled it out precisely:

It must be paid in one year, weekly, beginning payments with the first weekly installment at the beginning of the month of July: so that what each one owes will be paid back to the Bank by the first installment date of the same month in the following year, and while the *azogueros* have a six-month grace period, which is more convenient for them, the Bank also will have [the funds] with which to continue the same aid the following year.[37]

35 Ibid., p. 6.
36 Cañete y Domínguez, op. cit., p. 137.
37 *Real cédula de incorporación*. Bear in mind that loans were approved in January of every year.

In sum, in the operations of the Potosí bank two principal differences can be distinguished: first, it gave cash in silver to the miners for the *piñas* of metal they brought to cash in, regardless of the quantity. In addition, it extended credit for the purchase of equipment and tools as well as for mercury.

The merging of these two operations considerably reduced the role of private financiers (called *aviadores*, or silver traders, in the language of the times) in mining activity. That is, even with the difficulties arising from obtaining collateral for credit linked to mercury, the Potosí system was favorable to the small producers, as is shown by the large and growing number of small operators who came to exchange their production at the bank.[38]

In Oruro the situation was different, as has been mentioned. There was no bank of this type, and the *mercaderes de plata* played a prominent role in the silver business. As in Potosí, mercury was sold on credit; but in contrast, payment was not practical for small producers, except with cash.

The difficulties did not come so much from the need for adequate collateral, which in general the producer could satisfy with property (conditions no different from those in Potosí), but because the volume of silver a small Oruran producer brought to the *caja* often was not enough to produce an ingot.

The usual procedure was for the large producer to pay for the mercury when he brought in his *piñas*: after the ingots were cast, he paid what he owed for the mercury and the taxes (*diezmos* and *cobos*). The producer had the choice of paying in ingots, if the volume justified it, or of changing them for minted coins, with which he could make payments smaller than the value of an ingot.[39] Payment could be made only if one brought enough silver in *piñas* to produce at least one ingot.[40] There was no assaying by sight as in Potosí, and therefore it was impossible to cash in less than one bar of ore. All these limitations obliged the small producer in Oruro to obtain cash by selling his *piñas* to the financiers, or, perhaps, to a larger producer.

The Orurans never managed to overcome these limitations. In an 1808 report sent to Viceroy Liniers, for example, the ministers of the *caja real* of Oruro indicated that the topic continued to provoke the same irritation as in the previous epoch: "If the miner postpones [cashing in] his silver until

---

38 See, for example, *Libro diario y manual en que constan todas las compras y ventas verificadas en este Banco de Rescates de Platas de la villa de Potosí*, AGN, Buenos Aires, Potosí, legajo 26, Libro 4, Sala XIII-6-5-3.

39 The ordinances stipulated that the ingots weigh between 130 and 200 marks (1 mark = one-half pound). Usually, the bars registered in the books weighed more than 150 marks.

40 The account books that recorded the mercury trade confirm that credit was granted only to the biggest buyers. Even though the form of payment is not recorded in either the *Manual de azogues* or the *Libro real tesorero*, this can be inferred from the table of arrears. In no case are payments from small purchasers in arrears; the opposite is true of the larger ones.

he accumulates the amount needed to cast a bar, he would not find anyone to pay him for his ongoing needs, to trust him for mercury, coca, iron, money, and everything else."[41]

The documentation shows that the Oruro *caja* was far from being a convenient and fast place to cash in silver. It often lacked enough cash in coin to reimburse miners for the bars of cast silver, although this was in fact a relative thing: miners who enjoyed the good will of the official at the *caja* could make the exchange more easily than those who did not, who often had to wait.

The situation lent itself to high-handedness and corruption, and the corresponding protests accumulated in a number of documents. Even in 1808, the *cabildo* was still protesting about such questions to the viceroy:

In the mining district of Oruro where there is no exchange bank established, we completely lack a basis for financing; the miners suffer from incalculable delays, harm, and vexation because of the shortage of ready cash for the obligations and preparations imperative every week, since at the time of casting their bars at the *real callana* they find most of the time that the treasury is [too] exhausted to take them in their total legitimate import, and principally because the ministers look with too much indifference on the progress of mining, and manage arbitrarily, according to their inclinations, the taking of bars from any miner and the disgraceful turning away of the rest with the decisive unquestionable excuse that there is no money in the safe.[42]

For the rest of the materials necessary to produce silver, all financing was private. In this case, both large and small miners had to turn to the silver financiers. This implied financing costs considerably higher than those in Potosí. For an industry as risky as silver extraction, the presence of high financing costs left little margin for absorbing sudden drops in the silver content of the ores.

As shown in Table 8.1, after 1761 a decline began that, except for a brief recovery around 1770, continued inexorably for the rest of the century. This reflected the exhaustion of the richest lodes, the failure to find new ones, and the failure to introduce new technologies that might have compensated for these factors.[43] In the texts of the epoch it is reported that the last important discoveries took place before 1740.

The decrease in silver content of the ore combined with the absence of cheap credit strongly affected the financial power of individuals.

41 Letter from José Posadas Rubin and Joseph Gareson y Mesa, ministers of the *caja real* of Oruro, to Viceroy Liniers, November 19, 1808, in "Autos obrados con motivo de la representación que hizo el Cabildo de Oruro pidiendo para el fomento de la minería en esa jurisdicción, que las barras de plata se compren en las Reales Cajas de ella, al mismo precio que la Casa de la Moneda de Potosí," ANB, Sucre, Audiencia de Charcas, Expedientes de Minas, Tomo 91, doc. 749, fol. 24v.
42 Ibid.
43 In Mexico, on the contrary, there had occurred an intense technological change that permitted a marked increase in silver production. See Brading, *Las minas de plata*, op. cit.

An examination of the occupations of those who brought their *piñas* to be cast at the *caja real* reveals interesting data. Keeping in mind that the production cycle of silver ended with the casting, the percentage of mine owners who cast their production directly gives us an idea of the level of intervention by financiers in the operation. When the miners could not afford the full process, they found themselves with a choice of taking on more debts or selling their production to the silver traders, who then finished the process at the *caja real*.

The percentages of both types, for selected years, are as follows:

The figures in Table 8.2 permit us to appreciate the predominant trend in Oruro.[44] While in the 1750s more than 70 percent of the individuals who brought *piñas* to be cast at the *caja* were owners, after 1775 the percentage dropped abruptly to 20 percent, and in 1780 had reached a meager 6 percent.

In other words, in the three decades from 1750 to 1780, the silver traders replaced the mine owners in the commercialization of the metal.

This was clearly due to the financial difficulties of the mining entrepreneurs. With the rising costs of production – due to a progressive decrease in the silver content of the ore and to the greater depth of the excavations and consequent flooding – they had to turn to financial support in order to bring the production cycle to its final phase.

Because there was no discovery in Oruro of new and richer lodes that would have increased profits and improved the liquidity of the mining establishment, debts continued to grow along with the progressive involvement of the silver traders in the production process.[45]

This change had its problems. The miners' irritation grew in the face of a situation that they saw as highly prejudicial to their interests; nevertheless, the situation persisted with the same features through the succeeding decades, as many documents near the time of independence reveal. In the documents of 1808 the *cabildo* described to Viceroy Liniers what it considered the plundering of the miners by officials and traders:

It is enough to insinuate to V.E. that some miners have been seen with one or two bars in their house with not enough to hire a peon or buy daily food without begging for a short-term favor, or more ordinarily in such straits without sacrificing the intrinsic value of their *piñas* and bars, selling them at the deflated price that the scourge of traders call commerce, who are very quiet at the sight of this wealth on the counter at the cost of the noble exercise of mining. Even the miners themselves and the affluent exchangers find it necessary

44 "Libro real común de la caja de Oruro," AGN, loc. cit.
45 Long-term financing that would have permitted works of greater scope, like the opening of passages to reduce the costs of exploitation or to find veins of higher quality, was notoriously lacking in both Peru and Alto Peru. In Mexico, by contrast, capital was available for this kind of investment. On this last topic, see Brading, *Miners and Merchants*, op. cit. For Peru, see John Fisher, "Silver Production on the Viceroyalty of Peru, 1776–1824," *Hispanic American Historical Review*, 35 (1975), 25–43.

Table 8.2. *Occupation of individuals who brought*
piñas *to be cast to the* caja *of Oruro (by percent)*

Year	Mine owners	Silver traders	Others
1751	63.5	36.5	
1753	87.0	13.0	
1757	77.0	33.0	
1761	74.0	26.0	
1765	72.0	27.7	0.3
1767	56.8	41.6	1.6
1770	47.0	53.0	
1771	38.0	62.0	
1773	40.0	60.0	
1775	24.0	74.0	2.0
1777	22.6	77.4	
1778	21.0	79.0	
1779	18.0	82.0	
1780	6.0	92.0	2.0

to pay for porters and baggage to carry the bars to the *real casa de moneda* in Potosí, waiting anxiously for their punctual return in order to continue the production cycle of their operations.

And, further on:

The bar is a large coin authorized by the sovereign through the act whereby it is imprinted with the royal seal with its *ley* and weight; it being intolerable that its precious intrinsic value should suffer more or less the unfortunate eventual fate of the royal vouchers [*vales reales*], diminishing in the hands of the exchangers and usurers who have the cash that they continually cultivate in the royal treasury, in order to impose on the hardworking miner the necessity of accepting the low price of the trade.[46]

The solution proposed by the *cabildo* was to have more cash in the *caja real*, so the miners could cash in their bars without delay.

[The required solution is] for this higher government and subdelegated general superintendent to expedite the most executive providence providing the ministers of the foreign *caxa real* of Oruro for the regular conduct of the *gobierno intendencia* of La Plata that in advance without waiting, delay or arrears, and without room for the smallest motive of prejudice and complaint they take in purchase from the miners all the bars that are cast in the *real callana* itself at the price and current style of the *Real Casa de Moneda de Potosí* [Royal Mint of Potosí], taking them without predilection according to the order of their numbers as long as the cash in the treasury lasts.[47]

46 "El cabildo de Oruro al Virrey Liniers . . . ," op. cit.
47 Ibid.

The ministers, however, thought the *cabildo*'s proposal puerile; they felt that a *banco de rescates* ought to be established in Oruro, in the style of the one in Potosí.[48] This might indicate that the ministers were sympathetic to the smaller miners – who would be favored by a *banco de rescates* – or that they were in favor of the middlemen, and their proposal to create a bank was a dilatory tactic, given the predictably slow course a decision of this kind would take.

In either case, those principally affected by this suffocating dependency were the large miners. As the cost of production increased, their profit margin dropped, and there was a greater need for financing, or for cashing in the silver in advance and at a discount.

This displacement of miners by *mercaderes de plata* in the *caja* of Oruro was accompanied by an increase in the concentration of the mining sector itself; that is to say, fewer and fewer miners brought *piñas* to the *caja*. Silver production was concentrated in the hands of a few mine owners, at least after 1750.

In 1751, the three largest miners accounted for 60 percent of the silver cast at the *caja* by mine owners. The figures, in several important years, are shown in Table 8.3.[49]

To sum up, from 1750 to 1780, small miners were pushed out of business by larger ones, who in turn were displaced by traders. Presumably large miners had more financial resources than those with smaller volumes, and could continue to operate longer without having to borrow from the *mercaderes de plata*.

Among the names most often mentioned in silver production was that of the Herrera family. One of the oldest families in Oruro, in the 1750s and 1760s some of its members brought silver to be cast at the *cajas*. After 1771, by contrast, the name no longer appears in the records of casting, although it does in those of mercury purchases.

However, the owners of mines with the oldest records are the Rodríguez family. Their name appears linked to the history of the city from its founding, and they were the most important miners during the three decades immediately preceding the rebellion of 1781.

In 1765, the Rodríguez family cast bars with a value of 400,000 standard pesos, which represented 40 percent of the total production of Oruro. Until 1776, the annual volume they brought to be cast at the *cajas reales* remained at about 300,000 pesos. From then on the drop was steep: 82,000 in 1777, 45,000 in 1778, 95,000 in 1779, and only 3,000 in 1780.

The family's decline did not stop there: in 1782 its members were imprisoned, accused of having conspired against the crown during the rebel-

48 Ibid.
49 "Libro real común de la caja de Oruro," AGN, loc. cit.

Table 8.3. *The three largest miners' share of the silver cast in the* caja

Year	Percent of total
1751	59
1753	56
1756	41.7
1764	79
1766	66
1773	82
1777	89
1778	87
1779	100
1780	97

lions. The same fate befell a descendant of the Herreras who was allied with the Rodríguez family.

The last chapters of the book will narrate the vicissitudes of these and other miners during the crucial months of the Indian attack on the town of Oruro in 1781. By this time, what had once been a proud competitor of Potosí and the second-most-important urban center in the *audiencia* of Charcas had bidden farewell to its rich mining past.

9

The end of an epoch:
the Indian uprisings of 1780–1781

The forty-one years of Oruran history from 1740 to 1781 culminated with one of the most tragic and violent chapters in the life of colonial Spanish America: the great rebellion led by Tupac Amaru (José Gabriel Condorcanqui).

The bloody events that occurred in Oruro in February, March, and April 1781 were, in fact, a regional occurrence within the context of the great uprisings that spread from the south of present-day Peru to the north of what is now Argentina from the middle of 1780 to the middle of 1782.

In fact, throughout the century there had been frequent conflicts and mutinies against the officers of the crown, especially against the *corregidores*. In 1730, for example, there was a rebellion in Cochabamba.[1] In the same year, Velar de Córdoba headed the previously mentioned uprising of Oruro, which in one way marked the division of the factions of subsequent years; similar movements occurred in 1742 in Tarma and Jauja, led by Juan Santos Atahualpa.[2] In 1750 the *corregidor* of Huarochiri was murdered; in 1776 the same fate befell Jerónimo Sagasti, *corregidor* of the province of Chumbivilcas.

These movements were not always repressed with violence. At times the authorities even yielded to demands for lower taxes.[3]

Thus, by 1780 the colonial officials were already familiar with local mutinies and uprisings.

Nevertheless, those of 1780–1 were exceptional for their brutality on both the Spanish and the Indian sides. In the latter case, there was a striking contrast between their conduct in periods of peace – when their submission and tolerance for abuse was at times difficult to comprehend – and the

---

1 The list of rebellions is long. Starting in 1700, the curve reaches one peak in 1730. Thereafter it declines, starting to rise again in 1740, more slowly at first, then accelerating until the peak of the 1780s. See the graphs and tables presented by Scarlett O'Phelan Godoy, *Un siglo de rebeliones anticoloniales* (Cuzco, Centro Bartolomé de las Casas, 1988), pp. 296–307.

2 Frederick B. Pike, "Religion, Collectivism and Intrahistory: The Peruvian Ideal of Dependence," *Journal of Latin American Studies*, 10 (1978), 239–62.

3 Mendiburu, *Diccionario*, vol. 2, p. 46.

violence with which they responded to the call to rebellion made by their leaders. From an inability to protect even their smallest rights they passed, with surprising ease, to the organization of active centers of rebellion, throwing themselves into pillage and savagery previously unthinkable.

Although precise statistics are lacking, we know that the casualties in the rebellions of 1780 were very high on both sides. In La Paz alone, according to the diary of Sebastián de Segurola, it appears that the siege cost the lives of a third of the city's population, which was around 20,000 at the time.[4]

The casualties suffered by the indigenous population and the rebels were doubtless higher than those on the side loyal to the crown, and probably amounted to between 100,000 and 140,000. On the loyalist side an accurate estimate would be in the tens of thousands.[5]

In addition to the loss of human life, the uprisings had major economic repercussions. Not only were all kinds of property destroyed, and the land devastated in the areas where the fighting took place; but to this must be added the enormous expenses of defense, which reached about 2.65 million pesos, a figure that exceeded the annual revenues of the viceroyalty of Peru.[6] Moreover, resources were lost in the affected areas.

The extent of the uprisings was considerable. The first began on November 4 in the province of Tinta, under the direct leadership of Tupac Amaru (José Gabriel Condorcanqui). During the year there were also disturbances in other localities, including Arequipa (ninety leagues from Cuzco) Moquegua, Huancavelica, Huaras, Pasco, and La Plata. It is not clear whether these uprisings were part of the same network of interests and loyalties that clustered around Tupac Amaru.[7] Other insurgent movements, however, such as those of Chayanta, La Paz, Challapata, Oruro, and Sorata, showed clear signs of similarity to the November 4 insurrection.

4 Sebastián de Segurola, "Diario de los sucesos del cerco de La Paz," in Vicente Ballivián y Roxas, ed., *Archivo boliviano: colección de documentos relativos a la historia de Bolivia en la época colonial*, vol. 1 (Paris, A. Franck, 1872).
5 Rafael J. Sahuaraura Titu Atauchi, *Estado del Perú, año de 1784*, Francisco A. Loayza, ed. (Lima, 1944), p. 14. This author calculates about a hundred thousand Indians killed, while David Forbes, *The Aymara Indians* (London, Taylor & Francis, 1870), p. 6, estimates some forty thousand Spaniards killed. M. Hernández Sánchez Barba estimates that at the end of the eighteenth century the total population of the present-day republics of Peru and Bolivia was approximately 2.2 million; "La sociedad colonial americana en el siglo XVIII," in J. Vicens Vives, ed., *Historia de España y América*, vol. 4 (Barcelona, 1961), p. 339.
6 Guillermo Céspedes del Castillo, "Lima y Buenos Aires: Repercusiones económicas y políticas de la creación del virreinato del Río de la Plata," *Anuario de Estudios Americanos*, 3 (1946), 743–4, 818. This author estimates that the receipts for the period 1773–6 were 10,186,713 pesos (of eight *reales*).
7 O'Phelan Godoy, op. cit., p. 274, points out that among the indigenous population, those who devoted themselves to various forms of commerce were greatly affected by the increase in taxes introduced by the Bourbon reforms. I reached a similar conclusion in my work, "Levantamiento de masas en Perú y Bolivia," op. cit.

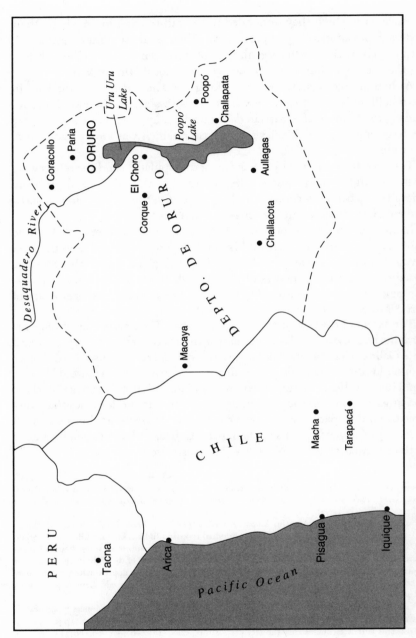

Map 3. Regions in upheaval during the Oruro uprisings

What were the most important factors contributing to the resentment and ire of the indigenous community? According to the testimony of the Indians themselves in subsequent court cases, the *mita* and the *reparto* were a constant source of conflict, as were the attempts to register migrant Indians temporarily established on the outskirts of towns and cities. Other factors less easily classified must also be added, as will be seen in the later analysis of the declarations of the Indians who were subjected to legal proceedings.[8]

In mining zones like Oruro – even though the *mita* was not present there – the deterioration of the social and economic situation of the Indians was linked to the decline of mining itself; judging from the documentation available, the indigenous peoples of the Oruro area grew desperate in the years preceding the uprisings.

In areas where the *mita* was in force, it had given rise to serious consequences after its adoption by the Spanish crown. The mines were dangerous and physically debilitating,[9] and, in general, when attempts were made to use paid, free-market labor, the cost was high given the technology in Alto Peru. The preceding chapter described that in Oruro free-market labor cost between eight and twelve pesos per week (as against seven pesos paid in Potosí) where in turn the *mitayos* were paid only three pesos per week.[10]

José Gabriel Condorcanqui, the new Inca

In the opinion of Pedro de Angelis, who in 1837 published for the first time the official papers relating to the rebellion of 1780–1 that are archived in Buenos Aires,[11] the rebellion of Tupac Amaru was above all a response to the extortions of the *corregidores* and the immunity they enjoyed in the *audiencias*.

Proud in character and irascible by nature [José Gabriel Condorcanqui] looked with rancor on the degradation of the indigenous people. . . . He had frequented the universities of Lima and Cuzco, where he learned enough to stand out among his peers. He was

---

8 See Chapter 12.
9 The indigenous population displayed a palpable decline after the year 1500. In 1561, according to the first royal census, the number was 1,106,672 for the Peruvian area. The lowest population figure (350,000) was reached in 1754, although afterward the numbers increased notably, but with ups and downs. See David Noble Cook, "La población en el Perú colonial," *Anuario de Estudios de la Universidad Nacional del Litoral* (Rosario), no. 8 (1965), 93; and Nicolás Sánchez Albornoz and José Luis Moreno, *La población de América Latina: bosquejo histórico* (Buenos Aires, 1968).
10 See also, Chapter 8, note 27. For a detailed study of remunerations in Potosí, see Tandeter, op. cit.
11 Pedro de Angelis, *Colección de obras y documentos relativos a la historia antigua y moderna de las provincias del Río de la Plata* (Buenos Aires, Plus Ultra, 1971).

not content to be a *cacique*, which was a hereditary position in his family; he sought to be recognized as the legitimate descendant of the old dynasties of Peru and had already managed to assume again the title of "Marqués de Oropesa" which had belonged to his ancestors.[12]

Nevertheless, the indigenous aristocracy and many *caciques* (or *curacas*) (Indian district chiefs) among the insurgent indigenous peoples were actively opposed to Tupac Amaru. As for the Indians of the community at large, their behavior varied; although the overwhelming majority of personal declarations by the Indians who were subsequently prosecuted evince a "desire for revenge that welled up spontaneously in the hearts of all" (in the words of Pedro de Angelis), in not a few cases one perceives an uncritical allegiance, forced perhaps by imperative circumstances and the climate of violence that had been unleashed.

According to the same source, Tupac Amaru had been frustrated in his attempts to suppress the *mita* and the *repartimientos* through peaceful and diplomatic means.[13] Only after this failure came violent rebellion. Arriaga, the *corregidor* of the province of Tinta, who was famous for his excesses against the Indians, was lured into a trap and assassinated on November 4, 1780.

Tupac Amaru, or "the Inca" – the name by which José Gabriel began to be known to the insurgent population – led his troops to Cuzco, where he overcame a force of militiamen loyal to the crown. Not a great triumph from a military point of view, the victory nevertheless kindled the fires of rebellion, extending it to distant regions.

But the winds of the rebellion were already blowing with considerable force in other areas of the viceroyalty. In the middle of 1780, in the province of Chayanta – under the jurisdiction of the *audiencia* of Charcas and located between Oruro and Sucre – the indigenous *caudillo* Tomás Catari had started a regional seditious movement. When Catari was captured, the *corregidor* Alós was taken in the village of Pocoata and held as a hostage until Catari was released.

After this test of strength, Catari began an effective propaganda campaign, writing secret letters to all the provinces inciting them to a general rebellion.

In this manner the agitation grew uncontrollably. Tupac Amaru tirelessly crisscrossed the areas around Cuzco, publishing edicts in which he summarized his objectives:

D. José I, by the grace of the Incan God, king of Peru, Santa Fe, Quito, Chile, Buenos Aires, and continents of the south seas, duke of the superlative, Lord of the Caesars and

12 Ibid., vol. 7, 193–4.
13 With the support of some members of the clergy in the viceroyalty of Peru, he had sent messengers to Madrid to meet with officials of Charles III. A confused situation put an end to these negotiations, after which Tupac Amaru, pressured by some of his followers, decided to opt for violent action (ibid., pp. 194–5).

Amazons with dominions in the great Paitití, distributing commissar of divine mercy for a public treasury without equal, et cetera.

Whereas it was agreed in my counsel by the prolix junta on repeated occasions, both secret and public that the kings of Castile have usurped my crown and the domain of my people for nearly three centuries, burdening my vassals with unsufferable taxes, tributes, lances, customs, tariffs, duties, stamps, tithes, *quintos*, assessments, viceroys, *audiencias*, *corregidores*, and other ministers, all equal in tyranny, selling justice at auction with the clerks of this authority, whom the more you push the more he gives, entering into this the secular ecclesiastical employees, without fear of God; ruining the natives of this kingdom as if they were animals; taking the lives of those who did not know how to steal, all deserving of the most severe revenge. Because of this, and because of the outcry of all that has risen to the Heavens, in the name of Almighty God, we order and command that none of said persons pay nor obey in any thing the intruding European ministers, and they must have full respect only for the priesthood, paying them the *diezmo* and the *primicia*, as it is given directly to God, and the *tributo* and the *quinto* to your natural king and lord, and this with the moderation that will be made known, along with the other laws to observe and keep. And for the prompt remedy of all the above-mentioned, I command that the oath made to my royal crown be repeated and published in all the cities, towns, and places of my domain, giving me part with complete truth of the ready and faithful vassals for the same reward, and of those who rebel for the punishment that they deserve, remitting to us the sworn oath, on account of which we are led.[14]

The most complex aspect of this has to do with the makeup of the two opposing groups. Many rank-and-file Indians avoided joining the rebel troops, and many *caciques* remained loyal to the Spaniards or tried to play the role of intermediaries and peacemakers; this last might be explained by the fact that in many instances they owed their social and economic positions to their good relations with officers of the crown.

On the Spanish side, the allegiance of the clergy was also variable. During the prolonged conflict that Tomás Catari had with the *corregidor* Alós over his right to be *cacique* – before he was sent to prison by the *audiencia* – he was supported in his demands by Father José Gregorio Merlos, curate of the doctrine of Macha. The Spanish chronicle, cited by Pedro de Angelis, describes him hostilely as

a priest of corrupt and scandalous conduct, a shameless and bold personality who was arrested by the *oidor* Pedro Cernadas in his own house and deposited in the Recoleta in shackles and later in the public jail with all the precautions required for the crime he was accused of and the constant attempts made to free him by the rebels.[15]

In the province of Tinta, at the same time, there was also a conflict developing between the *corregidor* Arriaga, later killed by order of Tupac Amaru, and the bishop of Cuzco, Monsignor Moscoso.

As for the other powerful groups on the Spanish side, according to testimony of the time[16] Tupac Amaru was confident of gaining their support,

14 Ibid., pp. 418–19.
15 Ibid., p. 197.
16 Francisco A. Loayza, *La verdad desnuda* (Lima, 1943).

particularly in Cuzco. Some of them responded to him at the beginning, such as the Ugarte brothers, the recognized leaders among the members of the *cabildo*. In Oruro there was a similar alignment on the part of the Rodríguez brothers and the Herrera family.

The meaningful support of these groups of Creoles – which is what they called themselves, as distinguished from the peninsular *chapetones*, who in general were staunchly opposed to the uprising – depended to a significant degree on the indigenous masses' capacity for mobilization, as demonstrated by Tupac Amaru. His unquestioned charisma launched this force against the detested figures of the *corregidores*. Furthermore, to the indigenous population – including the migrant Indians – to support the "new Inca" meant to become members of a movement endowed with great power. The hope that it would put an end to the long period of injustice and suffering increased the tendency toward violence, plunder, and reprisals.

As a first step, Tupac Amaru decided to accomplish an "exemplary" action that would light the torch for future confrontations. He took the *corregidor* Arriaga prisoner and tried him on charges of abusing the functions of his office, after which he sentenced him to execution. Tupac Amaru decided to mark this act with special pomp: the *corregidor* was hung in the central plaza of Tungasuca, surrounded by an armed corps of Indians and whites, in a ceremony observing all the formalities relating to such an execution. This reinforced the image of authority that the rebel leader was trying to convey, even though in one of his first declarations the authority of the king of Spain was still recognized.

After this affirmation of his leadership he became, especially for the wandering indigenous peoples who were not closely linked to local *curacas*, the undisputed sovereign.

The repression

After the execution of Arriaga and the related events in Chayanta, where the protagonists were the Cataris, the rebellion spread to different regions in the viceroyalties of Peru and Rio de la Plata. Although no direct connection can be proven, this coincided with the declaration of war between Spain and England.[17] The port of Buenos Aires was temporarily closed and trade was interrupted with the provinces of the interior, provoking a situation of general unease on top of the anarchy produced by the uprisings.[18]

The alarm was sounded in the two viceroyalties, and both the viceroy of

17 In 1778 France and Spain were allied with the newly independent United States against England, their traditional rival. Between 1779 and 1782 Spain reconquered Menorca and besieged Gibraltar without recovering it.
18 Andrés Carretero, "Importancia de la revolución de Tupac Amaru" (prologue to the work of de Angelis, op. cit.), p. 191.

Peru, Agustín de Jáuregui, and that of Rio de la Plata, Juan J. de Vértiz, finally authorized military repression. Jáuregui arranged for the *visitador general*, Don José Antonio Areche, to go to Cuzco and take absolute control of the war and finances; Vértiz confirmed the decision made by the *audiencia* of Charcas, which had appointed Lieutenant Colonel Ignacio Flores – until then governor of Moxos – commander general of the provinces of Alto Peru. Thus the conflict took on the profile of a declared war; and although this produced in the Spanish forces the determination to eradicate the movement at its roots, it also reinforced the combative spirit of the Indians and their allies.

Flores was given broad powers to work freely and without subordination to the *audiencia*. This gave him plenty of headaches because he was hindered in his mission on several occasions by the resentment of the *oidores*. His opinion of them was, of course, hardly pithy:

[*Los oidores*] criticized his tardy conduct, calumniating him as cowardly and indecisive, on the basis that he did not take part promptly and assuming that if he had taken the offensive against the rebels he would have been able to extinguish the boldness of the many through the defeat of a few.[19]

The Catari brothers

The conflict between Flores and the *audiencia* revealed its magnitude in the context of the confused events surrounding the death of Tomás Catari. Without informing Flores, the *audiencia* ordered the secret arrest of the indigenous *caudillo*, going against the express requests for prudence from the viceroy himself.

The news was received with much celebration in the city of La Plata, where it was assumed that the detention of the leader would dishearten the followers. But the escort accompanying the prisoner was attacked on the hill of Chataquilay, and both the rebel chief and his captors were killed in the fight.

Terror then struck the residents of La Plata, which was surrounded by more than seven thousand Indians under the command of Dámaso and Nicolás Catari, brothers of the dead man.

The *oidores* tried to conceal their culpability in authorizing such a rash act, but Flores set out to expose them. The city then divided into two opposing factions – something seen in other besieged cities such as Oruro – weakening its capacity for decisive action in the face of the threat of invasion.

From the Indian camp, the Cataris sent threatening letters to the city, revealing their assumption that they had forces and resources superior to those of the besieged city.

19 Carretero, op. cit., p. 214.

Inside the city, resentment began to rise against Flores, who decided not to attack the Indians. He probably doubted, with good reason, the level of military capability of the citizen militias; but also, in the opinion of his opponents, his nature predisposed him first to seek diplomatic negotiations with the rebels.

The *director de tabacos* (tobacco inspector), Francisco de Paula Sanz, visiting the city of La Plata by chance, decided to organize a retaliatory expedition on his own initiative. On February 16, 1781, with only forty-eight men under his command, he reached the Cerro de la Punilla and boldly engaged the Indians in combat. His little army was quickly forced to retreat, but the event served to accelerate the city's determination to launch a final attack against the rebels. This was undertaken on February 20, with a resounding victory for those loyal to the crown.

After this, nearly all the Indians in the province of Chayanta were frightened and apparently "repentant" – according to the interpretation of the Spanish chronicle[20] – and this resulted in the Indians of the *común* handing over many of their own leaders, among them Dámaso and Nicolás Catari themselves.

The exceedingly cautious behavior of Commander General Flores was heavily criticized at this time. It was thought that if he had proceeded with more urgency against the Indian attack, uprisings in neighboring provinces such as Chicha and Lipes might have been prevented.

Tupac Amaru's apogee and fall

There is no doubt that the war tactics of the indigenous rebels at first disconcerted the Spaniards. The impressive initial show of their capacity to mobilize concealed the confusion that reigned in their ranks and the general lack of communication – when not actual lack of cooperation – among their leaders. In the face of the decisive attacks of the loyalist militias, these organizational weaknesses became dramatically apparent.

Tupac Amaru himself had his effectiveness undercut by these problems. According to Pedro de Angelis,

Several attacks by the rebels have failed because of the inexperience of the leaders in whom Tupac Amaru had placed his trust. His wife made him return to Tungasuca to calm his nerves after he heard the news of the attack by the troops from Lima.

The absence of Tupac Amaru, although temporary, was accompanied by great reverses. His troops, which had not been able to penetrate Cuzco, were turned back from Puno and Paucartambo. These reverses and the Lima expedition, which was advancing with redoubled effort, made him realize the full import of the danger of his inaction, and how important it was for him to set forth as soon as possible.[21]

20 Ibid., p. 220.
21 Ibid., p. 217.

In spite of its weaknesses, the rebel movement was becoming too powerful in the eyes of the more or less affluent segments of the population who, in different areas overtaken by the revolt, had acted at least potentially as allies of the rebels. Nevertheless, as will be shown in the case of Oruro, these very people, some of whom had instigated or supported the uprisings, and who had even mobilized the Indian population for their own interests, began to feel threatened by the violence unleashed by the rebels.

Because of this, Tupac Amaru was not able to retain his grasp over certain important people in Cuzco. He relied, instead, on the growing support of his own community, which led him to become excessively optimistic about the possibility of a military victory against the forces of the crown.[22]

In spite of the enthusiasm and excitement his presence aroused in the Indian settlements he visited – before whom he wore the royal insignias of the Incas on his clothing – he was obliged to withdraw from the siege of Cuzco for the second time. This was probably a result of the unpredictable local support and of his lack of military experience. When he received news of the arrival of Valle's loyalist forces he decided to retreat, and fell back to the province of Tinta, where the Spanish leader overtook him and defeated him near Tungasuca.

Taken prisoner with his whole family, he was brought to Cuzco, where he suffered an atrocious torture in view of his followers:

On Friday May 18, 1781, after having closed off the plaza with the militiamen of this city Cuzco . . . they brought out from the Society[23] . . . José Berdejo, Andrés Castelo, a *zambo* [a man of mixed black and Indian blood], Antonio Oblitas . . . , Antonio Bastidas, Francisco Tupac Amaru, Tomasa Condemaita, *cacica* of Acos, Hipólito Tupac Amaru, son of the traitor, Micaela Bastidas, his wife, and the insurgent José Gabriel . . . Berdejo, Castelo, the *zambo* and Bastidas were simply hung. Francisco Tupac Amaru, uncle of the insurgent, and his son Hipólito had their tongues cut out before they were thrown off the steps of the gallows; the Indian woman Condemaita was garrotted on the scaffold. . . . Then they brought the Indian Micaela up to the scaffold, where in sight of her husband they cut out her tongue and then garrotted her, and she suffered infinitely because her throat was so slender that the screw could not strangle her, and it was necessary for the executioners to finish killing her by tying nooses around her neck and pulling in both directions and kicking her in the stomach and breasts.

The event finished with the rebel José Gabriel [Tupac Amaru], who was brought out into the middle of the plaza; there the executioner cut out his tongue and, bereft of children and wives, they put him on the ground, tied his hands and feet with four nooses, and with these attached to the cinches of four horses, four *mestizos* pulled in four different directions, a spectacle that had never been seen in this city. I don't know if it was because the horses were not very strong, or because the Indian was really made of iron, but they could not completely divide him, after they had been pulling for a long time until they had him up in the air so he resembled a spider. This took so long that the *visitador*, moved

22 On the support received by Tupac Amaru and the motives for the rebellion there have been diverse opinions. It is not my intent to discuss these questions here, but rather to defer them for a later work.
23 Jesuit college where the *visitador* Areche observed the execution.

by compassion, so that the poor wretch would not suffer any longer, dispatched a command to the Society, ordering them to have the executioner cut off his head, and they did so. Then they took the body under the gallows, where they cut off the arms and legs. They did the same to the women, and they cut off the heads of the rest to send them to different towns. The bodies of the Indian and his wife were taken to Picchu, where a pyre was built, onto which they were thrown and reduced to ashes, which were scattered to the winds and thrown into the stream that runs through there. Thus ended the lives of José Gabriel Tupac Amaru and Micaela Bastidas, whose pride and arrogance reached so far that they were named kings of Peru, Chile, Quito, Tucumán, and other places, even including the Gran Paitití, and other nonsense in this vein.

On that day a growing number of people gathered, but no one cried out, nor was one voice raised; many remarked, and I among them, that among such a large gathering there were no Indians to be seen, at least not in the dress they usually wear, and, if there were any, they would be disguised with capes or ponchos.

Several things happened that seem to have been willed and carried out by the devil, to confirm these Indians in their abuses, omens, and superstitions. I say this because, having had very dry weather and calm days, that day dawned so overcast that the sun could not be seen, and it was threatening to rain everywhere; and at twelve o'clock, when the horses were pulling apart the Indian, there was a strong gust of wind, and then a downpour, that made everyone, even the guards, run for cover. This has been what made the Indians say that the sky and the elements felt for the death of the Inca, whom the inhuman and impious Spaniards were killing with such cruelty.[24]

The preceding and well-known passage of Pedro de Angelis, apparently taken from the account of a priest who was a witness to the torture, allows us to omit longer references to the unusual degree of cruelty that occur in these accounts. As we will see later, particularly in the chapter devoted to the invasion of Oruro, the behavior of the Indians and the rebels toward their opponents did not differ greatly in terms of brutality and reprisal.

The other rebel centers

Another such case occurred in the region of Puno, which covered part of the *corregimientos* of Lampa and Chucuito on the western and southwestern borders and the south of Lake Titicaca. This area was devastated by enraged rebel groups who by January 1781 had practically taken over all the rural zones. The local leadership came in this case from *caudillos* of the zone, although later they received considerable aid from Diego Tupac Amaru, brother of the *caudillo*. From February to May the rebel forces laid siege to the city of Puno, obliging the two royalist commanders, Orellana and Del Valle, to abandon it and retreat to Cuzco.

The *cacique* of Puno, allied with the royalists, left a detailed chronicle of his confrontations with the other *caciques* and rebel *caudillos*:

The immense and furious army with which the enemies came to attack this city filled the Indians of the nearby villages with arrogance when they passed through, and they did not doubt that they would take it, because they only took into consideration their prodigious numbers, and doubtless did not imagine the resistance that was being prepared against them. Possessed of this confidence, their anger burst forth and they committed unprecedented atrocities; especially in Coata, where on the same day they exterminated 11 Spaniards and mestizos who they could get their hands on, without regard to sex, with complete freedom and safety because I happened to be occupied at the moment in the defense of this city . . .

[Entering with his men into the village of Juli, near Chucuito, taken by the rebels:]

Our men, when they entered the village, found the plaza and the streets inundated with blood, and corpses lying everywhere, without there being any rhyme or reason for it . . .

[In Chucuito itself:] After the cavalry companies left, the Indians came in and, since they encountered no resistance, they committed atrocities that have no precedent among men. They killed more than 400 Spaniards and mestizos, of both sexes, without even sparing suckling babies.[25]

At the same time, with little difference, the Indians of this other part of Azangaro and Lampa, redoubling their efforts, returned to attack the village of Capachica . . . [and] cut the throats of every Spaniard and white person they could get their hands on. So that, now in these parts there is no one except those who had time to find safety in the city which today forms a kind of little island of felicity in the midst of a sea of rebellion that surrounds it on all sides.[26]

But Puno, that "little island of felicity," also fell soon afterwards. The preceding description, dated April 1781, is the work of a chronicler who, in other passages, criticized with the same severity the errors of the Spanish government – in particular the excesses and abuses of the *corregidores* – which lends evenhandedness to his account.

These reports indicate, again, that the extreme cruelty of these confrontations did not belong to one side exclusively. Little can be added to illustrate the prevailing climate of violence after the description of the torture of Tupac Amaru, the massacres described by the *cacique* of Puno, or the following passage of Segurola:

The mocking and cruelty committed by the enemies against us, both those they took alive and those left dead in the field, cannot be spoken of without the greatest pain, horror, and compassion; the most common way in which they manifest their anger against the Spaniards, is that of cutting off their heads, arms, and legs, and tearing pieces off their bodies, dancing around the corpses every time they get one.[27]

Oruro itself was another focal point of the uprising. Although a detailed description is in later chapters, the following will permit us to place events occurring there in the general context of the uprisings.

Two centers of rebellion converged in Oruro and the surrounding areas: one lay in the neighboring province of Chayanta, where a chronic state of insurgency had been present since the mid-1780s, and where the long con-

25 "Relación del cacique Puno, de sus expediciones, sitios, defensas y varios acontecimientos . . . ," in de Angelis, op. cit., pp. 478–85.
26 Ibid. (2d ed., 1910), pp. 395–6.
27 Sebastián de Segurola, "Diario de los sucesos del cerco de La Paz, op. cit., vol. 1, p. 66.

flict between the *corregidor* Alós and Tomás Catari occurred. The other region in conflict included several areas near Oruro, for example, Pocoata.

The situation in Chayanta had generated a state of apprehension in Oruro; coming on top of the news of the rebellion of Tupac Amaru in Cuzco, it induced the authorities to organize several militias in the middle of December 1780. Apparently the army maneuvers performed by these groups aroused profound distrust among various people, especially among Indian groups living on farms in the outlying areas, who suspected a campaign to take them as hostages.[28]

Tensions increased little by little until on February 10 a bloody mutiny erupted in the city under the leadership of the Rodríguez brothers, who, as mentioned, belonged to one of Oruro's affluent families and one of whom owned a mine on the outskirts.

The rebel movement successfully took control of the city, notwithstanding conflicts that arose among the insurgents. As is shown in detail later, during the first phase of the revolt the participation of Indians and mestizos was very important, and the city was continuously invaded by large crowds who raised their demands from one day to the next. Soon the authority of the Rodríguez brothers themselves and their ability to control the Indian forces was undermined by this pressure. In March 1781 the Indians were finally repelled when the Creoles and Europeans closed ranks once again against the growing threat of the indigenous people, who by this time were attacking both groups indiscriminately.

The neighboring region of La Paz, and that extending south and east of Lake Titicaca, were also centers of rebellion. The siege organized by Julián Apaza, an Aymara Indian who adopted the name Tupac Catari, was the most important military event in the progress of the revolts.

The first siege of La Paz lasted 109 days, from March 14 until June 30, 1781. The second lasted 75 days, from August 4 to October 17 of the same year. The inhabitants lost most of their farms and property, and the shortage of food drove up prices of basic products to exorbitant levels. In addition to this, they were also obliged to supply food to the troops of the first auxiliary army that camped in El Alto, headed by Ignacio Flores. When Flores had to retreat without having taken control of the situation, the city found itself in circumstances even more serious than it had weathered during the months of the previous siege. The goal was to resist until the auxiliary army was in a position to renew its defense; but illness, lack of food, and low morale overcame the inhabitants. It fell to Sebastián de Segurola to defend the area until the Spanish colonel José Reseguín finally managed to defeat of the rebels on October 17, an action followed by the capture and death of Tupac Catari.

28 *Informe sobre los tumultos ocurridos en Oruro entre marzo y abril de 1781*, AGN, Sala IX-7-4-3, legajo 2, no. 3.

According to estimates made by the defenders, about 10,000 Spaniards – inhabitants of La Paz and adjoining towns – died in combat or of hunger (La Paz had a population of about 23,000 at the time).

The Indian offensive was blessed in this case with rare organization and perseverance. Throughout the two sieges, 80,000 to 100,000 Indians manning positions on the neighboring hills attacked the city night after night, firing guns and hurling rocks from slingshots. At the same time, they penetrated the walls of the defense trenches, taking the guards by surprise at all hours.[29]

In addition, the Indians easily concealed the number of casualties in their own ranks, removing their bodies after each battle and disguising their defeats by singing and dancing.[30] At the headwaters of the Choqueyapu River they built a dike and on October 12 they released it, flooding the region and destroying farms and livestock worth an estimated two million pesos.

All of this is testimony to the leadership abilities of Julián Apaza,[31] who was ably seconded by his wife, the famous Bartolina Sisa. On April 5 she personally accompanied the *caudillo* in his attack on the defending garrison. The chronicles relate that Catari had a chapel built in El Alto, from which he directed operations and attended mass "with his wife and his *oidores* in the manner of a *cabildo*,"[32] in imitation of Spanish pomp.

On June 30, 1781, Ignacio Flores took Bartolina Sisa prisoner and brought her to La Paz. Catari tried to negotiate with all the means at his disposal for her freedom, but in vain. According to one interpretation, the man who had once risen up as a feared and respected *caudillo* started to lose some of his mental stability after his wife was imprisoned:

[In Julián Apaza] we can see the signs of a painful interior drama. . . . Many of his letters and little notes, as well as his orders, of which there are many in the Archives of Seville, convey the *caudillo*'s personal tragedy. The two major causes of this terrible bitterness were without doubt the loss of his son and his wife by different means. . . . Bartolina was a prisoner of the royalist authorities, subjected to unspeakable abuses and pressures of every type. . . . Julián knew of this and his actions in the second siege of the city contributed to the efforts to obtain her liberation.[33]

José Reseguín defeated the rebels in October, pursuing Catari in his retreat until he captured and killed him. According to one chronicler of the

---

29 Gladys Seda Reyda, "El asedio de la ciudad (basado en el informe del tesorero de la real hacienda, Miguel Antonio de Llano)," in *Aportes documentales sobre la rebelión de Tupac Catari* (La Paz, UMSA, 1972). For a recent study of this subject, see María Eugenia del Valle de Siles, *Historia de la rebelión de Tupac Catari, 1781–1782* (La Paz, Don Bosco, 1990).

30 Ibid., p. 4.

31 The Spanish chronicles downgrade his image, portraying him as a drunk and a madman.

32 Seda Reyda, op. cit., p. 5.

33 Teodosio Imana Castro, "De lo pasional en la vida de los caudillos indígenas de 1780," in *Historia y Cultura: Revista del Instituto de Estudios Bolivianos*, 1 (1973), 128–9.

siege, "the appearance of the head of Tupac Catari produced substantial relief and high hopes, as he had been drawn and quartered by four horses by the troops of commander José de Reseguín, who came to the aid [of the city] for the second time."[34]

An interpretation of the Indian uprisings of 1780–1

It seems obvious that resentment of certain aspects of the colonial system persisted in the indigenous community. However, the role played by the consolidation of the renewed Caroline administration also bears consideration. An inevitable consequence of its plan for modernization – which included measures that represented a growing threat to nearly all peoples – was a generalization of the conflicts. Everyone became affected or feared they would be, from powerful Lima businessmen and aristocrats to the poorest farmers and tradesmen.

These measures, in fact, had been drastic: corrupt or inefficient officials were fired, payment of taxes was demanded, and usurpers were obliged to return lands they had obtained illegally to their rightful owners.

Although most of these changes produced greater efficiency and control of the bureaucracy, frequently the population reacted with displeasure. In the case of the indigenous peoples, this was highly visible. If, as has been mentioned, one of the principal causes of the rebellions was the desire to prevent illegal appropriation of land,[35] the Indians might have counted on more protection from a new bureaucracy that heeded the law than the one that held power for decades before.

Other confusing situations existed in the area of Indian trade. Many Indians who engaged in business were protected by laws under which the *alcabala*, a sales tax, did not apply to them as long as they were the direct producers of the goods they were selling. When customs was established as a separate branch of the administration, many Indian traders had to pay the *alcabala* for the first time, either because they were trading in goods they had not produced or because the customs officers were trying to raise taxes on commercial activities of every kind. The spontaneous response was an angry rejection of the tax increases.

Various reforms in this part of Spanish America, with the considerable level of arbitrariness many of these measures included, were a consequence of the work of the *visitador*, or inspector, José Antonio de Areche, appointed by royal decree on March 11, 1776.

The *visitador* arrived in Peru in June 1777, and through his strict conduct made his presence felt immediately, predictably provoking resistance.

34 Seda Reyda, op. cit., p. 5.
35 "Carta de Mata Linares a Escobedo," no. 7, Cuzco, March 14, 1785. Archivo General de Indias, Audiencia de Cuzco, legajo 35.

The crown required him to increase the funds in the treasury to finance the war with England. Under pressure from this demand, Areche availed himself of the existing bureaucratic mechanisms to grease the machinery of tax collection. As a result excesses were committed in the collection of taxes – especially among the Indians – generating general discontent.

The increase of the *alcabala* on local products and foodstuffs provoked a strong reaction, as did the order for a census of Indians, *cholos*, and mulattoes, the aim of which was to ensure the proper payment of tribute by them. This put mestizos and Indians on an equal footing, creating great social unrest.[36]

The installation of customs offices in many places where there had been none also gave rise to conflict; in Arequipa, the severity of the collections ordered by customs director Juan Bautista Pando provoked resistance on the part of nearly the whole population. In January 1780 subversive posters appeared, and the conflicts did not cease until March, when they culminated in the destruction of the customs house, the flight of Pando and his family, and the lowering of the alcabala to its previous rate.[37]

Dissatisfaction grew at an alarming pace, and many groups who felt aggrieved joined forces with a view toward resisting the reforms. Artisans, businessmen, disgraced members of the old bureaucracy, *corregidores*, and land usurpers all raised their voices in protest and did everything they could to hinder the implementation of the new measures.

Another revolt that arose from this situation was that of Lorenzo Farfán de los Godos, in Cuzco. Members of the old administration took part in it on one side (probably being fearful of losing their jobs) and on the other were the silver merchants, who objected to the increase in taxes.[38]

To counter the pressure coming from the central government, members of dominant local groups attempted to mobilize lower sectors of society. This occurred in several of the uprisings of 1780–1, for in the face of the relentless advance of the new Caroline bureaucracy, the most affluent groups in the colonial population came to support the demands of the Indians, even though these were not always relevant to the rejection of the pressures of taxation.

As has been seen, frequently the protests of the Indians—who were involved in commerce in large numbers—were directed against the customs agents. Nevertheless, it began to be apparent that the violent outbreaks tended to soften many of the new administration's resolutions and even, in some cases, to stop certain measures.

Consequently, many leaders and agitators of local groups affected by the reform decided to encourage the Indians' rancor and resentment. One ef-

36 Andrés de Carretero in de Angelis, op. cit., p. 188.
37 Ibid., p. 189.
38 Oscar Cornblit, "Levantamientos," p. 110.

fective vehicle for accomplishing this was the diffusion of rumors, and this was certainly done with no misgivings.

In the middle of 1780, then, rumors about mass movements were continual. This, against the background of popular discontent that the same opposition groups were instigating, created fertile ground for the general rebellion that broke out a short time later.

Of course, this perspective is given by time and knowledge of the outcome. Those who participated interpreted what happened in light of the needs of their respective groups. For example, the *corregidores* maintained that the movements started at the instigation of the priests of the indigenous communities; the latter, in turn, accused the former of commercially exploiting the Indians in their *corregimientos*. The bureaucrats accused both the priests and the *corregidores* of the same offenses.[39]

The migrant Indians

Another significant thing to consider is that the rebellions spread like wildfire through those regions that presumably had the largest number of "migrant" Indians; that is, the zones of La Paz, Chuquisaca, and the provinces of the bishopric of Cuzco surrounding Lake Titicaca.

This migration was linked partially to the *mita* system, since a portion of the *mitayos* did not return to their birthplace after fulfilling their obligation. They chose to remain near the place they had worked, taking odd jobs, working as paid miners, or wandering about in search of a living. Members of this last group usually settled in villages and cities, or else moved into zones not occupied by the Spanish administration. It is difficult to estimate how many there were, since most of them did not appear in the registries, in avoidance of the personal tax.

In Oruro, of course, there were no Indians working in the *mita* system, in spite of the initial request made by the city's founders. In the middle of the century, when the mining situation began to turn precarious, many mine owners again urged the authorities to include these Indians in the *mita* system, although they did not obtain a general measure on the matter. In fact, the Conde de Superunda, then viceroy, stated in 1750 that "the decree imposing compliance with the regulations of the *mita* on foreign Indians [*forasteros*] was a change whose introduction required great caution. Going against tradition, it might bring with it somewhat disturbing consequences."[40]

Although the term *forasteros* was a census category that included Indians who were sendentary and had land, doubts persisted as to the number of Indian migrants it included.

39 Ibid., pp. 110–11.
40 "Relación que escribe en Conde de Superunda, Virrey del Perú," in *Memorias de los virreyes que han gobernado en Perú durante el coloniaje español* (Paris, Bailly, 1859), pp. 90–1.

The truth is that when the chronicles allude to *indios forasteros*, they refer undoubtedly to the least integrated group. Feyjóo de Sosa, for example, principal accountant of the treasury in Lima, describes the conduct of these Indians in the following manner:

> I express it that the Indians of this capital are all *forasteros*, since this is how it is observed in the cities of Cuzco, Arequipa, and Villa de Potosí. These transmigrations make them wandering and errant, and consequently the provinces are deserted and depopulated . . . they are called *forasteros* because they come from remote and strange provinces, seeking refuge and aid for their needs; so that it can be verified that this whole nation lives wandering and errant being the most peregrine in its lands and possessions.[41]

In Oruro as well as in the other regions, the participation of these migrant Indians was significant, according to an assessment made during Amat's viceroyalty.[42]

Caciques or curacas

Also relevant to analysis of the Indian uprisings is the role played by the headmen – *caciques* or *curacas* – of the communities. These were leaders of mestizo or Indian origin who, when the Inca empire was overthrown and the coercion of the central power disappeared, became petty lords in their own territories.[43] Soon the colonial administration drastically limited their influence, however, leaving as their basic tasks the collection of personal taxes from the Indians and the assignment and registration of them to their *mita* obligation. To some extent they retained diminished judicial powers and some privileges such as exemption from the personal tax and the *mita*, as well as a salary and usufruct of land and water.

Indians of noble origin had preferential rights to the position of *curaca*; around 1770 there were about 2,300 of these in the viceroyalty of Peru, that is, 1.5 percent of the tributary Indians. It was not unusual for these *caciques*, given their influence in colonial business, to have some type of agreement with the Spanish administrative system. The frequent lawsuits relating to rights to *cacique*ships demonstrate that the post was in great demand and conferred economic and political benefits.

41 "Parecer que dió Don Miguel Feyjóo de Sosa," Biblioteca Nacional, Madrid, Ms. 13,368, fols. 30–30v.
42 Manuel de Amat y Junyent, *Memoria de gobierno* (Seville, Escuela de Estudios Hispanoamericanos, 1947), p. 236. The influence of the migrant population is recognized in the literature, even when some authors state that the "landless foreigners" (*forasteros sin tierras*) were those who specifically constituted this nomad mass. See Ann M. Wightman, *Indigenous Migration and Social Change: The "Forasteros" of Cuzco, 1520–1720* (Durham, N.C., Duke University Press, 1990), pp. 52–7. If the records distinguish "landless foreigners" from the rest, in the literature of the period they were called, with great ambiguity, simply *forasteros*. On this subject, see also Nicolás Sánchez Albornoz, *Indios y tributos en el Alto Perú* (Lima, IEP, 1978).
43 Cornblit, "Levantamientos," pp. 88–90.

Also significant is that most of the Indians belonging to the aristocracy of their race had fought against the rebels, as in the case of the Indian leaders Pumacahua and Choquehuanca. Their group accused Tupac Amaru of being a usurper and a bastard, denying his claims of descent from the Incan royal family. This stance was decisive in the failure of the rebellion, especially when the twelve *ayllus reales* of Cuzco also opposed the rebels and collaborated with the army forces in the defense of the city.[44]

The *curacas*, for the reasons already described, generally remained faithful to the Spanish during the uprisings, although in many cases there were changes of allegiance during the conflict under pressure from the rebel masses. The dynamics of the process nevertheless determined the emergence of new rebel commanders who showed themselves to be great leaders at the moment of greatest revolutionary agitation.

In the context of the alliance between the local upper classes, who feared for their privileges, and the dispossessed and displaced Indians, Oruro was, even more than Cuzco, one of the most conspicuous nuclei of rebellion. A large proportion of members of powerful groups led the revolt against the authorities. That important mine owners like the Rodríguez brothers and their allies risked taking their dangerous alliance with the Indians so far can be traced not only to the threat of higher taxes but also, without doubt, to the financial constraints weighing on them, particularly pressure by lenders. They ran a very great risk, however, for after they openly joined forces with the most dispossessed groups and the Indian population, the latter soon began to exhibit extremely violent behavior that approached limits beyond which the mine owners were unwilling to venture. Only by later withdrawing from their chance allies and shielding themselves behind the authority of the local *curacas* were they finally able to control the massive mobilization of the Indians.

44 "Carta de Mata Linares a Gálvez," Cuzco, March 19, 1786, Archivo General de Indias, Audiencia de Cuzco, legajo 35.

10

Oruro in the economic and geopolitical context of the epoch (c. 1780–1781)

The uprisings of the Indian groups and rebels of Peru took place during the reign of Charles III (1759–88), precisely when the modernization methods of the Bourbon monarch were at their apogee. The administration's initial reforms had already been introduced by the first kings of the new dynasty (Philip V and his successors, Ferdinand VI), but during the reign of Charles III it was possible to combine experience in administrative reform with the sometimes brilliant work of ministers and officials such as Aranda, Floridablanca, Campomanes, Jovellanos, Cabarrús, Olavide, and José de Gálvez.[1] The Caroline administration made a notable effort to bring things up to date and to introduce French influences. They originated projects to foster industrial growth, bureaucratic efficiency, and the consolidation of military power.

In the case of Peru and Alto Peru (the latter had been incorporated in 1776 into the new viceroyalty of Rio de la Plata) all this implied profound changes, both in the internal structure of society and in external relations with other regions of Spanish colonization. Still, by the beginning of the 1770s, Lima, capital of the viceroyalty of Peru, occupied a strategic and economically privileged position in the empire, partly as a supplier of resources for the crown and partly as a commercial distribution center for the mining settlements of Alto Peru.

This situation gradually declined throughout the eighteenth century, particularly because of the overwhelming threat presented by Buenos Aires. This was the cheapest port for the importation of European products, which were subsequently sold in the markets of Charcas and Chile. Metal from

---

1 On social, economic, and political events in Spain during the last part of the eighteenth century, see Raymond Carr, *Spain* (Oxford University Press, Clarendon Press, 1966), pp. 60–78; Richard Herr, *The Eighteenth-Century Revolution in Spain* (Princeton, N.J., Princeton University Press, 1958); and Juan Beneyto, *Historia de la administración española e hispanoamericana* (Madrid, Aguilar, 1958), pp. 439–504. On the Spanish government's administrative reforms and French influence on this process, see Arthur S. Aiton, "Spanish Colonial Reorganization under the Family Compact," *Hispanic American Historical Review*, 12 (1932), 269–80. The career of José Gálvez is well described by Herbert I. Priestley, *José de Gálvez, Visitor-General of New Spain* (Berkeley and Los Angeles, University of California Press, 1916).

Alto Peru also began to be exported from there. The importation of products via Buenos Aires was less costly due to the greater safety of the maritime route and cheaper overland routes.[2]

Lima had managed to retain its predominance during previous centuries, but by the eighteenth century the growth of Buenos Aires was a permanent fact, especially because its traders were willing to use any means, legitimate or not, to exploit its natural advantages. This situation culminated with Charles III's decision to create the new viceroyalty of Rio de la Plata on August 1, 1776. With this measure, Alto Peru came under the jurisdiction of Buenos Aires. Groups importing European products and those exploiting minerals suffered the most damage in the viceroyalty of Peru. This was not the case with those connected to local production, for example makers of coarse textiles for local consumption by the common people. The principal and almost only bastion of the so-called *bayetas de obraje* until 1790 continued to be Cuzco,[3] whereas Buenos Aires provided European products.

The crown's motives for creating the new viceroyalty had been principally strategic. The king wanted above all to consolidate Spain's position along the Rio de la Plata, eliminating the Portuguese threat and improving defensive preparedness against the British, whose presence loomed larger day by day.

Because the Portuguese had abandoned Rio Grande and Colonia del Sacramento, opposite Buenos Aires as a result of the secular conflict begun in 1680,[4] the Spanish decided to unite all available resources to finance an expedition led by Pedro de Cevallos in 1776. Thus, on top of the loss of the Alto Peru market, Lima had to weather enormous financial pressures to support a war.

After the victory against the Lusitanos and the establishment of the viceroyalty of Rio de la Plata, Spain, allied with France and the English colonies of North America, embarked on another costly war against England from 1779 to 1783.

---

2 This process is studied in the already cited work of Céspedes del Castillo, "Lima y Buenos Aires."
3 Pedro V. Cañete y Domínguez, *Guía histórica, geográfica, física, política, civil y legal del gobierno e intendencia de la provincia de Potosí (año 1791)* (La Paz, Armand Albar, 1952). Marie Helmer, "Documents pour l'histoire économique de l'Amérique du Sud: Commerce et industrie au Pérou à la fin du XVIIe siècle," *Revista de Indias*, 10 (1950) 522–4.
4 The conflict over the colony of Sacramento dated from 1680, when the governor of Rio de Janeiro, Manuel de Lobo, following orders of the crown of Portugal, erected a fortress with this name in the eastern district of Rio de la Plata. The fort was reconquered a few months later by José de Garro, governor of Buenos Aires; but the following year it was returned to Portugal following diplomatic negotiations. Newly conquered by Spain in 1705, it was nevertheless returned to the Portuguese by the Peace of Utrecht in 1715. Similar transfers from one crown to the other took place in 1724, 1750, 1761, 1762, 1763, 1776, and 1777. In this last year, after the final reconquest of the fort by Pedro de Cevallos, and after the signing of the Treaty of San Ildefonso, Spain remained in possession of the eastern territory, ceding other lands to Portugal in return.

Economic description of Oruro around 1780–1

The geopolitical transformation and the modifications in the economic life of Peru and Alto Peru thus provide a contextual framework for analyzing the uprisings in the zones mentioned earlier. The movements in each region, however, demonstrate their own peculiar characteristics and courses of development.

In order to understand the case of Oruro, for example, the production situation of the province around 1780–1 must be taken into account. Desolate and infertile, it had not been able to supply its own needs since antiquity. As a consequence, the neighboring province of Cochabamba was its major supplier of foodstuffs.[5] The welfare of Oruro, then, as the base of a prosperous trading situation, was of vital importance to the residents of Cochabamba.

During the rebellion of 1781, the siege imposed by the rebels cut the route to Oruro. The natives of Cochabamba hastened to organize a rescue expedition of militiamen, who were much more worried about potential damage to their city's economy than about the loss of human lives.

In the opinion of one official from Cochabamba:

Whether it has to do with their alliance with other provinces or the immediate influence of Oruro, they are still threatening second attacks and onslaughts from which no one goes in or comes out to buy the produce of this province, which provide the base for the circulation of money for other uses and necessary transactions: so that more than three months have passed with no customers, with the risk that the grain will spoil, and more so finding ourselves so close to the harvest of the current year.[6]

As for mining production, the trajectory of its declines has been described in the preceding chapters. It is interesting to compare the opinions of two travelers of the epoch who, just a few years apart, saw very different economic situations. Alonso Carrió de la Vandera ("Concolorcorvo"), in his famous "Lazarillo de Ciegos Caminantes," was already reporting signs of mining decline around 1773, since most of what was being smelted at that time in the city was produced in adjoining areas: "The large hill right next to the city itself, so convenient for the exploitation of its metals, had run out of ore with enough silver content to be worth the cost of working it because of the lack of water in the *lavaderos*."[7] In spite of this, he still apparently saw some traces of Oruro's prosperous past: "This city is next to

---

5 Dalence, op. cit. This author estimates that around 1830 the province of Oruro produced half of the potatoes it consumed. Nevertheless, one must bear in mind that the prostration of the province was complete during this period and its population much diminished.

6 Manuel Parrilla, "Escrito," Cochabamba, April 24, 1781, AGN, Buenos Aires, Sala IX 7-4-3, legajo 2, no. 1, fol. 50v.

7 Alonso Carrió de la Vandera (Concolorcorvo), *El lazarillo de ciegos caminantes*, op. cit., p. 179.

Potosí in size, because it has *cajas reales* and more than six hundred bars of two hundred silver marks are melted in them each year."[8]

Eleven years later, Francisco de Paula Sanz refers only to the city's geographical location and its lack of fertility, without even mentioning mining, which was, by that time, at its lowest point of the century:

> This city is really located almost halfway between Potosí and La Paz, closer to the latter city than to the former; but it is situated on an extensive plain, whose arid fields produce no crops and are not capable of doing so; even for livestock this country has little offer, being as infertile as it is dry; and consequently it only has enough livestock for subsistence.[9]

In 1787, the description of Oruro contained in the *Diccionario geográfico-histórico de las Indias Occidentales ó América* presents a picture of thoroughgoing demographic and productive decline:

> The crops produced are potatoes, quinine and a little barley: they raise small livestock and manufacture a lot of gunpowder as the land is very nitrous, but not as much as in past times when their gold and silver mines were flourishing; today they are in a state of extreme decline, most of the area washed out and difficult to remedy for lack of slope [*sic*] to the land; thus the population continues to decrease, there being about 8,000 souls in the whole province.[10]

Finally, in the last years of the eighteenth century, a detailed report was made by Anthony Zachariah Helms, who passed through Potosí and Oruro on his trip in 1791 from Buenos Aires to Lima. His objective was to assess the state of mining in the region,[11] and his report speaks eloquently for itself:

> Four miles before reaching Oruro, the valley is totally covered for three miles with a crust of salt mixed heavily with saltpeter. The mountains in this region are exceptionally rich in metals, not only according to old reports, but from direct observation; and according to some investigations, among the few who have taken charge of the rich old mines, the beneficiaries can make high profits.
>
> But one can verify from persons who worked some of these mines, as for example the royal tobacco administrator did [a reference to F. de Paula Sanz], that the labor costs exceeded the profits. . . .
>
> In consequence of the [horrifying?] rebellion of the Christian Indians that occurred less than eleven years ago in the viceroyalties of Rio de la Plata, in Oruro, as in most of the cities of both viceroyalties, nearly a majority of the wealthiest part of the Spanish population was killed, and the greater part of the city was sacked and destroyed. Others, who were lucky enough to escape with their lives, emigrated with whatever money they had concealed in hiding places, some to other provinces but most to Europe. They must have

---

8 Ibid.
9 Francisco de Paula Sanz, "Carta al Virrey Loreto," Buenos Aires, August 24, 1784, AGN, Buenos Aires, Intendencia de La Paz (1783–5), Sala IX 5-5-4, legajo 3.
10 Alcedo, *Diccionario*, pp. 400–1.
11 A. Z. Helms visited this area in 1791, sent by the Spanish crown as part of the Nordenflicht expedition, to examine the possibilities of improving production technology in the principle mining centers of Peru and Alto Peru.

had millions, gained from the exploitation of the riches of the mines: the present consequence is that for lack of means, mining is completely finished.

I found there only one place actually in operation, which was profitably exploiting the residues of two local mine scrap heaps with crushers with two drop hammers, like those of Potosí, as proof of the richness of the minerals that were formerly mined there. The profits were so substantial that the owner made a profit of 500 pesos a week after paying salaries and expenses.

This man had earned 234,000 pesos in nine years simply from the old residues, without having to reactivate any of the rich old mines.[12]

The description of this practically lone miner, an intelligent but phantasmagorical remnant of other epochs of splendor, closes the period of Oruran silver production, which for a brief moment had competed with the richness of Potosí.

We should add that, as a product of his research, A. Z. Helms considered the mines of Oruro to be potentially richer than those of Potosí, which probably explains their capacity to produce silver without the help of *mitayo* labor. By that time, however, Oruro had already forgone any possibility of establishing more efficient production methods, and its economic decline appeared inevitable.

The *Corregimientos* around 1780–1

As we have seen, one of the main arguments against the *repartimientos* was the obligation imposed on the Indians to buy high-priced articles that for them were useless or nearly so. This compulsory manner of increasing consumption was supported not only by the *corregidores* but also by those who traded in these goods. The elimination of the *repartimiento*, therefore, would result in conditions as unfavorable and bothersome as its maintenance had produced.

The figure of the *corregidor* was nevertheless becoming an obstacle to the Caroline administration's desire to centralize and increase the efficiency of the bureaucracy. The right to appoint *corregidores* was taken away from the viceroys and transferred exclusively to the Council of Indias in Spain,[13] provoking protests from the viceroys. As one can see in the lists of appointees, however, only in the second half of the eighteenth century did the *corregidor* come to be considered as a functionary, rather than as a supplier of resources through the sale of jobs. In fact, at the beginning of the reign of Charles III, the appointments no longer specified any kind of special remuneration to the crown except the normal tax called *media anata*.[14]

12 Anthony Zachariah Helms, *Tagebuch einer Reise durch Peru, von Buenos Ayres an dem grossen Plataflusse, ueber Potosi nach Lima, der Haupstadt des Koenigsreichs Peru* (Dresden, 1798), pp. 126–7 of the English translation: *Travels from Buenos Ayres by Potosí to Lima* (London, 1806.)

13 See the "Relación del estado de los reinos del Perú que hace el Excmo. Señor don José Armendaris, marqués de Castel-Fuerte," in *Memorias de los virreyes que han gobernado el Perú durante el coloniaje español,* III, op. cit., p. 58.

14 See "Títulos de los corregidores," Archivo General de Indias, Lima, legajos 633–7.

That a *corregidor*'s salary did not depend entirely on the crown was an important obstacle to the plan to integrate the position into the bureaucratic system. As a result, the regulations were much stricter than for other functionaries. Thus, members of the bureaucracy were not usually appointed to this post; furthermore the appointment lasted only five years, and renewal was difficult. It was, consequently, a short-term privilege.

The job of *corregidor* was, because of all this, one of the weakest links in the colonial administration, and it was destined to disappear. An opportunity for change presented itself with the establishment of the system of *intendencias* throughout the Spanish empire, which reached its final planning stages in the late 1770s.[15] The functions of the *corregidor* were finally absorbed by those of the *intendente*, a position instituted in Peru in 1784.

Areche's visit, mentioned above, was related to this measure. In his report to the crown he harshly attacked the institution of the *corregimiento* and recommended that the *repartimiento* be abolished. In a letter to Gálvez in 1780, he reported, "It is neither easy nor possible to improve the basic government of the Province of Peru, nor your treasury, while its leaders or *corregidores* are merchants."[16]

This would indicate that although the *repartimiento* was abruptly abolished after the rebellion, the idea had circulated in colonial administrative circles previously.

The 1770s in America saw a series of measures tending to increase bureaucratic efficiency. One of these recognized the need for care in selecting future functionaries, as is apparent in the appointments of *corregidores* who took office after the coronation of Charles III. Even then, however, there were still no systematic procedures for electing members of the administration, much less *corregidores*. One sure way to get an appointment was to demonstrate some link with the high officials of the Council of Indias. Frequently as well, a *corregimiento* was offered to a military man as a reward for service in the army.[17]

An additional proof that the government was not satisfied with the recruitment of *corregidores* – after the first reforms imposed by the Ordinance of *Intendentes* in the viceroyalty of Peru in 1784 – is that only nine of the fifty-nine subdelegates appointed had previously been *corregidores*. None of the *intendentes* or the *tenientes asesores* had held the office.[18] In the viceroyalty

15 Lynch, *Administración general española*, op. cit., Chapter 3.
16 "Carta de Areche a Gálvez," no. 195, Lima, May 16, 1780, AGI, Indiferente General, legajo 1713.
17 Moreno Cebrián, op. cit., has established percentages that show the predominance of soldiers among the seekers of this office. For 1760, and referring to the six *corregimientos* of Peru, he finds that more than 43 percent of the hopefuls were soldiers. But this percentage diminished among those who were successful, to 33 percent. In 1761, for three *corregimientos*, 40 percent of hopefuls were soldiers, and more than 53 percent of those named were. The rest were *letrados*. See Morena Cebrián, pp. 146–53.
18 Mendiburu, *Diccionario*, vol. 4, p. 458.

of Rio de la Plata, only four of the thirty-nine people mentioned on J. Lynch's list[19] had previously been *corregidores*, and they were probably appointed because they had proven military or administrative expertise.

In this way, positions within the state machinery came to be filled by an ever-more-efficient bureaucracy. The division and specificity of functions became more pronounced and, fundamentally, the law was observed with new vigor. This gave rise to a new standard in the assessment of personal effort on the job and posed a threat of job loss for many officials.

Such modernization also threatened powerful groups in each region. For example, mine owners and merchants now had to pay taxes, as did the *corregidor*. His traditional role completely contradicted the new direction of events.

Of course, the *corregidor* had earned the enmity of many sectors of society, particularly the Indians, due to the *repartimiento*. Nevertheless, it is interesting to note that hostility toward the institution was general and independent of the level of abuse or corruption with which the *corregidor* had exercised his role. Viceroy Guirior, for example, pointed out in his memoirs of the government:

Although I have already described to your Excellency the corruption provoked in the provinces by the present disorder in trade . . . I see at the same time that the *repartimientos* have always existed there but have not produced such damaging and lamentable manifestations. . . . On the contrary I find that the *repartimientos* . . . were carried out with obvious moderation . . . in places where the people's resentment has reached just the same extremes.[20]

Thus, the correlation between the abuses of the *repartimientos* and the disturbances they provoked is not so clear. It is nevertheless understandable that the introduction of patterns of consumption and the discipline of unfamiliar work in a community that frequently patterned its way of life around subsistence would give rise to agitation. Inevitably, then, the *corregidor* – due to the characteristics of his position – was the target for the complaints and antagonism of the indigenous people.

In addition, for the common bureaucrat, the *corregidor* was not an official of the crown, but simply a merchant under another guise. Much resentment was provoked by his quickly gained wealth; indeed, his earnings often greatly exceeded what a high-ranking royal official could earn.

Even the clergy of both high and low rank had reason to be antagonistic about the constant conflicts over questions of patronage or jurisdiction. A typical case was the confrontation mentioned earlier between Bishop Moscoso of Cuzco and the *corregidor* Arriaga of Tinta: Moscoso wanted to

19 Lynch, op. cit., pp. 273–81.
20 Virrey Guirior, "Memoria de gobierno," in *Relaciones de los Virreyes y audiencias que han gobernado el Perú* (Madrid, 1892).

apprehend some inhabitants of the town of Yauri, but the *corregidor* and his lieutenant opposed him, alleging that the question did not come under church jurisdiction.[21]

The lesser clergy, on their side, had intimate ties with the indigenous population, as can be seen in the Oruro uprisings.

21 Francisco A. Loayza, *La verdad desnuda* (Lima, 1943), p. 30.

11

The Oruro uprising

The account from which the history of the uprising of the city of Oruro in 1781 as traditionally told is called "Diario del tumulto,"[1] apparently an eyewitness account by a person present at the events who signed anonymously as "a priest." It is a letter report to an addressee who is also anonymous and living elsewhere, in which the author wants to offer his own interpretation of what happened. In his text, he alludes to "another diary," written doubtless by Bishop Menéndez, vicar of the principal church in Oruro (although he does not expressly mention his name), who was an unconditional ally of the Rodríguez family. According to the author, the bishop's version was an anti-Spanish libel whose falsehoods he would try to refute by contributing his own version – which, of course, he saw as impartial and objective.

The vicar of the cathedral, Bishop Menéndez, did not sign his diary, but did not go to great pains to conceal his authorship either.[2] The diary is to all appearances written in support of the Rodríguez party. The author's concern basically centers around the defense of his actions and the limitation of his responsibility for the death of several Spaniards, which later earned him a stiff sentence.

Also well known is the transcription by Pedro de Angelis[3] who, although not citing his source, clearly bases his text on the first of these accounts, relieving it here and there of some of its author's excesses of interpretation.

In order to reconstruct what happened during the Oruro uprising we have also consulted the unpublished testimonies of the Indians arrested and tried at the end of the rebellion. We have also used the subsequent confessions of the residents of the city – both Creoles and Europeans – some of them

---

1 "Diario del tumulto acaecido en la villa de Oruro en 10 de febrero de 1781 con motivo de la sublevación de Tupaj Amaru," *La revista de Buenos Aires, historia americana, literatura y derecho*, 22 (1870), 270–312.
2 Also transcribed by *La revista de Buenos Aires*, directly after the previously cited diary, with the title "Relación trágica de los funestos y ruidosos acaecimientos de la Villa de Oruro," pp. 312–25.
3 De Angelis, op. cit., pp. 221 and following.

court witness accounts and others made under presumption of complicity with the Indian invasion.[4]

The precipitating factors

As already described, events in Oruro followed the wave of Indian uprisings expanding in neighboring regions.

News of the bloody events in the provinces of Chayanta and Tinta, and the edicts of Tupac Amaru in 1781, had put the residents of the town on maximum alert.

In parallel developments, at the end of December 1780, the *cabildantes* again played out the familiar scene of replacing the municipal authorities. The *corregidor* at the time was Ramón de Urrutia, from the faction opposed to the belligerent and powerful Creole Rodríguez clan. The Rodríguez family had been in control of the city and its municipal jobs since 1760 – directly or through their allies – in a situation similar to that of the Herreras in the middle of the century. Furthermore, the two families were by this time linked by intermarriage.

The dramatic events of the uprising and the prominent role played in it by Jacinto and Juan Rodríguez suggest that the family had lost economic power in recent years; this drove them to make changes in their political tactics. In other times they would have been able to oust disloyal *corregidores*, but the new situation forced them to accept that Urrutia was going to keep his job. Perhaps because of this, they took unusual risks in the formation of new alliances, such as the pact with the indigenous people that led to the bloody events in the city.

The European chronicler described his view of what happened in Oruro as follows:

It has been ten years since there has been in this city a total regression in the mining works so that in the present situation there was not a single mine that was formally in operation, nor could they pay even what was necessary for its maintenance and operation, these being the only things that sustained the vicinity, whose total decline has put its miners and *azogueros* in such lamentable condition that those who are counted as owners, and among others they owned huge amounts of property like the said Rodríguez, Herrera, and Galleguillos, with other residents, all find themselves in a state of arrears discovered in many thousands to the king and other persons without being able to pay because they have no means with which to continue working their mines, because the *habitadores* [financiers or *aviadores*] of these people who regularly and even I would say solely are the *chapetones*, now no longer wanted to give them the same supplement since many of them went bankrupt helping these miners, who, desperate for not having anything with which to work,

4 "Testimonio del expediente de diligencias practicadas para averiguar los tumultos meditados contra Oruro (remitido por don Mariano Vargas y Rodríguez)," Buenos Aires, 1789, AGN, Sala IX, 7-4-3, legajo 2, no. 3. I have included only some of the testimony contained in this rich and extremely long document.

not finding any other way to save themselves, and to cancel their debts with the *chapetones*, it seems to have fomented this rebellion.[5]

This is why, at the end of 1780, rumors and fear overtook the residents. According to one source, what weighed most heavily on their spirits were "the fatalities that occurred in the Provinces of Chayanta and Tinta with an edict issued by the Insurrectionary Tupac Amaru in which he ordered all the *corregidores* and *chapetones* [killed] because his intent was to leave not one remaining in this nation."[6]

The chronicler alluded to the edicts that Tupac Amaru had issued between November 1780 and January 1781,[7] and to the profusion of letters sent to his captains, the disturbing contents of which circulated with increasing effect.

Fearful news was also arriving from the neighboring province of Chayanta, where the Indians took as hostages the *corregidor* Alós and his bill collectors.[8] As mentioned, this conflict had been going on for several years, and the demands of the indigenous leader, the well-known Tomás Catari, apparently enjoyed the support of the royal officials of La Plata, at first, and of the priest of the area of Macha, Father Merlos.

The disruption reigning in these bordering regions led Urrutia to form militias, with the intent to defend or dissuade. To this end, he called residents over thirty-four years of age to shooting practice on Thursdays and Sundays in the city fort.

The diary of the chronicler who was a partisan of the Creole party differs on this point from the pro-European author. According to the latter, the residents of the city

enthusiastically learned the teachings of their skilled European instructors in the handling of arms. Some, of course, did not like it, either because they sided at first with the rebel Tupac Amaru, whose coming they eagerly awaited, or because they truly were his trusted [allies] in this city [as became known later]. These people only went to another drill, to undermine the teachers and disciples and form different critiques of their operations opposed to the crown, at the same time that they insolently put up posters opposed to the crown, censuring the government of the *corregidor*.[9]

The diary attributed to Bishop Menéndez affirmed, on the other hand, that the edicts of Tupac Amaru, in which he declared his intent to "liberate the naturals and Creoles from the slavery and the hostilities they suffered at the hands of the Europeans,"[10] had plunged Urrutia's partisans into fear and confusion.

5 "Diario del tumulto," op. cit., pp. 283–84.
6 Ibid., p. 271.
7 See Chapter 9.
8 As shown in Chapter 9.
9 "Diario del tumulto," op. cit., p. 272.
10 "Relación trágica," op. cit., pp. 312–13.

According to the pro-Creole chronicler, all the inhabitants had rallied enthusiastically at first to Urrutia's summons, regardless of what side they were on, above all because they were offered payment for attending the exercises. In his opinion, it was the European Spaniards who began to get alarmed when they realized the diligence and enthusiasm with which the Creoles were learning to use the weapons. They reportedly began "to show fear that if the Indian advance really happened, the Creoles would have to rebel first, [and] that they would have to rebel against the Europeans.[11]

The organization of these militias provoked anxiety and waves of rumors in Oruro: on the one hand, it was said that the Europeans were using the troops to get rid of some prominent Creoles. Immediately, the opposite opinion was also heard: that it was these same prominent Creoles who were taking advantage of the campaigns to eliminate their European competitors.

The municipal elections of 1781

This is how things stood at the end of 1780, when everything converged once more on the city's traditional source of friction: the January 1 elections for the posts in the *cabildo*. Nothing seemed to have changed: two irreconcilable factions were fighting over the jobs of *alcaldes de primer voto* and *segundo voto*.

By Christmas Eve, everyone's attention was focused on the electoral confrontation, obscuring the importance of the Indian threat inside the city limits.

The pro-European diary commented that on Christmas Eve a poster had appeared in which

after threatening the *chapetones* with the assassination that they later carried out, and after insulting D. Fernando Gurruchaga of Vizcaya, the outgoing *alcalde ordinario* (a job that had been performed that year with utter justice, rectitude, and prudence) with declarations damaging to his person and justice. It also warned the council of the *cabildo* to avoid electing European *alcaldes*, because if this happened, they would not last 8 days since they would rise up and kill them for being robbers and to avoid this travail they should elect specifically the Señores Rodríguez as *alcaldes*.[12]

Election day arrived, and the candidates of *corregidor* Urrutia managed to defeat those of the Rodríguez family, which had held the most important positions in recent years.[13]

The diary of Bishop Menéndez makes not the slightest allusion to the municipal elections, passing directly to the events of February. But the pro-European chronicler, understandably, contributed a detailed account:

11 Ibid., p. 313.
12 "Diario del tumulto," op. cit., p. 272.
13 See "Registros de pagos de media anata" (Chapter 7).

When the day of the circumcision of the Lord arrived in this year (1781), [the *corregidor* Urrutia] proposed to the council that they name as *alcaldes* subjects endowed with good habits, and lovers of justice, so that thus they could carry out their jobs with the maturity and judgment intended by the Royal Laws. To this effect he proposed the *licenciado* D. José Miguel de Llano y Valdez, patrician (Creole), D. Joaquín Rubín de Celis and D. Manuel de Muguruza, Europeans, the second of these married in this city to a Lady of highest nobility and endowed with the advantages of nature and fortune; looking always for the *vara* to leave the house of the Rodríguez, who were trying to make it eternal as in the house of Judah, and that neither they, nor any of their partisans or domestics be elected, finding yourself informed, the first of which in the space of 38 years that these subjects have possessed these jobs without ever permitting others to be appointed because of their ambitions to govern. The second, for the injustices, extortions, and violence they perpetrated on all kinds of people with the incorrigible despotism to which this city has become accustomed, as also by the great omission, and no zeal that they had to avoid the offenses of God, and to punish the public criminals, since if the authors of these were their servants, allies, comrades, far from sentencing them to any of the penalties prescribed by law, they favored them, and fomented and altogether vouched for by said *corregidor* as an eyewitness.[14]

The same chronicler goes on to relate that, in spite of pressures by the Creole Rodríguez family, the municipal *varas* fell to the partisans of Urrutia, putting an end to the prolonged period of Rodríguez control.[15] One of the Rodríguez brothers, Don Jacinto, reportedly suffered a painful attack of colic that afternoon because of his anger at the election results. Don Juan, meanwhile, hurried off to his mines after warning his followers not to take part in any celebrations of his rivals' victory.

The next day, according to the pro-European chronicler, the connivance with the Rodríguez family of the vicar of the city's principal church, Bishop Menéndez, became known. By ancient custom, once the new authorities were confirmed by the *corregidor* in the council room of the *cabildo*, all the members walked in solemn procession to the principal church to hear the mass of thanks. This was done on January 2, 1781, but when everyone arrived at the doors of the church, they found them closed. The sacristan came out to tell them there would be no mass that day since no one had paid for it. This was an unprecedented insult to the holders of the municipal *varas* from a church leader, and it presaged a storm on the horizon.[16]

The expedition of Manuel de la Bodega

Meanwhile, the military exercises continued to exacerbate the tension between the two sides and to reinforce the rumors and mutual distrust. In this strained climate, word arrived on January 15 of the death of Tomás

14 "Diario del tumulto," op. cit., pp. 272–3.
15 The "thirty-five years of domination" of the house of Rodríguez mentioned by this writer are reduced to eighteen by Pedro de Angelis who, in the remaining paragraphs, faithfully copies the rest of the account. The economic predominance of the Rodríguez family became apparent from around 1760.
16 "Diario del tumulto," op. cit., p. 274.

Catari. The event encouraged the *corregidor* of Paria – a neighboring province of Chayanta, the center of the Catari rebellion – who with excessive optimism believed the time had come to go back to his *corregimiento* to collect back taxes. With Catari dead, he assumed that the Indians in nearby settlements would once again heed the laws of the crown.

Thus the *corregidor* Manuel de la Bodega unknowingly set out toward his unfortunate martyrdom; he asked Urrutia for militia support from Oruro, but was denied, as Urrutia was as afraid of provoking indigenous reprisals as of annoying his rivals. Bodega then rashly decided to march on Paria with only thirty men he armed himself – having apparently recruited them in Oruro – and set out first to the village of Challapata. A document describes the end of this absurd campaign:[17]

With this escort [Bodega] marched to the village of Challapata [in the province of Paria], which he reached on August 16, 1781, at four in the morning, and took prisoner five Indians who carried proof that they were the principal accomplices and moving force [of the resistance against his authority and against the payment of tribute] without encountering the least resistance among them; led on by this, the *corregidor* seems to have pondered the idea of accrediting or initiating there the trial against these criminals in order to turn them over afterwards to Chuquisaca; but the peaceful situation he thought he had for this operation turned out to be deceptive, since about four o'clock in the afternoon they discovered a troop of a thousand Indians advancing in two columns with different banners, one red and the other black. They came to a halt on a nearby hill in complete silence, and very soon, with additions of greater numbers, sounding mournful horns in signal, they charged the village and the *corregidor* and his men were surrounded, and he tried to take cover in the plaza; and in this short space of time he found himself left with only twelve men and two Negroes, since the rest of his group had already taken flight.

[After the *corregidor* fled to take refuge in a church, the Indians followed him and went in, breaking down the doors], and finding the *corregidor* on his knees to the King of Kings and Lord of Lords, they impetuously seized him, and, caught in the midst of the mob, he was taken out to the plaza by now more dead than alive, having been hit with a stone in the temple while still inside the church, and he was beheaded by the hand of his own slave . . . with whose head [the *corregidor*'s] they walked about publicizing the victory through the whole village shouting uproariously. . . . As for the others who were in hiding before the combat, being Creoles, mestizos, and *cholos*, the rebel leader himself, after they were rounded up, gave them their liberty and even a pardon so they could go, although on foot, back to their homes; from which we infer that all the fury of this rabble was directed solely against the Europeans or Spaniards who these resembled. With such a horrible event as this, this city finds itself in a state of major consternation, since it is surrounded by the Province of Paria, and the part remaining adjoins Sicasica which likewise, although it has

17 Document dated Oruro, January 30, 1781. Included in the "Relación de los funestos acontecimientos ocurridos en el día 15 del presente mes de enero de 1781 en el pueblo de Challapata jurisdicción de la provincia de Paria, con su corregidor Don Manuel de la Bodega, y el 26 de dicho mes en la de Carangas con su corregidor dn. Matías Ibáñez," in Paz, *Guerra separatista*, op. cit., pp. 240–4. This document raises to eighty the number of soldiers recruited by Bodega, as compared with the thirty cited in the "Diario del tumulto." Pedro de Angelis interpolates the figures, indicating that "fifty men were recruited at his expense" (op. cit., p. 224). This confirms that the *corregidores* covered expenses of this type from their own pockets.

not reached such extremes, is surely just waiting for an excuse for something similar to happen.[18]

Conquer or die

Bodega was not the only European to be deceived when it came to the Indians. Three centuries of daily coexistence had not taught the Europeans to understand the needs or behavior of the Indians. When the indigenous universe demonstrated its astonishing distance and inaccessibility, Creoles and Europeans began to suspect how little they had penetrated it.

Scenes like the one at Challapata were repeated by the dozens between 1780 and 1782: a group of Indians who until the day before had behaved submissively and even obsequiously or who, in the worst of cases, had passively resisted the obligation to pay tribute, would change their manner so rapidly that the Europeans could not gather their wits and make an effective, authoritative response.

A reading of sources from the prior epoch leads to a similar interpretation. There we find cases of indigenous violence, but not the organizational capacity to sustain and spread it. The profuse documentation amassed by Creoles and Europeans during the preceding years tended to concentrate on their internal quarrels.[19] There are, of course, protests by *caciques* – always about taxes – and more direct allusions (when not actually lawsuits) to the highly criticized behavior of the *corregidores*. Nevertheless, a profile of the Indian as violent and merciless such as the one that emerged between 1780 and 1782, was far from usual in earlier documentation. Even at a distance one is still impressed – though not as much as the Spanish themselves must have been – by the sudden transformation of these tribute-paying, submissive Indians into columns of thousands of silent, armed combatants, guided by their own banners and trumpets, standing on a hill to then charge without mercy on the despised city of the whites.

It is probable, however, that the archival documents omit, misrepresent, or simply ignore part of the changing reality of the years preceding the uprisings. The eyes of European Spaniards and even of the Creoles were not trained to observe the internal world of the indigenous population; and those who did see what was happening – several parish priests, for example – took sides with the rebels. It is hard to believe that no signs of the vengeful upheaval building in the parishes filtered through to the Spaniards, or that the latter could be so blind to the accumulated zeal for revenge in blood and fire produced by these unknown people in reaction to injustice and punishment.

18 "Relación de los funestos acontecimientos," op. cit., pp. 240–4.
19 Except for previous uprisings, restricted to specific zones, or the exceptional one of Juan Santos Atahualpa.

The inhabitants of Oruro were no exception – even the Creole faction, which supposed itself capable of controlling the Indian uprising – and thus the residents of the city prepared the stage for their own odyssey. The documentation presented in this and the next chapter, in addition to the sources already mentioned, consists in many cases of the opinions of the attacking Indians.[20]

The simplicity with which they explain their principal motives for taking the city is impressive: to kill, annihilate, cut the throats of the whites, rob them of their property, and "die or conquer," according to their own declared slogan. These motivations had remained latent for a long time; only a situation like that in the 1780s could have allowed such a full expression of their vehemence.

The final outcome also takes us by surprise: the absolute defeat, the trials of the leaders, the open denunciations of leaders by their followers in order to save their own lives or lighten their sentences, the return to submission and to observance of the laws of the Europeans – and, a few decades later, of the emancipated Creoles. The enigmatic world of the Indian, subject to its own laws, turned in on itself again. It did not matter that it increasingly came to include *cholos* ("civilized Indians") and mestizos, in accordance with the complicated but flexible system of castes; an inside and an outside always endured. A large part of the later history of Latin America was marked by these features, perhaps even until the present.

Vigil, rumors, and crossed signals

In Oruro, the horrible end of Manuel de la Bodega caused consternation. Restlessness mounted after the event due to a disturbing rumor that the Indians in the surrounding areas seemed convinced that the city had supported the *corregidor*'s expedition. According to the chronicler,

With this event the Indians of Challapata, Condo, Poopó, and other neighboring towns were convinced that the *corregidor* Urrutia had assisted Bodega with arms and men to kill them and from that day on they menaced the city and its *corregidor*, threatening to lay waste to it and kill all its inhabitants.[21]

According to the pro-Spanish chronicler, the chaplain of the mining mills of Don Juan Rodríguez – the Franciscan, Fray Bernardino Gallegos, who in fact was found guilty and prosecuted after the uprising was over[22] – assiduously visited Oruro carrying messages from the Indians of Challapata

---

20 "Testimonios del expediente" (Juicios de Oruro), loc. cit.
21 "Diario del tumulto," op. cit., p. 275.
22 "Testimonio del quaderno Segundo de autos criminales obrados por don Sebastián de Segurola sobre la rebelión de la Villa de Oruro," Buenos Aires, 1789, AGN, Sala IX, 7-4-3, legajo 2, no. 2.

to the peasants living within the settlement limits. Their contents were alarmist, indicating that they were prepared to enter because they knew that *chapetones* and Creoles were holding military practice. Urrutia indicated his displeasure to the priest, which apparently only gave him more incentive to continue his activities. Clearly, according to this source, most of the letters attributed to third parties and containing sensational news about Indian agitation came from the pen of Fray Bernardino himself.

The interpretation of the author of the pro-Creole diary, on the other hand, gives all the credit for the rumors to a spontaneous indigenous uprising. According to Bishop Menéndez,

We knew that the assembling and crowds on all the roads was ceaseless and to this effect the transient Indians hindered passage and interfered so that in order to get by one had to give them money. At the same time we were receiving letters from said Indians in which they said that since soldiers were going out from the city to avenge the deaths that had been executed, they were beginning to gather in order to defend themselves. Also they said that Tupac Amaru was just outside La Paz and kept conquering provinces so that he would be recognized as King of all Peru.[23]

Confusion grew daily, with public and secret meetings in the *cabildo* following one another without any satisfactory decision being reached. The main problem was the exhausted funds of the public treasury, since – according to the pro-Spanish chronicler – "nothing was resolved because there was no money in the *caja de propios*, or to put it better because there was no such *caja*, since for many years in these parts Don Jacinto Rodríguez had had absolute control over its deposits."[24]

Finally, the treasurer of the *cabildo*, Don Salvador Parrilla, offered 2,000 pesos of his own money to begin defraying the costs of maintaining troops and purchasing the paraphernalia of war. On February 4, three hundred men were called up at a salary of three *reales* a day, and officers were appointed, both European and Creole.

The four companies thus formed lost no time in demonstrating their differences, in accordance with the different composition of their memberships. The Spanish chronicler particularly denigrates the company formed on the initiative of Don Manuel Serrano, which in his opinion was made up of "the most infamous riffraff of the place [and having as its] Lieutenant Don Nicolás Herrera, whose praises his perverse deeds will supply to you . . . as well as the deeds of his Sergeant, Don Bernabé Pineda."[25] According to this source, Herrera had acted in a scandalous manner: "As he is accus-

23 "Relación trágica," op. cit., p. 312. Note the allusion to foreign or transient Indians. The writer here describes them as subject to the subversive command of the parish Indians, but this conflicts with assessments given in later accounts, where a more directive role is attributed to them.
24 "Diario del tumulto," op. cit., p. 276.
25 Ibid., p. 276.

tomed to plunder, one night he did not let the soldiers come into his quarters, locking the doors [because each captain was in charge of paying his troops at night], and he kept all the money for the salaries."[26]

Nicolás de Herrera was not judged the same way by Pedro de Angelis. He cautiously characterized him as "quarrelsome" – adding later that Herrera had been one of the most active spreaders of anti-Spanish rumors – and he omitted the story about the soldiers' pay.[27] In Bishop Menéndez's diary there is no direct mention of Herrera's participation.

On February 6 events began to gather momentum. Once more, opinions about developments unfolding in the uprising were contradictory. According to the Creoles – going on the word of Bishop Menéndez – the "papers" being circulated around the city in the name of Tupac Amaru were exasperating the Spanish, who also viewed the Creoles' enthusiasm in learning how to use arms with apprehension:

They began to show fear that if the Indians were really advancing, the Creoles would rebel first, that they would have to rebel against the Europeans; but there were others who in any case were sure of victory for their side, basing their argument on the cowardice of the Indians and Creoles, and the superiority of their arms and bravery, and in fact encouraged by this they fortified themselves with all kinds of firearms, bullets, and powder, buying them at exorbitant prices from the Creoles themselves. At the same time the *corregidor* ordered all the Creoles to hand over their firearms and [said] he would keep them in his house so that in case of any new developments the Europeans could get them and use them . . . and with this the arrogance and aggressiveness against the Creoles increased.[28]

According to the version of the Spanish chronicler on February 6 there was another irregular situation in the barracks when Don Clemente Menacho, a Creole in charge of one of the companies, went to collect the payroll money at the house of the *corregidor* himself. There, apparently, he was humiliated when both Urrutia and the distributor let it be known that he had not returned what was left over from previous payments. The next day, his company did not want to provide musicians for the tattoo, a disobedience repeated on February 8 by Serrano's company.[29]

Pedro de Angelis also attempts a conciliatory paragraph in this case, preferring intelligently to summarize the general state of mind he assumed was prevalent:

The troops thus in their quarters, there was a lot of dissent over the small subordination of the soldiers, the illegal behavior of the officers in the administration of their remuneration, and other reasons that arose more out of their state of mind than from well-founded complaints.[30]

26 Ibid., pp. 276–7.
27 De Angelis, op. cit., p. 226.
28 "Relación trágica," op. cit., p. 313.
29 "Diario del tumulto," op. cit., p. 277.
30 De Angelis, op. cit., p. 226.

The uprising of February 1781

Until at least the middle of the twentieth century a historiographical debate persisted about the events and participants that made February 10, 1781 one of the first "national dates" for Oruro, and for the Bolivian republic in general.[31]

Events unfolded in the following manner: by the afternoon of February 9, the city was buzzing with rumors. Among the Creoles it was whispered that that night the Europeans had decided to dismiss the four companies in the barracks, and that this had prompted the *corregidor* to put them under lock and key; it was also rumored that

[the *corregidor*] had spoken privately with the Negroes who were also quartered in the same house with the Creoles, giving two knives to each of them [and that] a *chapetón* asked them in the barracks if they had confessed yet, that in the house of the *corregidor* and next door to the barracks there were three ladders against the wall and that under his bed there was a cellar dug at right angles to the Creole barracks.[32]

All this created so much apprehension among the Creoles that there was no way to get them to return to the barracks; only by "begging them on his knees" and promising them that from that night on he would share their quarters was the *corregidor* able to get them to return.[33]

What happened during the night before the 10th is told only in the diary of the pro-Europeans. Here is the first mention of the famous harangue of Sebastián Pagador, considered by nineteenth-century Bolivian historians as an early but unequivocal expression of the Creoles' zeal for independence. It seems a little strange that the event was not recorded in Bishop Menéndez's diary.

According to the pro-European diary,

on the ninth at ten o'clock at night several soldiers went out who were quartered in Serrano's company, shouting and screaming for help from the other companies and when asked what the matter was Sebastián Pagador replied for all, saying aloud: Friends, countrymen and comrades, be assured that the most perfidious treachery against us is being planned by the *chapetones*; this news has just been brought to me by my daughter. On no other occasion will we ever have to give such clear proof of our honor and love for country as this one. Let us not be concerned with our lives, let us sacrifice them in defense of our country, converting all the humility and submissiveness with which until now we have suffered the tyranny of the *chapetones* into anger and fury in order to tear them to pieces and if possible be done with this accursed race.[34]

In a polemic that took place in 1920 but was kept alive for many years by its participants, the historians Adolfo Mier and Marcos Beltrán Avila,

---

31 See the polemic between Adolfo Mier and Marcos Beltrán Avila, in Beltrán Avila, *Jacinto Rodríguez y Sebastián Pagador: El 10 de febrero y el 6 de octubre. Opiniones* (Oruro, M. C. Gamarra, 1944).
32 "Relación trágica," op. cit., p. 313.
33 Ibid., p. 314.
34 "Diario del tumulto," op. cit., p. 277.

Mier defined Pagador as "the genius behind the Oruro uprising of 1781," and as the representative of the heroic attitude of the city of Oruro. He based his opinion on the story told by Pedro de Angelis in his "relación histórica." Mier was refuted by Marcos Beltrán, who understood that Pagador was only a subaltern adjutant of Jacinto Rodríguez; in his judgment the latter was the real leader and driving force behind the events in Oruro.[35] Although Pedro de Angelis took note of the document just quoted – and apparently was the first to transcribe the famous "harangue" in its entirety – he touched it up conveniently. For example, he underlines the motivation "for love of country," omitting the previous phrase, which alludes to "our honor." Likewise he ignores the strong expressions in the document about "tearing the *chapetones* to pieces" and "finishing off this accursed race once and for all."[36]

Continuing with the pro-Spanish diary, which Pedro de Angelis follows at this point almost without modification, at the same time that Pagador was making his proclamation, Nicolás Herrera entered the house of the patrician Casimiro Delgado, a very rich man of the town, "exaggerating the oath of the *chapetones* with the most vivid colors his malicious intent could paint."[37] According to this source, Pagador, who was considered little more than a servant of the Rodríguez family, had heard Don Jacinto say "between mouthfuls of coca and *chicha*" that the *corregidor* wanted to hang him and his two brothers. He used this unfounded statement to fuel his arguments to stir up the Creoles, taking advantage of the existing climate. The same source is no less kind to Nicolás Herrera, whom he calls a "robber and highwayman."

Nicolás Herrera knew that a few days before many bars and bags of silver had been deposited in the house of the Spaniard José Endeiza.[38] With the threat of Indian invasion, Endeiza and three other Spaniards decided to place all their belongings and money in the house of Miguel Salinas, a trader in merchandise from Castile, figuring that from there they could defend themselves in case of attack. Endeiza's three friends were Juan Blanco, Francisco Palaquelos, and Pedro Lagrara; later they were joined by others. Herrera knew about all these movements, according to the pro-European document and Pedro de Angelis's transcription.[39] Herrera and two "clerical guests" who were staying in his house at the time went outside and saw the disturbance. Rumors circulated about the "treachery" of the Spaniards; the women went to the barracks to ask the men to retreat in the face of the "threat of death" they believed was hanging over them.

35 See the polemic between Adolfo Mier and Beltrán Avila, op. cit., pp. 24–31.
36 De Angelis, op. cit., p. 226.
37 "Diario del tumulto," op. cit., p. 277.
38 The author of the "Diario del tumulto" asserts that the value of what Endeiza retained in his house was 500,000 pesos (p. 278), whereas de Angelis (p. 227) reduced the sum to 50,000.
39 "Diario del tumulto," op. cit., p. 278.

In the midst of this chaos (and perhaps taking advantage of it), Herrera and Pagador decided to visit the house of Jacinto Rodríguez to ask him to stand before a popular meeting. According to the European source, this had already been convened by the Rodríguez family. Fray Bernardino Gallegos had made a trip days before to Challapata, with the objective of calling together the Indians, mestizos, and mulattoes who worked in the mines, to get them to march on the city during the night of February 10. The priest proved to be an able propagandist, and his scheming added more fuel to the fire. For example, days earlier he had pretended privately to burn – nevertheless making sure his act became known – a supposedly secret letter that spoke of imminent invasion. This added to the prevailing state of alarm. According to the source, it was later proved that the priest had written the letter himself.[40]

By the middle of the afternoon of the 10th, the situation was already totally out of Urrutia's control. The soldiers were sacking the fort and refused to go to their quarters even though Indians could already be seen on the outskirts of town. The pro-Creole source does not state this explicitly, although he does admit that the Creoles had decided to meet en masse at the house of Jacinto Rodríguez after hearing rumors that he would be assassinated by the Spaniards, thus ignoring the defense against the Indians.[41]

When night fell trumpets were heard, and it was assumed that the Indians would attack; but when armed militiamen went to the hill of Conchopata, they found that it had been a false alarm. This, however, set the tragedy in motion.

By now ready to fight, the Creole militiamen returned and went to the center of the city. There, in the plaza, they attacked the house of the Spanish shopkeeper Miguel Salinas. The episode, predictably, is reported by each of the sources according to his own perspective.

According to the bishop's diary, the Creoles left the barracks following orders from the *corregidor*, but when they passed the Plaza del Regocijo, several *chapetones* began to fire on them from a corner house – that is, from Salinas's shop. In the face of the attack, the document continues, the Creoles responded by throwing stones at the balconies, but, finding themselves at a disadvantage, "they threw several flaming torches and started the fire . . . and surrounded them on all four sides."[42]

The pro-European chronicle tells the events in a different manner, assuring us that the rocks were thrown first. At this, the Spaniards responded with salvos from their guns "into the air," from the balcony, without wound-

40 Ibid., pp. 280–2.
41 "Relación trágica," op. cit., p. 314.
42 Ibid., p. 315.

ing any of the Creoles.[43] Then, the house was surrounded and harassed until the morning of the next day:

The Creoles were affronted, and full of pure rage, they kept slinging stones against the house and balconies. The men who gathered, nearly 4 thousand, set fire to the house, and the women who came were many and they occupied themselves with a continuous barrage of the strongest and most solid stones, which they brought from the mines; and thus they kept up the battle, until after three in the morning.[44]

Although the chronicler mentions only Creoles, the presence of men armed with slingshots and of women – if true – would indicate that Indians and mestizos were among the attackers.

The bishop's diary confirms what happened, relating that the next morning it was found that only four or five Creoles had been wounded, while not one *chapetón* or black escaped the house alive. They died so horribly, it says, "that first they were burned, and then they were finished off with stones and lances so it was not possible to recognize them except by their clothes."[45] To justify what happened, the bishop adds this surprising paragraph:

Here it is essential that the reader take into consideration the Divine hand, which so prodigiously and clearly favored the Creoles over the misfortunes suffered by eleven *chapetones* and five slaves. The former were massed at a short distance of twelve paces without any protection against the bullets, and the latter were inside a room into which no stone or fire ever entered, only reaching the edge of the balcony. After they were dead it was recognized that though their feet and hands were burned it was because they left the shelter of the wall and went to adjoining houses on the roofs that were burning and only by this miracle can the innocence of the Creoles and the malice of the Europeans be known although at the time of dying and the pardon they asked assured that it was the *corregidor*'s fault.[46]

That terrible Sunday ended with few illusions that the *corregidor* could control the situation. He understood that he was facing an uprising of unpredictable consequences and that he did not carry any effective power in the city. Nevertheless, he tried to play his last card: to convince Jacinto Rodríguez and Nicolás Herrera of the need to pacify the anger of the Creoles, *cholos*, and Indians. Rodríguez did not deign to answer any of the messages sent to his mills; when the *corregidor* went personally to Herrera's house, he found him playing cards with his two companions – one of whom, according to de Angelis, was the priest of Sorasora, D. Isidoro de Velazco – and was unable to interrupt the game with his request for help. Herrera indifferently answered that the situation was already out of hand and it was too late to do anything about it.[47]

43 "Diario del tumulto," op. cit., p. 286.
44 Ibid., p. 287.
45 "Relación trágica," op. cit., p. 315.
46 Ibid., pp. 315–16.
47 "Diario del tumulto," op. cit., p. 287.

The invasion

On Monday February 12, Oruro awakened to desolation and tragedy: smoke and the smell of the charred bodies of the Europeans, who had been dragged in front of the public hall, bore brutal testimony to the night's events.

An attempt by the priests to calm people's anger by carrying the holy sacrament in a public procession met with indifference from the majority and hostility from some. The new day, far from bringing calm, seemed to presage increasing violence. In the morning the prisoners in the jail were set free, and in the afternoon people began plundering the burned house after hearing about the great "spoils of war" hidden there.[48]

According to Bishop Menéndez, who in his diary always refers to himself in the third person as "the vicar," he went on his own initiative to the house of Jacinto Rodríguez, since the latter was "the person most loved and respected among the secular Creoles," in order to ask him to calm everyone down. According to this report, they both went to the *cabildo* after calling the people to assemble there, and from its balcony, Rodríguez was named *corregidor* by popular acclaim. The bishop, according to his own version, took advantage of the opportunity to speak paternally to the crowd assembled, exhorting those present to be obedient. But threatening voices were raised against Urrutia, on whom the suspicions of European Spanish treachery centered. The bishop appealed to the magnanimity of the crowd and begged them to pardon the offenders.

Apparently a difficult negotiation ensued between the bishop and the leaders of the people concerning the conditions of expulsion of the hated *chapetones*. It must be mentioned that in this account, the bishop skillfully describes his own participation, presenting himself as arbitrator. It is impossible to know if his efforts to moderate were real or not; according to his version the crowd demanded that the Spaniards be disarmed and exiled from the city if their lives were to be spared. The bishop states that he was not put in charge of collecting the arms of the pardoned Europeans.[49]

The European version, although more concise in this part of the story, confirms everything related by the bishop except the popular demand for the confiscation of arms:

Between 8 and 9 that day everyone went down to the jail and, opening the doors, they threw out all the prisoners and then they left shouting "Long live our *justicia mayor* D. Jacinto Rodríguez." Shouting "viva" and "victory" they marched clamorously down the street playing drums and bugles and got him from his house and made him march all around the four sides of the *Plaza Mayor.* . . . I don't know if it was before or after this that the vicar [bishop] of the city came out on the balcony of the *cabildo* to admonish the Creoles, asking them what it was they wanted or demanded in their favor in order to quiet down. And

48 Ibid., p. 289.
49 "Relación trágica," op. cit., pp. 315–18.

they answered all as one, we want D. Jacinto Rodríguez for *justicia mayor* [*corregidor*]. Let the *corregidor* and the rest of the *chapetones* leave this place in exile, in our sight.[50]

Contrary to expectations, however, the popular acclamation in favor of Rodríguez did not save the situation. At midday, according to the pro-European source, several groups of Indians arrived armed with bugles, slingshots, and nooses, apparently with the intent of guaranteeing the defense of the new *corregidor*. With horror of nature they saw that, after paying him homage at his domicile,

> and telling him with many embraces and hand-kissings that they had come to defend his life; and he gave them money in thanks, they went running riotously off with the Creoles to see the dead; but the sight so enraged them that they discharged their fury again against the mangled corpses . . . and every Indian bloodied his arms and bathed them in that innocent blood.[51]

After paying homage to Rodríguez the Indians went to the houses of Manuel Herrera, Clemente Menacho, and Antonio Quirós, to "search the houses where there was money, in order to loot them, and the places where the *chapetones* were hiding," asserts the pro-European document.

The bishop, meanwhile, was beginning to suffer the burden of his efforts at conciliation. He had to intervene personally to defend the life of the Spaniard Juan Antonio Martínez, in whose house he was at that moment undertaking the confiscation of arms. The Indians obeyed his orders, but they searched every corner of the house. Considering the terror of the Spanish occupants of the house, the bishop agreed to take them with him and give them immunity in the principal church.[52]

The author of the European diary accuses the bishop of having given the confiscated arms to the Indians, but reports that this did not satisfy their demands. As their violent attitude continued to grow, Bishop Menéndez made a curious decision that better describes his partisan zeal than his conciliatory talents. In the not-very-charitable words of the European diary:

> The priest, who had no more devices left to deal with this trouble, decided to climb to the top of the *Rollo* [the symbol of the founding of the city, which was erected in the center of the Plaza Mayor of every Spanish settlement] to preach discipline in the public plaza. As this made him seem laughable and ridiculous to both the Creoles and the Indians, they became much more insolent and shot at him three times with a slingshot, until they made him come down.[53]

In his diary the bishop omits any description of this humiliation and emphasizes only the noisy and threatening attitude of the Indians.

50 "Diario del tumulto," op cit., p. 289.
51 Ibid., pp. 289–90.
52 "Relación trágica," op. cit., pp. 317–18.
53 "Diario del tumulto," op. cit., p. 290.

After the bishop's failure to pacification, the priors of the communities of Augustans, Franciscans, and Mercedarios tried in turn to hold a neighborhood procession led by the figure of San Cristo de Burgos. This had no impact on the people either. The ceremony was attended mainly by "most of the old women," and its presence was requested only in front of the shop of the Spaniard Francisco Resa to try to ward off looting by the Indians. Again, the Indians reacted to the religious images with scorn:

The procession marched in fact to this place but before it could accomplish anything the Indians began to show evidence of their apostasy of the Catholic religion, which until then it was thought they had professed, since they shouted out that this Image was nothing more than a piece of cactus, and how it had been painted to deceive them.[54]

Such quotations, describing the Indians' indifference and openly anti-Christian sentiments, are often found in other sources.[55] This corroborates the presumption of a superficial evangelization and of the survival, in the form of a complex religious syncretism, of their ancestral beliefs.[56]

Nevertheless, related events do not indicate much religious zeal on the part of the insurgent Creoles either; they were frequently associated with acts of rebellion against the church's teachings. Although this can be partly attributed to a reaction against the European predominance in the clergy, the disrespect to priests clearly identified with the rebel band – as in the case of Bishop Menéndez – obliges us to consider nonpolitical causes for this rejection.

As for the bishop's situation, he insisted hour after hour that his authority over the Indians was only nominal. This became clear when, as he attempted to go to the cemetery to give a Christian burial to the dead, the Indians stopped him with threats; according to his version, he somehow did the job by himself, but not without risking his life.[57]

Meanwhile, the entrance of indigenous people into the city continued uninterrupted. According to the calculations of the European chronicler, which are perhaps exaggerated, in the space of six hours, four thousand of them had gathered. They came in from the outskirts, then went up and down the streets in groups blowing their trumpets and launching stones with slingshots. Some of them marched carrying flags, and many Creoles, according to the same source, came from all corners of the city to welcome them with embraces.

54 Ibid., pp. 290–1.
55 "Juicios de Oruro," loc. cit.
56 See, in this regard, Frank Salomon, "Ancestor Cults and Resistance to the State in Arequipa, ca. 1748–1754," in Steve J. Stern, ed., *Resistance, Rebellion and Consciousness in the Andean Peasant World, 18th to 20th Centuries* (Madison, University of Wisconsin Press, 1987), pp. 148–65.
57 "Relación trágica," op. cit., p. 318.

The outbreak

On Tuesday February 13, Oruro awoke to complete occupation by the Indians. Both diaries tell of the profound upheaval that began to unify Europeans and Creoles in the face of this multitude of armed and warlike Indians.

Although Rodríguez still had confidence that he could contain the disorder, discouraging signs began to appear. Accompanied by a committee, he went out in the morning to try to control the plundering of the shop of the European Manuel de Bustamante. There he found that neither his exhortations nor those of the bishop who, as usual, did not leave his side, were producing the desired effect. Not only did the looting continue, but the Indians, on realizing that the *alcalde de primer voto* was present in the committee, immediately demanded his head when they understood that he had allied himself with the *chapetones*. The *alcalde* managed to escape, but the unwise behavior of the Creole leaders indicated that the outbreak had begun.

The Indians used a slogan on this occasion that was later repeated in other documents. According to the Spanish chronicler, at the same time that they were condemning the alcalde and demanding his head, they shouted, "'*Comuna, comuna, comuna!*' – A word they used when they wanted to rob or kill, as if they were saying, 'all for one.'"[58]

This expression seems to be associated, however, with the idea of the "community," understood as the popular base of an indigenous settlement. The bishop uses a related expression in his diary when he describes that "from that afternoon on [Monday, February 12] *mancomunes* [associations, or commonwealths] of Indians began to enter."[59]

On February 13 Jacinto Rodríguez decided to validate his appointment, convoking an open *cabildo*. As he passed in front of the principal church, he had to act as mediator in an argument between the bishop and a large number of Indians crowded against the front door. They suspected that the deposed *corregidor* was hiding inside the church; the bishop assured them that this was not so and that the only refugees were "four *chapetones* who had already confessed." The Spanish chronicler indignantly interprets this as an indirect signal by the bishop to the Indians to assault the refugees:

The Indians, who did not want to be told otherwise, became enraged, and full of fury they broke in, overcoming the strength of the church, they opened the crypt, and the Indian women, braver than the men, went into the deepest recesses of this gloomy cellar . . . and brought out a coffin in which a corpse had been laid, [and] ordered it opened, believing the *corregidor* was shut inside it. . . .[60]

The bishop tells the story in a similar manner, but without admitting that he handed the Europeans over to the Indians. He relates that the pressure at

58 "Diario del tumulto," op. cit., p. 291.
59 "Relación trágica," op. cit., p. 318.
60 "Diario del tumulto," op. cit., p. 292.

the doors of the church had become unbearable; for three hours he talked and wept before them, but by then the stones were raining against the church walls, "and it not being possible to contain them because their insolence mounted at every instant, especially that of the women, who in order to separate the vicar from the doors, tore his habit to shreds, knocked him to the ground twice, and kicked and punched him with their hands and feet."[61]

He reports that he decided to distract the attackers, proposing that they search the church. Meanwhile, he went to save the Eucharist and signaled the Europeans to flee over the adjoining rooftops, where they were quickly discovered and killed.

Allusions to the fierceness of the Indian women abound in other sources. In sieges of cities, they provided logistic support as stone carriers for the slingshots and as bearers of arms and supplies. Once inside the occupied strongholds, however, they participated equally in the fighting, encouraging the men with their ferocity and denying clemency much more regularly than the men.

One of the fugitives from the principal church was the European Manuel de Bustamante. When he was captured, because he was known to be protected by the *corregidor* in spite of his origins, the Indians went to Jacinto Rodríguez to obtain the execution order. He decided that the Spaniard should be locked up in the public jail, which enraged the Indian, who reportedly said, "'You have called us to kill *chapetones*; and now you only want them to go to jail. Well, it does not have to be this way.' And shouting the accursed '*comuna, comuna,*' they carried out that disgraceful murder."[62]

From that moment on, both chroniclers describe the deteriorating situation in equally dispirited tones. The lists of attacks grew ceaselessly; the immunity of churches and convents was ignored, and those who took refuge in them were dragged out and brutally killed. Those Creoles who looked like Europeans "by their dress and faces" began to find themselves in a difficult position.

On the morning of Wednesday, February 14, the convent of La Merced was surrounded by a large crowd of Indians, many of whom climbed on its roofs and towers. Making a tremendous din, they entered and found a Spaniard under the Virgin's cloak and another disguised in women's clothing, recognizable by his shoes. They killed both of them immediately, and before the wailing of the widows they claimed to have received orders from Jacinto Rodríguez. After a fruitless search of the homes of the Europeans – who had fled, in most cases, with only the clothes on their backs – they searched for the black slaves and also the dogs, and killed them "with rabid thirst."

Jacinto Rodríguez, meanwhile, began to take many of the European fugi-

61 "Relación trágica," op. cit., p. 319.
62 "Diario del tumulto," op. cit., p. 293.

tives into his houses, since they were the only places by this time that offered immunity from attack. It was nevertheless foreseeable that at some moment Rodríguez's protection would cease to be sufficient. The effective authority of the Creoles had expired and the city had, without any doubt, been conquered by the Indians.

That night the Creole leaders came to a decision: with money from the *caja real*, they would pay off the Indians, at the rate of one peso a head, on the condition that they retreat from the city. The Spanish chronicler relates this development with indignation, asking, "Who would not be astonished at this idea? To pay assassins and robbers at the Monarch's expense because they came to rob and kill at [the Creoles'] orders?"[63]

The bishop, in turn, relates that the measure was a last resort, because the Indians had already become as aggressive with the Creoles as with the Europeans:

There were by now so many Indians and the city was so thoroughly dominated that they commanded men and women to dress up [like Indians] and chew coca; and the residents were so fainthearted and obedient that they did not refuse for that day and several days following to take off their own clothes and put on Indian dress, going out of course into the street to manifest their blind obedience. And this was so general that only the priests and monks did not copy them. At the same time . . . they only convened [in the name of] "*comuna*" and in all the houses, bakeries, and shops, they complained of going three or four days without food, asking for and receiving whatever they wanted.[64]

Thus on Thursday, February 15, the Creoles decided to meet the Indians in the outskirts of town to promise them the payment. The bishop, always quick to adhere to the forms of conciliation, delivered a strange speech, according to the pro-European chronicler:

My sons, I as your Priest and Vicar and in the name of this whole city give you due thanks for the fidelity with which you have come to defend us, killing the vile *chapetones* who wanted to take the lives of all the Creoles in treachery; a thousand and one times we thank you and we beg you to retreat to your houses, since the *chapetones* already lie dead, as you have seen and done, and in case you have incurred any discommunion or censure, let all of you make an act of contrition in order to receive absolution.[65]

While the bishop reports his participation without quoting his speech, he agrees with the above version, confirming that "the vicar" delivered a Christian exhortation to the Indians that lasted an hour, about the favor they had done for the city.

The Indians negotiate a retreat

The Indians, however, were more interested in material restitution than in divine absolution. After the bishop's speech, they pressed Jacinto Rodríguez

63 Ibid., p. 296.
64 "Relación trágica," op. cit., p. 320.
65 "Diario del tumulto," op. cit., p. 296.

to formally declare that their demands be heard: in the first place, that the lands of the Europeans be from then on returned to the community ("*al común*") of the Indians; furthermore, that the tributes and *diezmos* be abolished. "The priest, the prelates, and councilmen of the *cabildo* conceded everything, filled with pure terror before more than fifteen thousand Indians, all armed with sticks, stones, and slingshots,"[66] the Spanish chronicler writes.

In the middle of the negotiations, a rider approached the crowd; he had come from the province of Tinta with a message from Tupac Amaru. The latter recommended to his followers "that they regard the temples and priests with much respect and veneration, that they do no harm to the Creoles, and pursue only the *chapetones*."[67] In addition, the messenger informed everyone that the rebel chief was ready to go to La Paz, news that aroused cheers of joy from Indians and Creoles alike.

Curiously, the pro-Creole diary of the bishops makes no mention of this; but Pedro de Angelis does, and adds a suggestive remark about Manuel de Herrera:

[After the message was received] . . . the infamous name of the tyrant was shouted repeatedly, and was heard again in the plazas and public streets by every class of people with greatest rejoicing, everyone running with banners and other demonstrations of jubilation, which Don Manuel de Herrera imitated from the balcony of his house, waving a white handkerchief and accompanying this action with the same words as the others, which were: "Long live Tupac Amaru," words the people kept reciting, filled with joy.[68]

The news provoked the Creoles to reconsider an alliance with the Indians. Meanwhile, distribution of the payment continued amid general confusion; the bishop reports that the Indians

crowded around pushing and shoving so that no matter how hard the Judges tried, there was no way to keep them in order, and so in the end the silver coins were thrown to whoever could catch them first. More than twenty thousand pesos were spent this way until noon when this form of gratification came to an end [and then] they went back into the city on the pretext of getting their *guapis* or bundles.[69]

It then became difficult to dislodge them by peaceful means. Inside the city once more, the Indians felt they were masters of the will of the residents. According to the Spanish chronicler, Jacinto Rodríguez appeared in public dressed in indigenous robes embroidered in gold, "consenting perhaps to be Tupac Amaru's viceroy."[70]

According to the vicar this demand had come from the Indians themselves, who furthermore

66 Ibid., p. 296.
67 Ibid., p. 297.
68 De Angelis, op. cit., p. 297.
69 "Relación trágica," op. cit., p. 321.
70 "Diario del tumulto," op. cit., p. 298.

had published a pamphlet in their language, ordering that no Creole accompany them, that unless they were recognized first they would be killed, and they would guard the city so there would be no more thievery, assuming that only the Creoles robbed, and they suffered the blame without having taken advantage of anything.[71]

As we shall see later, records of subsequent court trials indicate that the Indians' claims were not entirely false.

With everyone back in the city, the bishop reports, there were repeated cases of "drunkenness, looting of churches, and, since no more Europeans could be found, [the Indians] began to kill Creoles and beat them with whips for utterly ridiculous reasons, such as for loading guns and wanting to defend themselves from one another."[72]

According to the troubled bishop there were no limits to the Indians' brutality, which ranged from bringing dogs to tear apart and eat the corpses to indiscriminate pillaging of every house in the area. Five Indians died at the hands of their own kind over the spoils of war, presaging a threat of general fighting.

On the afternoon of this interminable Thursday, Juan de Dios Rodríguez, Jacinto's brother, arrived in Oruro accompanied by forty Indian chiefs from Paria. As they passed through the city, according to the Spanish diary, they wrenched the royal arms from in front of the post office building, "and trampling and destroying them, to indicate that the reign of our king and lord Don Carlos was already finished."[73]

Far from calming the anger of their comrades, the new arrivals shrewdly coerced the city's frightened landowners into deeding their land over to the indigenous communities.[74] It is not unlikely that Juan de Dios Rodríguez had made a pact with the *caciques* of Paria whereby the ceding of land was a condition for the evacuation of the city. Among them was the prestigious Indian chief Lope Chungara, *cacique* of Challapata. After a firm order from him, two or three of the most rebellious Indians were executed by their own forces; the rest, in absolute obedience, agreed to begin evacuating the city at once.[75]

By Friday, February 16, the situation began to return to normal as the Indians slowly left the city. Tension remained high, however, because more than twenty thousand Indians who had come from Poopó were awaiting in the surrounding area, ready to storm the city on their own account. Lope Chungara, with Juan de Dios Rodríguez's permission, took advantage of this situation to extract more land and *estancias* for the indigenous communities.[76]

71 "Relación trágica," op. cit., p. 320.
72 Ibid., p. 321.
73 "Diario del tumulto," op. cit., p. 298.
74 Ibid., p. 299.
75 Ibid., p. 299.
76 "Relación trágica," op. cit., p. 322.

A troubled truce and a new attack

The retreat of the indigenous forces meant only a brief interval of peace for Oruro, since a few days later the unresolved internal disputes among the inhabitants made their appearance anew. After the first inventory of the looting had been made, it was found that the Indians had not been the only beneficiaries. According to the European chronicler:

The reward of every *cholo* was to say that he had killed 2 or 3 *chapetones* and they showed off what they had taken during the looting, saying they had fair title to it since they had earned it in wartime; but seeing the insolence with which they publicly used and sold the stolen articles, people went to tell Don Jacinto about it. He appointed 4 or 6 men to go and collect the stolen goods; they did so, and this caused a second tragedy, since all the thieves demanded the return of what they had justly earned, and [said that] if this were not done they were going to start killing them, so they thought it prudent to return to each one what they had stolen."[77]

The bishop confirms this version, adding that the men appointed by Jacinto Rodríguez went beyond the call of duty, "taking whatever seemed to them to be stolen to the house of Don Jacinto, which included a great deal that belonged to the owners of said houses, and this gave rise to an interminable and insoluble dispute."[78]

As we shall see in the chapter on the trials, quite a few residents of Oruro remained under suspicion in addition to the *cholos* accused by both chroniclers. The mutual accusations began to gather momentum. The Creoles insisted that in neighboring cities similar treachery by the *chapetones* had been verified. The latter claimed that the Creoles had organized a campaign of defamation against the deposed *corregidor*. Many voices were raised in criticism of both Creoles' and Europeans' open purchases of stolen merchandise at ridiculously low prices – for example, bars of silver for only four pesos.[79]

The bishop's behavior especially was criticized by the Europeans, above all after a ceremony of "pacification" he celebrated on Sunday, February 19. According to the Spanish chronicler,

he gave the people a lecture full of errors, mixing lax, scandalous, and rash propositions and doctrines into it, and even saying that they were not obliged to return what they had robbed and sacked on the night of Saturday the tenth. . . because they had earned it in wartime and let them make an act of contrition and be absolved.[80]

March 8 was Juan de Dios Rodríguez's birthday; according to the European chronicler, he invited prelates, priests, and prominent citizens of the city, "and anyone who refused to drink was seized by Rodríguez and his

---

77 "Diario del tumulto," op. cit., pp. 300–1.
78 "Relación trágica," op. cit., p. 322.
79 "Diario del tumulto," op. cit., p. 304.
80 Ibid., p. 302.

servants and speaking in the voices of Indians, they said in imitation of them, '*comuna, comuna!*'"[81]

The rejoicing of the Creoles did not last long, however. Early the next morning, Indians entered and took the city by surprise. The only account is that of the European diarist: according to him the specific objective of the invasion was the Rodríguez house, which managed to erect defenses by calling on neighbors for help. For a moment the internal hostilities were suspended in order to unite against what was now understood to be the common enemy.[82]

It was a sensible move, but insufficient to ward off the threat gathering on the horizon: the repulsion had not intimidated the Indians, and they were preparing to attack the city again when the time was right. The roads leading to the city were cut off "without permitting food or supplies to be brought in, since they took the lives of the drivers," while the attackers reorganized their forces and reinforced their numbers.

The attacks have so far been described from the point of view of its citizens; the Indians had their own perspective.

81 Ibid., p. 304.
82 Ibid., pp. 304–5.

12

The voice of the rebels

As we might expect, none of the invading Indians left voluntary written testimony about the uprising. Fortunately for historical reconstruction, the trials held after the revolt produced detailed accounts in which the Indians being prosecuted expressed, in some cases with astonishing candor and bluntness, their motivations for joining the movement. Furthermore, letters and written orders exchanged by the Indian chiefs, and those sent between them and their subordinates, reveal the expectations of the movement's leaders. From these sources it is possible to follow the thread of the insurrections of March and April 1781 that followed the February invasion.

The eviction of the Indians from Oruro, accomplished after the difficult negotiations that have been recounted, did not put an end to their aspirations, as the Creoles and European Spaniards had naively hoped.

All February, March, and April insurrections were finally broken up, and this probably owed less to the royalist forces[1] than to the lack of coordination among the Indians. As in other areas, the perception of defeat spread among the rebel Indians with the same speed as had the call to revolt. The Indians of the community surrendered en masse as soon as they knew of the defeat of their advance guard by the army sent to put the rebellion down. In most cases, the chieftains were not taken prisoner; rather, they were handed over by the Indians themselves.

In spite of the *escribano*'s monotonous transcription – in most cases accomplished with the aid of a translator – it is not difficult to imagine the pathetic character of these scenes. After months of blind trust in the coming of the "new Inca" and the expected overthrow of the colonial regime, the Indians were not absorbing their defeat and its consequences. Foreseeing the terrible reprisals that approached – the bloody executions of Tupac Amaru and Tupac Catari were exemplary models – the proud community once more assumed its submissive mien before the royal officials.

Not all the witnesses were ready to abandon their principles, however. Although they were in the minority, many Indian captains and lieutenants

1 Campbell, *Military and Society*, chapter 6.

161

spoke boastfully before the judges in spite of the consequences of imprisonment, repeating their stories and proudly reiterating their war cry, "die or conquer."[2]

Most of the Indians decided to seek the pardon of the victors, especially after having witnessed the moderate attitudes of Viceroys Vértiz and Jáuregui. In spite of this – or perhaps because they felt their lives were safe because of the viceroys' attitudes – they were not shy about telling the judges their true motives.

Thus, many of the things the Indians said were monotonously repeated: they had been summoned to raze the city of Oruro, to burn it, to kill all its inhabitants (except the Indians living inside the city limits), to loot the houses and stores, and to put an end to the payment of tributes and other obligatory taxes. When the testimony referred to the first invasion, in which the Indians had counted on the support of the Creoles, it was clear that the latter were exempt from the Indians' vow to kill.

As for the tributes, many Indians stated that they would not resist future payment, when Tupac Amaru reached Oruro in person and liberated the region. Clearly, however, this was one of the most sensitive and least negotiable items: the astute *cacique* Lope Chungara, who had controlled his men so skillfully, was assassinated soon afterward by a mutinous group of Indians for publishing an edict demanding continued tribute payments to the crown.

Although the names of many local Indian leaders are mentioned often in the testimonies of their followers, a few stand out especially as leader of the March and April invasions. In the insurrection of March 19, the captain of Sillota, Esteban Calisaya, is mentioned, together with Matheo Guaca and Santos Mamani of Challapata. Mamani was the indisputable leader of the attacks of April 1 and 2.

It is difficult to establish whose commands these local leaders were obeying. According to subsequent statements by Santos Mamani, who was the Indian *alcalde* of the *ayllu* of Andamarca in Challapata, spokesmen for Tomás Catari came to his parish to urge his followers to stop paying the taxes, thus starting the outbreak of hostilities with the *corregidor* of the province. According to his own testimony in the trial of May 1781, transcribed by the *escribano*:

[The Indians sent by Tomás Catari] . . . brought to his village some papers containing the order not to pay taxes to the *corregidores* . . . and persuading the whole community of Indians of this, they made them all believe this entirely, and so [the Indians] resisted paying it, although their *corregidor* had agreed to reduce it as ordered by the superior courts, and he urged the *alcalde* [that is, Mamani] to encourage his people to make that payment, threatening to fine him twenty-five pesos if he did not do it, and having sent someone to ask

2 These two highly revealing terms were always expressed in that order.

him to do this, Mamani, fearful he would have to pay the fine, resisted, and he became angry with him, and when the *corregidor* went to the town of Challapata in January 1781, he ordered him taken prisoner together with Lope Chungara, Carlos Cañaviri and Joseph Quispe, and their imprisonment enraged the people of his town and they killed their *corregidor* and many of those who accompanied him.[3]

We may infer from this that the movement was influenced by the Catari brothers – Tomás, its principal leader, and Dámaso and Nicolás, his lieutenants.

It later became known that the forces led by Santos Mamani, Guaca, Calisaya, and other local leaders were preparing a concerted action with Indians from other *corregimientos*, in particular those from Sica Sica. This region abutted La Paz on the northwest, which was soon afterward besieged by Julián Apaza (Tupac Catari). Many letters were sent by the latter and his lieutenants to the Indians of Sica Sica between February and April 1781, which, as we know from the trial records, were later brought to Oruro by the Spaniard Dionisio Bolaños. In all of them the communities were urged to join the movement; in one, Tupac Catari himself ordered that on sight of this paper all available Indian forces should gather in the hills of Calamarca: "Thus must all gather without exception because thus I Lord Viceroy and Catari command it."[4]

But the forces of Sica Sica did not seem ready to join Tupac Catari as quickly as he demanded. His messages became increasingly acerbic and were laced with threats to those who did not join immediately. All the missives are signed, "I, the viceroy," and in one of them dated in April – that is, in the midst of the siege of La Paz – the signature reads, "At this height of the battle, I the Lord Viceroy Tupacatari."[5]

Four of the Indians who testified in Oruro – three of them captains – acknowledge responding to Tupac Catari's command. Sebastián Santos,[6] fifty years old, was one of them. From the province of Pacajes, he was recruited by a local *cacique*, who brought him to the siege of La Paz. There he met Tupac Catari, who appointed him captain general. His file contains a copy of this appointment, which highlights once more the singular style of the proud *caudillo* of La Paz:

I Lord Viceroy Tupacatari, to the Captain General of the Town of Sicasica, Sebastián Santos, give power and license by all the property of the King Our Lord, that no one may stop me

---

3 "Testimonio del expediente de diligencias practicadas para averiguar los tumultos meditados contra Oruro, remitido por don Mariano Vargas y Rodríguez," Buenos Aires, 1789. AGN, Buenos Aires, Sala IX-7-4-3, legajo 2, no. 3 (testimonies taken in Oruro throughout 1781); declaration of Santos Mamani, fols. 233–235.

4 Loc. cit. (letter from Tupac Catari, no date, but supposedly written between February and April, 1781), fols. 176, 178–180.

5 Ibid., fols. 178–180.

6 The age of the Indians arrested or giving testimony, as noted in their own declarations, should be considered approximate.

from so ordering and whoever does not obey may be beheaded and strangled too, because now there is no justice or anything, only to the Captain General, and from the day of the Nativity the battle began and fourteen towns were devastated, and by this I give him license in my place for him to search everything as I command and that they obey him as they do my person, for being an old and upright and important man of noble blood, and at the end of this order I command, provide and sign that it be done, I sign my name, Viceroy Josef [*sic*] Tupacatari."[7]

Of the seventy-six testimonies selected in Appendix A, twenty-five mention Tupac Amaru and only three mention Tupac Catari. Nevertheless, it appears that the Oruro uprisings were more influenced tactically by the nearby *caudillo* of La Paz than by Tupac Amaru himself. Nevertheless, the latter's highly symbolic and emotional slogans remained popular in areas relatively distant from the rebellion's birthplace.

The material documenting the indigenous point of view on the Oruro upheaval of 1781 is too extensive to be summarized in this chapter.[8] We have therefore chosen several examples of the Indians' opinions about their own movement. The morass of orders and counterorders, comings and goings, and sudden changes of alliance evidenced in the letters and proclamations of the local leaders and their followers, forms a mosaic from which it is possible to extract extremely varied and surprising information.

The events of March and April 1781 can be summarized as follows: according to the statements made by the Indians, the motivations for the attack of March 18 and 19 and that of April 1 and 2 were similar, namely (as previously mentioned) to raze Oruro and kill its white inhabitants, and to stop the payment of tributes and other taxes. As for the Indians' entrance into the city on March 9, there is only one brief description, by a chieftain,[9] which adds nothing to what we have related in the previous chapter.

The arms used by the invaders were always rudimentary, judging by scattered remarks: slingshots, *live* – that is, the weapon for hunting vicuñas – whips, knives, sticks, lances, and an occasional spade. There is sometimes mention of "mouths of fire." In spite of their limitations, the sheer number of these tools made the attack quite dangerous in the hands of the most experienced Indians. Especially worthy of mention is the dexterity of the slingshot wielders. According to one witness,[10] during the attacks of March 18 and 19 more than seven thousand men and an equal number of women gathered at the siege of La Joya, where slingshots were concentrated for eight days. The Indians of Sillota had brought an enormous quantity of stones by burro for this purpose, which they discharged from the banks of the Río de la Barca.

7 "Testimonios," loc. cit. (appointment of a lieutenant by Tupac Catari), fols. 190–191.
8 This documentary material has been compiled over several years of research on this topic. Because of its variety and thematic richness I am studying it with an eye to a future monograph.
9 "Testimonios," loc. cit. (Declaration of the Indian, Andrés Colque), fol. 135.
10 Ibid. (Declaration of the mestizo, Eusebio Padilla), fol. 28.

It is difficult to estimate the number of Indian rebels. Witnesses and defendants repeatedly mention, in round numbers, ten thousand armed men at each uprising. Whether there was a strategy for combined attacks in the region must be analyzed in another context, in particular by comparing the missives of the principal leaders, which are frequently contradictory in content. The Indians in court repeatedly recited the same chant: Oruro would be just the beginning, and later they would fall on Chuquisaca, Cochabamba, and Potosí. These almost ingenuous ideas contrast with the realism of leaders like Santos Mamani, Esteban Calisaya, and Matheo Guaca,[11] who seemed to have a better notion of the risks of the enterprise. This would explain their frequent attempts to get their followers to avoid violence, especially noticeable in missives sent to the Rodríguez family before the first of the March invasions.[12]

The parish priests had a controversial role. Although some Indians accused them of betrayal,[13] one can see in the list of persons sympathetic to the insurgents in Appendix A that many are priests.

The attack of March 18–19 was detonated by the burning of the town of Quiriquiari by soldiers from Cochabamba. A non-Indian resident of Sorasora[14] relates that the Indians of that parish were very upset by the burning and began to organize, demanding revenge. The *alcalde* and the prominent citizens of Sorasora warned them against provoking the Cochabamba soldiers because they might also burn Sorasora, but to no avail.

The hopes of the Sorasora Indians centered on the aid they expected to receive from their brothers in Challapata. The indigenous *alcalde* of that parish was the famous leader Santos Mamani. With several captains, he approached the mill of Buenavista, a league from Sorasora, on March 9. The Indians were angry and it was impossible to calm them down. The chieftains gathered there, with Santos Mamani at their head, and took all the Spaniards and mestizos in the town prisoner.[15] This is how the rebellion of March 18–19 began. Although it is difficult to trace Mamani's route during the following few days, apparently he began to send letters and circulars from Sorasora to his fellow leaders in nearby districts, calling them to a show of force at the gates of Oruro. Mamani's strategy was not limited to these measures, however. Many of his missives indicate that he was also in constant communication during the first days of March with the Rodríguez brothers, of whom he constantly asked instructions on how to proceed. Everything indicates that the attack on Oruro was not part of his original plans. In fact,

11 Ibid. (Declaration of Santos Mamani and other minor chieftains), fols. 88, 89, 233–239.
12 Ibid. (Letter from S. Mamani to J. Rodríguez), fol. 58.
13 Ibid. (Dámaso Subieta), fol. 30.
14 Ibid. (Pedro Miranda), fols. 50–51.
15 Pedro Miranda was a white man; he was taken prisoner by Mamani, who named him his secretary and writer of proclamations.

his first move was toward Quiriquiari. When he returned to Sorasora, he found that its inhabitants had gone to Oruro, intending to attack.[16] According to these sources, Santos Mamani had no intention of destroying Oruro, even though he shared his fellow Indians' desire for revenge. The Franciscan priest José Antonio Cervantes relates an interview with the indigenous leader. In Mamani's explanation of his motives for joining the rebellion, his identification with the goals of the uprising are plain to see:

[Mamani stated] that the time had come for the Indians to be relieved from pain and for the Spaniards and Creoles to be annihilated, whom they called "*carao*," which in their language means "naked" because without paying tax nor doing much work they were the owners of what [the Indians] worked for under the yoke and paid many taxes for, and they had the comforts and the Indians were oppressed, hounded, and consigned to utter misery all their lives.[17]

The outcome of the revolt of March 18 and 19 was nevertheless disastrous for the Indians. Their attempt was frustrated by a surprise attack by the soldiers of Oruro, and by lack of discipline among the different groups from which their force was made up.

On March 20 Mamani wrote to the Rodríguez brothers, asking them to intervene at the La Plata *audiencia* in exchange for a laying down of arms.[18] Juan de Dios Rodríguez answered with a decree agreeing to the proposal. Everything seemed to be leading to a truce; however, the Indians in the neighboring parishes were not agreeable to it. Going against their chieftains, they continued to threaten the city, but again the city's defense proved more effective than their poorly coordinated attacks. In any case, they soon rediscovered the advantages of blockading the delivery of food. With the road to Cochabamba cut off, Oruro began to languish and its inhabitants grew desperate again. The demoralization reached its culmination with the second attack on April 1 and 2. But again the Indian forces were defeated, this time definitively, by the determined defense put up by the city's inhabitants – both Creoles and *chapetones* – under the military command of Jacinto Rodríguez.

Although recalcitrant groups remained on the outskirts, this defeat marked the beginning of the massive surrender of the Indians to the city authorities. Every day more chieftains were handed over by the parish Indians themselves. While this might have indicated another about-face by the Indians of the community, most of them – according to accounts from the subsequent trials – apparently had little confidence in the effectiveness of the attack.

In any case, the Indians' quick acceptance of a negotiated retreat and the mass petition for pardon from the Spanish authorities speaks of their final recognition that the cause had already been lost.

16 "Testimonios," (P. Miranda), fol. 57.
17 Ibid. (Fray J. Antonio de Cervantes), fol. 58v.
18 Ibid. (Letter of S. Mamani), fol. 65.

13

Picking up the pieces

The last Indian assaults on Oruro took place in April 1781. After a day of desperate combat on April 2 in which Creoles and *chapetones* (only eighteen of them, according to the chronicle) fought together to defeat 120 Indians, the latter "began to beg for mercy, promising to hand over the ones who were the cause of their revolt, and many of these were also being brought daily from the towns of Sorata, Challacollo, and Poopó and their environs."[1]

Jacinto Rodríguez and the Oruro militia leaders reached an agreement at this point with some of the chieftains, on condition that the Indian blockade be lifted. The rebels from Paria and Sillota did not concur, however, and continued to block the road, a situation that had become equally intolerable for the businesses of Cochabamba, Oruro's traditional supplier. On Palm Sunday, just a few days after this confrontation, Commander José de Ayarza, leader of the Cochabamba militia, invaded Oruro. He had just quelled the Indian uprisings in Colcha and Quirquiabi and his troops were leading a sizable herd of livestock that they had taken from the rebels.

With this booty, he entered the city, presumably expecting a triumphal welcome from its inhabitants. This was not forthcoming, however; they were received coolly by Jacinto Rodríguez's followers, who were afraid their own authority would be undermined by the troops. Ayarza did not seem too concerned about their lack of courtesy and decided to stay in Oruro with his men until the following Tuesday. In spite of their early departure, word that they had come to the aid of Oruro spread among the Indians, finally intimidating those who insisted on enforcing the blockade.[2]

Oruro was at last free from the Indian threat, but hardly anything was left standing in the city. This was true not only of its material condition but also – and principally – of its battered social relations. For the rest of the century what we can gather of its history pertains to trials, confiscation or restoration of property, and descriptions of the Indians' behavior during the uprising. Mining activity never had another chance, and the traditional

1 "Diario del tumulto," op. cit., p. 309.
2 Ibid., pp. 309–10.

struggle for municipal honors lacked the spark provided earlier by the warring political factions. The leaders of the rebel party were in prison or dead, and those loyal to the crown – beginning with the *corregidor* Ramón de Urrutia himself, who returned to Oruro after the rebellion had been quelled – remained totally subordinate to directives from the Charcas *audiencia*.

Almost at the same time that all this was unfolding in Oruro, the president of the Charcas *audiencia* wrote to Viceroy Juan José Vértiz: "It causes horror to recall the rebellions and disasters that they are constantly undergoing – the most painful of which is what is happening in the City of Oruro, whose unfortunate situation is to this day [March 15, 1781] unknown."[3]

On the same day Urrutia wrote to Vértiz about what had happened after his humiliating departure from Oruro that February. Lacking any support, he had gone to Cochabamba to ask for help from his *corregidor*, Félix de Villalobos; the latter refused because his own city was threatened by the same danger. Urrutia had then gone to Charcas, where he explained what had happened to the *real audiencia* and Commander Ignacio Flores.[4] There he waited for the end of the conflict, after which he returned to Oruro with no assistance other than the paternal directives of the higher authorities.

The main concern in the recently pacified city was the trials of the rebels and the participants in the conflict. During March and April the Indians were brought to trial, and after this Spanish control over the indigenous people became total once again. By express orders from the viceroys of Peru and Rio de la Plata, the death penalty and brutal mutilation were reserved for the chieftains, sparing the others, who were by then sufficiently cowed.

This was not the case for the rest of Oruro's inhabitants. Accusations of robbery and pillage extended not only to *cholos* and mestizos but also to prestigious families, and even to priests and monks. As might be expected, the Rodríguez brothers' star began to dim this time for good, and with it the fortunes of their most faithful allies, such as Nicolás Herrera. Urrutia, their old enemy, now protected by the legal authorities, was waiting for an opportune moment to be reinstalled in the *corregimiento*; but he had returned in the midst of a storm at least as difficult to tame as the one that had ousted him months before.

Not until the end of 1782 – nearly two years after the onset of the fighting – was Ignacio Flores, from his position as president of the *audiencia*, able to restore Urrutia as head of the *corregimiento*. The energetic commander decided to preside personally over the ceremony at the Oruro *cabildo*, in order to demonstrate the extent to which Urrutia was appreciated in high

---

3 Ignacio Flores to Viceroy Vértiz, Charcas, March 15, 1781, AGN, Biblioteca Nacional, legajo 190, doc. 1899.
4 De Angelis, op. cit., p. 754.

places. Flores's letters to Urrutia show great perspicacity, along with demands for tact and moderation that seem to have been taken from a colonial manual on "the art of governing." While it seems doubtful that Urrutia could have carried out even a small part of this advice, it is worth reading, for it shows that Flores had uncommon intelligence and a powerful instinct for conciliation that often caused his enemies to accuse him of indifference.

In a letter to Urrutia, Flores commented that he had seen in the *cabildo* on November 1, 1782, the day before he was to be confirmed in his post, "signs of unity and commendation [on the part of the *capitulares*] which, if in fact they are not a pretense, will remain in my memory as true and sincere gratitude."[5] Urrutia definitely had a hard job to tackle, and he may have taken it on out of a need to redeem his self-esteem. The inhabitants remained divided into a multitude of factions. Accusations rained on all sides in anticipation of the moment – to take place in 1784 – when the conduct of leaders and followers, laymen and clergy, would be judged.[6]

Central parts of the testimonies collected in 1784 are transcribed here in Appendix B. It is not surprising that they revolve around the generalized plundering of the city during the invasions. This case cited by several witnesses was considered one of the most scandalous: a black slave, Luisa María Calvete, admitted to having seized a bar of silver from an Indian who had just stolen it and, figuring she ought to return it to its owner, entrusted it to a monk, Fray Santiago Calatayud, of the Mercedary order. The monk, however, kept it for himself, and then refused to pay a commission to Calvete. Another monk from the same order, Fray Fernando Carreño, was accused by the authorities of his own order of having taken two stolen bars of silver to Cochabamba.

A complaint was levied against Jacinto Rodríguez over the previously mentioned instances in which those he had appointed to collect stolen property from private houses took advantage of the assignment to remove other property as well.

There is also frequent mention of the behavior of the troops from Cochabamba. After they entered the city as "liberators," they began to buy up most of the stolen goods, which they took to their own city to be sold at low prices. Another fact that nobody denied was the brutal attack on the houses of the Europeans in the *Plaza Mayor*, in which unidentified *cholos* and mestizos were mentioned as the principal culprits. Many seemed to have been impressed by the latters' boastfulness, as they publicly admitted to having stolen gold and silver and even to having gambled with it in dice games.

---

5 Ignacio Flores to Ramón Urrutia, Oruro, November 2, 1782, AGN, Biblioteca Nacional, legajo 191, doc. 1976.
6 Ibid.

Also widely mentioned was the favorable testimony of the soldiers at the fort regarding Ramón de Urrutia, recognizing that he had offered to stay with them in the barracks on the eve of the indigenous attack to assure them of his loyalty. Also discussed was the behavior of Bishop Menéndez, whom nearly everyone characterized as openly taking sides with the Rodríguez brothers.[7]

Finally, in 1784, the list of prisoners from the Oruro area was made known. Most of them were Creoles.[8]

The testimonies collected in Appendix B obviate the need for any additional commentary on the violence that closed this chapter in the history of Oruro and marked the end of an era. The Indian testimonies in Appendix A and those of the opposing side presented in Appendix B demonstrate similar degrees of intensity and blind destructiveness.

The forty-year period described here is populated with a parade of people in rancorous conflict with each other over domestic differences, most of them stimulated by zeal for bits of local power that were fought over as if honor and life were at stake. Evidence is rare of the moderating effect of mediation or intelligent renunciation; Viceroy Manso de Velazco tried, along with the two men he trusted, but as has been shown, his efforts met with little success.

During the rebellions of the 1780s, violence and extreme rivalry again appeared, although in this case blood was shed in a painfully unprecedented manner. Nevertheless, in the midst of the cruelty and disorder, a few sober voices were heard above the apathy and the collective compulsion for violence.

These solitary voices demonstrated their underlying power to penetrate and anticipate the intentions of their fellow men, and urged the avoidance of reactive behavior in the face of the unknown, incomprehensible, dominant, or simply strange. These voices, however, belonged to leaders of opposite factions during the bloody conflicts of 1780–2. One of them belongs to Tupac Amaru:

Dear Sir [Don Gregorio Mariano Sanchez, parish priest]: I received your letter and, informed of its contents I must say that neither time nor my work permits me to answer you at length, as the provocative sentiments of your letter deserve; and, putting it succinctly, I impress upon you that with respect to the fact that I am a lay person, as I am called, I can hardly require any parish priest to receive me with choir mantle, tall cross, and pallium, since I do not encourage such ceremonies nor do I need them. . . . From your expressions I understand that you have a lot of feeling for those robbers the *corregidores*, who with no fear of God impose unsufferable labor on the Indians, with their undeserved *repartos*, robbing them with their long fingers, and some of the parish priests do not refrain from collaborating in this shady business, who will be separated from their jobs like robbers, and then they will know my might and they will see if I have the authority to do it.

7 "Testimonio del quaderno segundo de autos criminales obrados por Sebastián de Segurola sobre la rebelión de la Villa de Oruro," Buenos Aires, 1789, AGN, Sala IX-7-4-3, legajo 2, no. 2.
8 See Appendix B.

This state has never permitted [the Indians] to know the true God, but only to contribute their sweat and labor to the *corregidores* and priests; so that, having personally made inquiries in most of the kingdom about the spiritual and civil government of these vassals, I find that all of them who make up the national people have no evangelical light because they lack operatives who would minister to them, this being due to the bad example they are given.

The example executed on the *corregidor* of the province of Tinta was motivated when I was told [by him] I was going against the church, and in order to contain the rest of the *corregidores*, this justice was necessary. My desire is that this kind of boss be eliminated entirely, that the *repartimientos* cease, that in each province there be an *alcalde mayor* from the Indian nation itself and other persons of good conscience, with no other mission than the administration of justice, Christian policy toward the Indians and other individuals, being paid a moderate salary, with other conditions which in time will be established. . . . This is the whole idea, for now, of my enterprise, leaving to the King of Spain the direct domain which he has had, without taking away the obedience which he is due nor the regular commerce, as the principal nerve center for the conservation of the whole kingdom.[9] (José Gabriel Tupac Amaru, letters to Dr. G. M. Sanz and to the *cabildo* of Cuzco, Cocotoy, and Campos de Ocororo, November 1780 and January 1781)

Another to Commander Ignacio Flores:

It seems to me appropriate to pass on to you the following few counsels: that it would be very good policy to win over one or two of the largest towns in your province with the gift of this or that distinction belonging to civil address, animating them with the title of friends and loyal subjects of the king. For whose good effect it would be very useful to enter into close friendship with their respective priests. And in the same way win over with benefice in all the villages some intelligent Indian woman or *chola*, who will be able to give you honest news about the designs of the Indians. . . . Since the Indians, in their plans, are not uniform and depend on many contingencies, it would be good to fall on them at the birth of their uprisings; and once well proven the intentions of their chiefs and accomplices, to punish them promptly with death, avoiding the dangerous jailhouse, but being very careful that their guilt is proven. If, as usually happens, the troops who serve the Province desert, do not respect justice and disrupt the order of society . . . it would be appropriate . . . to verify who the principal transgressors are and remove them.

. . . you will see to it that [the Indians] trust in the fairness of the Spaniards, which must be manifested in many ways. . . . I have been told that in a certain Province the *corregidor* was abused and persecuted by the Indians for having offered them a reduction in one part of their *repartimiento* and not having kept his word; I do not expect this infraction on your part, but take the example as illustrative.

I have asked his Highness the Viceroy not to allow the two thousand veterans who have arrived in Buenos Aires to pass through these provinces, considering the havoc they would wreak among the poor Indians. . . . Your honorable zeal will discover with time many other injuries and you will prudently avoid them. May Our Lord keep you for many years. (Ignacio Flores, regional commander and interim president of the *real audiencia* of Charcas, to the *corregidor* Ramón Urrutia, Oruro, November 2, 1782)[10]

It speaks eloquently of the situation that of the two testimonies with which we bring this work to a close, one should belong to the triumphant side and the other to the vanquished; and that they are the words of two of

9 De Angelis, op. cit., pp. 389–95.
10 Ignacio Flores to Ramón Urrutia, loc. cit.

the highest authorities in the conflict. Not in the events of the war but in a certain less tangible territory – like that of Viceroy Manso de Velazco in 1745, or of the old and wise Landaeta, or of Father Romero, who wrote so beautifully and had such a serene mind – these two figures in this history can be compared, attesting to the smallness of many of their own followers, and expressing with eloquence, finally, the different qualities of men.

Appendix A

Indian raids on Oruro, 1781: testimonies

People attacked by the Indians during the raids on Oruro
(January through April, 1781)[1]

Fernando Gurruchaga (European), *alcalde ordinario*
José Miguel Llano y Valdés (Creole), *alcalde propietario*
Joaquín Rubí de Cellis (European), *alcalde propietario*
Manuel de Mugurusa (European), *regidor*
Fray Antonio Lazo (Augustine), no information on origins (hereafter N/A).
José Endeiza (European), very wealthy
José Cayetano de Casas (N/A)
Pantaleón Martínez (Creole), shopkeeper
Juan Blanco (European)
Miguel Salinas (European?), wealthy shopkeeper (killed by the Indians)
Juan Pedro Jimenez (European?)
Juan Vicente Larrain (European?)
Domingo Pavia (N/A; ex-official *mayor* of the *caja de Oruro*)
Ramón Llano (N/A)
Antonio Sánchez (N/A)
Francisco Palazuelo (European)
Francisco Resa (European), shopkeeper, killed
Manuel de Bustamante (European), wealthy shopkeeper, killed
Miguel Estada (European?), killed
Vicente Fierro (European), wealthy miner, killed
Agustín Arregui (Creole), killed
Ventura Ayarza (European), killed
Pedro Martínez (European), killed
Francisco Antonio Cacho (European), killed

1 These two lists have been drawn up on the basis of another extensive compilation of materials referring to the economic occupations of the residents of Oruro up to the period of the rebellions. Here I present only nationality, occupation and – in the first list – cases of violent death at the hands of Indians. In a complementary study, the social position of miners and *azogueros* of the town (Creoles and Europeans) has been classified and cross-referenced with various data about their participation in the uprisings of 1781. In a future work I will present the results of this table, out of which have emerged some interesting angles for social analysis of this period of decay in the mining sector.

José Ballain (N/A), killed
José Ibarguren (European?), killed
Diego Azero (European?), killed
Pedro Lagrabe (European), killed
José Caballero (European), killed
José Sorzano (European)
Manuel Puch (European)
Francisco Polo (Creole), shopkeeper
Francisco Durán (European), killed?
José Arijón (European), killed?
José Isasa (European), killed
Antonio Geibum (European)
Vicente Garria (European), killed
Juan Antonio Martínez (European), miner
N. Ganderegui (European)
Esteban Amezcaray (European?), nominated for *corregidor* of Chayanta
Santiago Fernández Royo (N/A)
Ramón de Urrutia (European), *corregidor* of Oruro

People who appear in the documents as sympathetic to the insurgents

Jacinto Rodríguez (Creole), mine owner
Juan de Dios Rodríguez (Creole), mine owner
Bishop Patricio Gabriel Menéndez, priest of the principal church
Fray Bernardino Galleguillos (Franciscan?), son of a mine owner
Nicolás Herrera (Creole), mine owner
José Asurdui (N/A), officer of the Menacho company
Fray Feliciano Galleguillos, brother of Francisco
Isidoro Quevedo (Creole)
Manuel Herrera (Creole) brother of Nicolás, *alcalde provincial*
Rev. Isidoro Velazco, priest of Sorasora
Juan de Montesinos (Creole)
Antonio Quirós (Creole), lieutenant of the Menacho company
Rev. Manuel Amézaga, priest of Challacota
Nicolás Iriarte (Creole), lieutenant of the Menacho company
Juan Gualberto Mexía, brother-in-law of Menacho, lawyer of the *audiencia* of La Plata.
Miguel Portilla (Creole), soldier in the company of Menacho
Felipe Miguel Aseñas (N/A), *fundidor* and weigher of the *caja real* of Oruro
Francisca Orozco (N/A)
María Quirós (N/A), wife of Azurdui
Bernardino Ibáñez (N/A)

Table A.1. *Groups attacked by or sympathetic to the insurgents during the uprising in Oruro in 1781*

| | Attacked by | | | | |
	Miners	Financiers or businessmen	Religious Secular	Regular	Other
Creoles	2	2	—	—	—
Europeans	—	28	—	1	—
No data	1	9	—	—	—

| | Sympathetic to | | | | |
	Miners	Financiers or businessmen	Religious Secular	Regular	Other
Creoles	12	3	1	—	1
Europeans	—	—	—	—	—
No data	1	—	3	7	12

Manuel Pineda (N/A)
Federico Javier Navarro Velazco (N/A)
Casimiro Delgado (Creole), wealthy
Rev. Mariano Bernal, secular priest
Fray Joseph Bustillo, prelate of the convent of La Merced
Sebastián Rodríguez Crespo (N/A)
Fray Marcos del Ribero, order of San Juan de Dios
Fray Santiago Calatayud, convent of La Merced
Pedro Asquas (N/A)
Fray Fernando Carreño, convent of La Merced
Clemente Menacho (Creole), mine owner?
Isidro de la Riva (Creole?), mine owner, *alcalde* of Oruro
Diego Flores (Creole), mine owner
Manuel Serrano (Creole)
Gregorio Salamanca (Creole?), mine owner

Indian testimonies*

Seventy-six testimonies have been selected from this record, in which witnesses and defendants give descriptions of persons, places, objectives, and experiences during the invasions of Oruro.

* *Source*: "Testimonio del expediente de diligencias practicadas para averiguar los tumultos meditados contra Oruro (remitido por Don Mariano Argas y Rodríguez)," Buenos Aires, 1789. (AGN), Sala IX-7-4-3, Leg. 2, no. 3.

Table A.2. *Categories of those giving testimony*

	Indians	Mestizos	Mulattoes
Chieftains	21	—	—
Unidentified followers	46	6	—
Tailor	—	1	—
Mayordomo	—	1	—
Marginal	—	—	1

Sixty-seven of these testimonies were made by Indians, eight by mestizos, and one by a mulatto. Distinguishing Indians from mestizos can be difficult. Generally the mestizo spoke Spanish and differentiated himself from the Indian people of his town. Some mestizos acted as translators or scribes for the Indians (that is, they wrote down their edicts and proclamations), and also as messengers. It is not unlikely that this function was also filled by the more acculturated Indians (the so-called Ladino Indians, who knew both languages); on the other side, it is also likely that many mestizos were completely integrated into the indigenous sector. The problem persists, however, of which criterion to use in classifying them – cultural, ethnic, or linguistic?

Of the sixty-seven Indians, twenty-one were captains, *caudillos*, Indian *alcaldes*, and the so-called *tumultuarios*. Of the mestizos, one was a tailor and the other *mayordomo* of a silver mill.

Only four of the total giving testimony were women (all belonging to the group of Indian followers).

The information collected in the testimonies was categorized as follows:

A: Places that each witness or defendant named, including those they went to personally and those from which other Indians were summoned, or those mentioned as places of revolt or agitation (in capitals, the *corregimientos*; in lower case, the towns, ranches and annexes).

B: Leaders and chieftains most often named in the testimonies (many of whom later testified as witnesses).

C: Under this heading are two categories:

C-1: Any specific allusion to recuperation or restoration of what they considered to be still theirs, in spite of its having been confiscated injustly by the Spaniards, in their view (for example, land, mines, or mills).

C-2: Any general anti-Spanish allusion, which might also contain expressions about social or political recuperation.

D: Any allusion to what they wanted suppressed (basically, institutions understood to be socially or politically unfair, particularly tributes and *repartos*).

E: Eagerness for the spoils of war; here appear the references to sacking of property as a motivation for invasion.

F: References to death, destruction, fire, annihilation, and so forth, mentioned as a motive for invasion. In both E and F, these phrases have no connotations related to vindication; they are calls to sack and kill without any express justification.

G: Under this heading appear phrases revealing the witness's or defendant's attitude toward combat or aptitude for war.

    G-1: Phrases showing them to be recalcitrant, fierce, and threatening, even before the court, and those containing the slogan (clearly very widespread), "Die or conquer."

    G-2: Phrases showing the opposite attitude, that is, that they did not fight of their own will, that they retreated with great fear before the Creole–Spanish defense, or that they quickly (or finally) came to beg pardon for everything that happened.

H: Opinions against officials and clergy, and antireligious remarks in general.

I: Under this heading are references to Tupac Amaru (all were favorable; no critical comments appeared).

J: The same, with reference to Tupac Catari.

Results

C-1: (recuperation of own land and property): Of the 46 Indians of the community, only three mention this topic; but of the 21 chieftains, 10 speak of this as an essential motive.

C-2: (general allusions to reparation and anti-Spanish remarks): 4 Indians of the community allude to this, as do 2 mestizos. No Indian chieftain mentions reparation in these terms (or rather, on this point the leaders were more precise and referred concretely to lands or mills).

D: (injustices to be eradicated): Of the 46 Indians of the community, 15 make reference to this point, and of the chieftains, only 3. There is a mention by the mestizo *mayordomo*, but it is an allusion to an opinion of the Indians.

E: Of the 46 Indians of the community, 7 mention the spoils of war; of the 21 chieftains, 6 do.

F: Of the 46 Indians of the community, 23 allude to killing without quarter; of the 21 chieftains, 11 do. The mulatto also mentions this, as do the 2 mestizos who held special social positions. Of the remaining 6 mestizos, 5 mention this.

G1: 6 Indians and 2 chieftains indicate they are recalcitrant.

G2: 3 chieftains fought against their will.
H: 3 Indians, 1 chieftain, and 5 mestizos speak against officials and the
    clergy.

1. Thadeo Balcazar (mestizo)/Age 14/native of Carangaro-Pacajes/len. HC
   A. Paria, Quillota, Burguillos, Llamquene, Chocoña, Rivera
   B. Miguel Flores
   F. [The Indians said] "that it was appropriate to invade the town and
      annihilate it because they saw its townspeople as enemies" (3v).
      [They decided] "to kill them one by one, except for the [Indian]
      taxpayers" (4v).
2. Diego Agullan (Indian)/native of Aguas *est.*[2] Aguas Calientes/len. NHC
   A. Inuvina, Paria, Challapata, Toledo
   B. Diego López
   F. [They had the] "resolution to annihilate [the town]" (5)
3. Lorenza Barbosa (Indian)/native of *est.* S. Juan, Paria
   A. Paria, Ancoaya, Soracachi
   B. Francisco Mamani
   F. "to enter the village with troops and take the lives of all its
      townsfolk" (7v).
   I. "assuming that orders came from Tupac Amaru" (7v).
   H. "by now no one obeys the *alcaldes*, much less the priests" (7v).
4. Juan de Dios Chambi (Indian)/native of parish Caracollo-Ayllu Tanaco/
   len. NHC
   A. *Est.* El Chono, Carangas, Pacajes, Toledo, Carángaro, La Joya, Sillota,
      Paria
   B. Matheo Guaca, Diego Acquacho, "the Taquichiri."
   F. [They were summoned to] "invade this town and reduce it to ashes"
      (16).
   E. [Other Indians] "had taken an increasing amount of money, dry
      goods, local and Castilian clothing and with this interest he con-
      curred [*sic*] . . . and he came this morning to join [the looting]"
      (16v).
5. Francisco Aguado (I)/native of Parish Caracollo-Ayllu Tanaco/len. NHC
   A. Guayllamarca, Toledo, Sillota, Cumaguana, Mahosa.
   B. [illegible]
   F. [They came to] "ruin it and completely blow this town away" (17v).

2 Codes used in testimonies
  HC = spoke Spanish
  NHC = did not speak Spanish
  est. = *estancia*
  tum. = *tumultario*, or "tumult maker"

6. Tomasa Ramos (Indian)/*est.* Ivira-Chioza. Ayllu Cantauchique/NHC
   A. Toledo, Challacollo, Mohosa, Icho, Sicasica.
   F. [She heard the others say] "they were trying to do away with the city and ruin it" (21).
7. Santos Cutgene (Indian)/native of Toledo-Ayllu Collana/NHC
   A. Sillota, Challacollo, Guallamarca, La Joya, Toledo.
   B. Manuel (?) Guaca, Esteban Calisaya.
   C. [Summoned to] "destroy entirely and kill all its inhabitants [of the town] and the townsfolk without any reservations" (22v).
8. Cruz Choque (Indian)/native of Corque-Carangas/NHA
   A. Sillota, Paria, Toledo, La Joya, Challacollo, Challapata.
   B. Esteban Calisaya, Matheo Guaca.
   F. "They were eager to take over the town and take the lives of all its residents to which end they mounted the attack" (23v).
9. Micaela Orcoma (Indian)/native of parish of Toledo/NHC
   A. Paria, Sillota, Challapata, Carangas.
   B. Esteban Calisaya, Manuel Mamani.
   F. [They were summoned to] "reduce the city to ashes, entirely destroying its inhabitants" (24v).
   H. "It was appropriate for their success to cut off the head of His Mercy the Justicia Mayor and that [*sic*] of his two brothers, and to snatch the crowns off the priests" (24v).
   I. "and cutting off their heads [of the officials and priests] to send them to the rebel *cacique* Josep [*sic*] Tupac Amaru" (24v).
10. Casimiro Ramos (mulatto)/native of Salta/HC
    A. Guallamarca, Sillota, Toledo, Corque, Challacollo, Challapata.
    B. Marcos Onofre.
    F. [In Sillota] "the Indians were called together . . . to attack this town [Oruro] and do away with all its residents" (26).
11. Eusebio Padilla (mestizo)/native of Oruro (town)/HC
    A. Sillota, *est.* Calisaya, La Joya, Carangas, Pacajes, Challacollo, Toledo.
    B. "Matheo and Gregorio."
    F. [They were summoned to "cut off the heads of"] "all the Spanish residents, mestizos, Negroes and all the castes without leaving anyone alive except the tribute-paying Indians" (28v).
    H. "to come to this town [Oruro] to take the life of his Mercy *Señor Justicia Mayor* in the first place [Urrutia or Rodríguez?] . . . and cut off the head of the image of Our Lady of the Rosary that they worship in the Church of San Domingo" (28v). "An Indian who said he was a friend of His Mercy (idem) wanted to dissuade them and for that they killed him on the spot" (28v). "Oruro would only serve them as lunch once the principals were out of the way, who were the Rodríguez and then the Witch Our Lady of the Rosary with

whose cloak the city was protected, and setting fire to it and de-
molishing the temples and all the buildings" (30).

    I. [Once all the preceding was done], "they would leave the situation
pacified until the *cacique* Tupac Amaru arrived" (30v).

12. Dámaso Subieta (mestizo)/native of Corque/Carangas/HC
    A. Corque, Sillota, Caracollo.
    B. Dionisio Guanca, Calisto Sepita, Matheo Guaca.
    H. [An Indian from Toledo, at the insistence of the priest] "confessed
and took communion and for that they thought to kill him" (35).

13. Isidro Subieta (mestizo)/native of Corque-Carangas/HC
    A. Toledo, Sorasora, Challapata.
    B. Dionisio Guanca.
    F. [In spite of the attempts at pacification by Dionisio Guanca] "the
rest showed that they were resolved to enter and lay waste to everything" (37v).
    H. [The priest of Toledo] "contradicted totally [what they proposed
with respect to doing away with Oruro, so that] they said that he
was paid to advise them and betray them by giving them time"
(37v). [They said that] "all the priests were likewise paid to do the
same treachery that they precisely had to avenge and this voice was
so corrupt in the town that both old and young knew it" (37v).

14. Santos Cachi (Indian)/native of Sicasica (but lived in Oruro)
    A. *Est.* of Alcamóvar, Quillacota, Sicasica.
    F. [He knew that what they were planning was, once the town of Oruro
was ruined and annihilated, to rise up] "to despoil as much of it as
there was to covet" (41).

15. Joseph de Cano (mestizo?)/native of Oruro-Res. Sorasora/tailor/HC
    A. Sorasora, Challapata, Sicasica, Pacajes, Carangas.
    B. Francisco Banco, Antonio Herrera, Eugenio Alarmi, Manuel
Mamani.
    F. [The Indians, on both occasions, decided to entirely destroy the town
of Oruro without leaving any soul alive in it and setting fire to it]
(43).
    H. [The Indians of Sorasora and Challapata proposed] "advancing on
this town and doing away with it and taking the head of Colonel
Don Juan de Dios Rodríguez" (42v).

16. Ana María Arias (Indian)/native of Guancipata?/NHC
    A. Challapata, Paria, Sicasica, Pacajes.
    F. "The aim of the Indians was to annihilate the town [of Oruro]" (44).

17. Patricio Figueroa (mestizo)/resided in Poopó/HC
    A. Challapata, Sicasica, Condocondo, Macha, Pocoata.
    B. Juan Guanca, Mamani [which one is unclear].
    C. "They would have to stay by [*sic*] the mills and mines and he would

have to continue working on his own account with the silver and mercury of the *caja real*" (46v).

18. Antonio Campos (mestizo?)/resided in Poopó/mill *mayordomo*/HC
   A. Challapata, Paria, Quirquiravi, Sorasora, Venta de El Medio, Condocondo, Poopó.
   B. Santos Mamani.
   F. [He knows because it is public and widely known] "that the principal intent of all the Indians was to ruin and demolish this town [of Oruro]" (49).
   H. [To do the preceding] "without sparing even the temples and taking the riches and whatever they found [*sic*] in them" (49). [Likewise they schemed to trick Colonel Don Juan de Dios Rodríguez] (49) and kill him (49v).
   D. [They would do the preceding, under the pretext that the suspension of work that had occurred before this tumult in their mines and mills was very prejudicial to them] (49v).

19. Pedro Miranda (mestizo?)/resident of Sorasora/HC
   A. Sorasora, Paria parish, Sillota, "the inns on the road to Potosí," Quirquiabi, Colcha, Poopó, Salinas, Condocondo, Challapata, Urmini, Peñas, Machacamarca.
   B. Santos Mamani.
   G. [The aim of the insurrection was for the Indian community to remain absolutely in control of all the property and labor of the mining industry] (53v).
   F. [To this end, they planned to ruin and exterminate the town of Oruro] (53v).

20. Sebastián Cruz (Indian)/from Tayaquina-Sorasora/*alcalde.*
   A. Las Peñas, Condocondo, Sorasora.

21. Ventura Valencia (Indian)/native of Challapata-Ayllu Ilave/NHC
   A. Paria, Sicasica, Mohosa, Caracalla.
   I. [The *alcaldes* of Challapata] "warned the Indians of their partiality (composed of one or more *ayllus*) so they would quickly get ready, telling them it was by order of Tupac Amaru, who was currently fighting against the city of Cuzco and that it was necessary to help him" (75v–76v). [With respect to whether he believed that this order came from Tupac Amaru] "he answered yes and in light of this he had come [to Oruro] with the resolution that was expressed widely among [the Indians], the news that he would be crowned and rule these dominions" (76–76v).

22. Federico Javier Condoni (Indian)/native of Challapata-Ayllu Silca/ NHC
   A. Paria.
   B. Santos Mamani.

D. [They had] "the hope that when this *real caja* [of Oruro] and its ministers were ruined, there would no longer be collection of the royal tributes nor other royal rights" (78) [continues below].

E. "They came ready to take spoils from this town [Oruro] to alleviate their poverty and this was what encouraged the people to participate in the enterprise" (78).

I. [The foregoing needs would end with] "the arrival of Tupac Amaru whom they expected to improve their fortunes and asking him if he had given [credence?] to these lies he answered that he had taken it as the truth because all his friends had assured him of it and from seeing the movement taking place everywhere as well" (78).

D. [He was opposed to the *cacique* Lope Chungara] "because he had spread the word that . . . they had to pay the royal tributes of which they already thought that they and the rest of their *ayllu* would be free after they had performed the task of attacking this town" (78v).

G-1. [Because of the foregoing and while he denies having participated in this death] "he had taken satisfaction [in it and in that of the *corregidor*]" (78v).

23. Ventura Arroyo (Indian)/native of Las Peñas/NHC

A. Mohosa, Ichoca, Paria Sicasica, Challapata.

B. Diego Onofre, Damasio "Catarsi" (Catari?).

C. [Indians from other districts informed him that] "the natives were well dug in everywhere, successfully fighting the Spaniards" (79v).

D. "The natives had to be freed from paying tributes and other taxes" (79).

I. [The foregoing would occur] "when Tupac Amaru arrived [whom they would inform about their fight against the Spaniards] (79v).

24. Matheo Alejandro (Indian)/native of Las Peñas/NHC

D. [Another Indian told him] "that it would not be long until they would be free of *repartos* and tributes and other things with which the *corregidores* had them so oppressed and that it was an opportune occasion to make an effort to get some relief" (82).

I. [He was also told that in La Paz they were working for the foregoing and to] "achieve tranquillity with the arrival of the higher authority whom they awaited, Tupac Amaru." [He felt overwhelmed by Tupac Amaru] "who was said to be of royal blood" (82v).

25. Martín López (Indian)/native of Challapata-Ayllu Andamarca/NHC

A. Sorasora.

B. Santos Mamani.

G-1. [He agreed with the opinion of the Indians of Sicasica, in the sense that] "it was necessary to show their bravery and effort and [if] they achieved the ruination of the place . . . they did not doubt that they would have tranquillity in their villages and it would not be necessary to bother them anymore, for which reason he made the declaration of "die or conquer" (86v).

26. Santos Malco (Indian)/native of Challapata-Ayllu Ilave/HC
    A. Caracollo, Condocondo, Peñas, Poopó, Sorasora.
    B. Pascual Conchavi.
    C. "He rushed to undertake [the attack on Oruro] joining his whole community [premeditatively] with the motive of [obtaining] freedom" (87v).
    D. "In order to be free of paying tributes and other taxes" (87).
    F. "They had to totally destroy the town and its inhabitants" (87).
    G-1. "Although in the skirmish nothing had gone wrong, their desire was 'to die killing' or achieve their goals" (87v).
    I. [The tributes] "had to be paid to Tupac Amaru when he came" (87).

27. Thomás Mamani (Indian)/native of Challapata-Ayllu Quillacas/NHC
    A. Sorasora.
    B. Dionisio Chungara.
    F. [Dionisio Chungara asked him] "to help ruin and annihilate this town [Oruro]" (88).
    I. [The foregoing order, according to Chungara], "was from Tupac Amaru" (88).

28. Manuel Mamani (Indian)/native of Challapata-Ayllu Tacagua/NHC
    A. Las Peñas, Poopó.
    B. Adrían? Mamani.
    D. [He ratified the reason for the death of the *cacique* Lope Chungara] "for wanting to reestablish compliance with the royal tributes" (92).
    F. [Together with those of Sorasora] "they decided to destroy this town [Oruro]" (91).
    G-1. [Prominent Indians from Sorasora, after the defeat, took Indians from Challapata prisoner and handed them over to those of Oruro, he among them. Because of this], "he was so indignant that if there had not been so many people present at his capture he would have killed anyone who crossed his path" (91v).
    I. [They had orders from Tupac Amaru not to pay the tributes] (92).

29. Antonio Ramos Chaparro (Indian)/"aged"/from Ormini/NHC
    A. Paria, Sicasica.
    C. [In spite of his age, he participated in the invasion] "with an eye to taking possession of the lands which many years ago had been seized from them by the intruders, lands which since the olden days had belonged to the community of his people, and under the pretext of having come on the King's behalf, they had held them" (92v–93).
    G-1. [With his authority as an old man] "he prevented the reading in his village of the response that was sent from this town [Oruro] so

they would make peace, understanding that in that manner their lands would not be restored to them and he advised them not to accept any such agreement. [Thus] he decided to come and help his people in the war against this town" (93–93v).

30. Diego Mamani (Indian)/native of Challacollo-Ayllu Ilave/NHC

   A. Venta de El Medio, Paria, Ichoca, Sillota.
   C. "They thought that [the region of Oruro] was their territory" (95v). [He also said] "he had not thought anything against the King or against the Republic" (95v).
   D. [He believed, because all the Indians said so], "that there would be no more pressure from then on, with the *real caja* gone from this town" (95v).
   F. "and its population destroyed" (95v).
   I. [They assumed that] "Tupac Amaru was making war against the city of Cuzco [and he] would be very pleased with whatever the community did in his service and the compliance with his orders on which he assumed he was acting" (95–95v).

31. Thomás Cuizana (Indian)/native of Challapata-Ayllu Andamarca/NHC

   A. Caracollo, Sillota, Condocondo.
   B. Santos Mamani, Dionisio Chungara, Calisaya, Gregorio, and Pascual Condori.
   D. [The Indians themselves killed the *cacique* Lope Chungara] "for wanting to persuade them to pay the royal tributes punctually" (96v).
   F. [Calisaya summoned the people to] "invade and annihilate this town [Oruro]" (96).
   I. "believing the rumor that to attack the town was the order of Tupac Amaru" (96v).

32. Nicolás Colqui (Indian)/native of Challapata-Ayllu Tacagua

   A. Paria, Sicasica, Mohosa.
   B. Pascual Condori, Santos Mamani, Carlos Carnaviri.
   C. [They said that as a result of the invasion they would have more land] (98v).
   E. [They hoped that after the invasion] "they would pay less taxes and perhaps improve their fortunes considering what was said about the spoils that were to be taken" (98v).

33. Francisco Mendoza (Indian)/native of Challapata-Ayllu Ilave/NHC

   B. Francisco Mamani, Gregorio Ari.
   D. [He participated in the revolt] "on account of the continued payment of *repartos*, tributes, and many other things that burdened the miserable Indians, they only aspired to remedy this situation by following this path" (100).

34. Francisco Bilca (Indian)/native of Challapata, Ayllu Tacagua/NHC
    B. Dionisio Chungara.
35. Martín Cuellan (Indian)/native of Challapata-Ayllu Chungara/NHC
    A. Sicasica, Sorasora.
    D. [The goal of the invasion was] "to destroy the *caja real*, to be done with these tributes" (103v).
    F. [The strategy was to take the hills first] "so as to facilitate the entry of the others so they could set the fire that would initiate the ruin of Oruro" (103v).
36. Felipe Calani (Indian)/native of Challapata-Ayllu Chungara
    A. Sicasica, Sorasora.
    B. Casimiro Gutiérrez.
    D. "He believed he would be free of the tributes" (105v).
    I. "In agreement with the disposition of Tupac Amaru" (105v).
37. Thomás Condori (Indian)/native of Camaguana-Pacajes/Cap./NHC
    [This is an atypical case: I mention it as original. He went to war only to follow his wife who had betrayed him with another man. They forced him to attack but at the first shots he was afraid and ran away.]
38. Francisco Banco (Indian)/native of Camaguana-Pacajes/Cap./NHC
    A. Challapata, Las Peñas, Poopó.
    C. [After the invasion] "definitely they would give them the lands" (110v).
39. Antonio Herrera (Indian)/native of Sorasora/NHC
    A. Venta de El Medio, Sillota, Paria, Toledo, Challacollo.
    B. Santos Mamani.
    C. "The principal intent of everyone was that the mines and mills should operate for the community of Indians and that they should share the rest of the property" (114).
40. Andrés López (Indian)/native of Sorasora/NHC
    B. Ildefonso Condori.
    C. "The haciendas had to be distributed among the community" (115v).
    D. "It was commonly said that by killing the Spaniards and Mestizos the Indians would be free of the taxes of tribute and *reparto*" (116).
    F. "The time had come for all the Spaniards and mestizos to die" (115).
    H. "With several Spanish in prison, the witness personally threatened them with death telling them that the mill of Sorasora would no longer be run by *cholos*" (116).
    G-1. "When he was asked again if he really intended to kill any of them he answered that the *mayordomos* of that mill persecuted and punished him for no reason when he worked for them" (116).
41. Matheo Guaca (Indian)/from Challacollo/Cap/HC?
    A. Sillota, Paria, Toledo, Challapata.

B. Martín Calisaya.

G-2. For not having "proportion [predisposition?] to fight, he soon refused on this occasion [at the beginning of March, when M. Calisaya told him from Sillota to join. Later he was obliged to do so] (117).

42. Andrés Chinchi (Indian)/native of Challacollo-Ayllu Tanaco/NHC

A. Challapata, Sicasica, Pacajes, Paria, Caracollo.

F. [He offered to participate in the invasion of March 18 because he was assured] "of the desire to annihilate the town [Oruro] on the part of the Great Community" [of the different parishes named] (119v).

43. Bernabé Taquichini (Indian)/native of Challacollo-Ayllu Tanaco/captain/NHC

A. Toledo

F. "The objective was to destroy the town [of Oruro]" (121).

44. Joseph Chinchi (Indian)/native of Challacollo-Ayllu Tanaco/captain/ NHC

A. Challapata, Paria, Carangas, Pacajes, Sicasica, Chayanta.

B. Matheo Guaca.

D. [He said he had come believing the news he heard] "that the natives would be free of the taxes that they had to pay before" (122).

H. "and for this it was necessary to kill the Spaniards and it seemed to him it was the right time in light of the movement made against his *corregidor* in Challapata" (122v).

G-1. "and although in the battles that occurred he did not kill anyone, the definite emotion he felt was "die or conquer" because this was what the orders were from the Indians of Challapata" (122v).

45. Diego Aguacho (Indian)/native of Challacollo-Ayllu Tanaco/NHC

C. [In spite of the deaths that occurred, he is convinced of the need for the attack] "which in the end was to live in more comfort" (127).

46. Sebastián Guanachi (Indian)/native of Cunaguara-Pacajes/NHC

A. Sillota, Sicasica, Challapata.

47. Juan Flores Ibarra (Indian)/native of Ilacota-Pacajes/NHC

A. Quirquirabi, Macha, Pocoata, Poopó.

B. Santos Mamani.

48. Antonio Pacheco (Indian)/native of Las Peñas-Poopó/NHC

A. Iruma? Tatita?

49. Andrés Colque (Indian)/native of Sequipalca-Paria/Cap./NHC

A. Quirquirabi, Sillota, Challapata, Cullcupampa, Paria, Calaguailla, Cachicachi, Ancoata, Soracachi.

50. Bartolomé Mamani (Indian)/*est.* Sequipal-Paria/NHC

B. Andrés Colqui, Asencio Mamani.

F. [He said he came to the town of Oruro for the first time under the command of Captain A. Colqui and the second time under A. Mamani], "with the intention of doing away with all the residents since from the counsel they had it was the suitable thing to do" (138).

   I. "since to do the contrary would be to do badly by Tupac Amaru" (138).

51. Asencio Mamani (Indian)/(origin N/A)/Cap.

   A. Cocota, Mohosa, Sicasica, Sillota.

   F. [The community impressed on them that they had to do away with the residents of this town of Oruro] (138v).

52. Sebastián Santos (Indian)/age 50/Callapa-Pacajes-Ayllu-Collana/captain

   A. Chuñavi, Las Yungas.

   B. Bernardo González, Tupac Catari.

   C. [They ordered him to] embargo all the haciendas that the Spaniards had in Las Yungas, collecting all their fruits without letting them be wasted and used up" (186).

   F. [They were going, each with their own people] "with the resolution to do away with the Spanish Creoles [of La Paz?]" (186v).

   J. [Tupac Catari named him Captain General], "giving him the title" (187).

53. Manuel Condori (Indian)/Ayo Ayo – Sicasica – Ayllu Goillana/captain

   A. La Paz, Sicasica.

   B. Nicolas Laymiguauca, Marcelo Colle, Felipe Laura, Juan Calle, Santiago Quinto, Anselmo Morales.

   E. [Tupac Catari ordered him, after the invasions of La Paz] "to collect and bring to him all the treasure [of Carangas] that was found in its *cajas reales*, which he refused to do" (188v). [Also the aim of the entrance into La Paz was] "to take possession of all its treasures."

   F. [and furthermore] "to do away with all its residents and ruin it entirely" (189).

   J. [In Ayo Ayo Julián Apaza – Tupac Catari ordered him to continue with the invasions that had already been made in this city] (188).

54. Antonio Mamani (Indian)/age 25/Ayo Ayo-Sicasica – Ayllu Ancata

   B. Tupac Catari.

   J. [He was a soldier in Tupac Catari's troops, participating in 7 invasions].

55. Manual Cama/age 40/Venta de El Medio-Paria/*tum.*

   A. Challapata, Colcha.

   B. Santos Mamani, *El alcalde* Uchasara?

   G-2. [He states he did not go to the battle of his own will but on orders of the Indian *alcalde*] (198).

   L. Handed over as "principal tumult maker" by the Indians of Venta
       de El Medio.
56. Lucas Guaigua/age 50/Venta de El Medio?/*tum.*
   B. Alcalde Uchasara, Santos Achacollo.
   D. [He assumed that they would be free of the tributes] "news of which
       came to Indians like raindrops" (199v).
   F. [They had as their aim to take over the haciendas and property of
       the residents of Oruro] (199v).
   L. Handed over as a "tumult maker" by the Indians of Venta de El
       Medio.
57. Francisco Churqui/age 50-plus/native of Cullcupampa-Oruro/*tum.*
   A. Irooma, Pisagueri, *est.* Tutucala.
   B. Esteban Cuchillo, Alejo Mendoza, Manuel Beltrán, Mateo Sipi,
       Nicolás Cuchillo, Nicolás Tutucala, Miguel Favian.
   F. [The goal was to do away with and ruin the inhabitants of the town
       of Oruro] (202).
   G-1. Nicolás Tutucala [was determined?] "especially to take the life
       of Clemente Menacho" [captain of one of the Oruro companies]
       (202).
   I. [The other goal was] "to wait for 'Tupamaro' who as King was going
       to eliminate their poverty" (202).
58. Alejo Mendoza/age 30/native of Cullcupampa, Paria Parish/*tum.*
   A. Iruuma, Cullcupampa, Pisaqueri, Challapata.
   B. Esteban Cuchillo, Nicolás López, Miguel Fabri, Pascual Tomas,
       Nicolás Tutucula, Dionisio de Tal.
   E. [The goal of the invasion of Oruro was to get the riches] (203).
   F. [and kill its inhabitants] (203).
   I. [The foregoing was the order of Tupamaro], "for whom they waited
       for hours and in the consultations and meetings of the Indians they
       spoke of nothing else except this rebel who they assumed was al-
       ready king" (203v).
   L. Handed over as a "tumult maker" by the Indians of Cullcupampa.
59. Cruz Favian/age 26/*est.* Cullcupampa-Paria parish/captain/15/V.
   A. Icotoca? Mohosa, Iruuma.
   B. Esteban Cuchillo, Alejo Mendoza.
   F. [The goal of the invasion was to] "do away with the inhabitants"
       (204v).
   G-2. "For having been captain of his ranch and for having come with
       his people to attack this village [they arrested him], . . . although
       he did not enter because he found himself with those who were flee-
       ing" (204v).
   E. [More on the goal] "and to get their houses and riches [belonging
       to the residents]" (204v).

I. [What was expressed in the goals] "was the order of Tupac Amaru" (204v).

L. Handed over as a "tumult maker" by the Indians of Cullcupampa.

60. Andres Cuchillo/age 40 plus/*est.* Cullcupampa-Paria parish/*tum.*

A. Paria parish, Caracollo.

B. Miguel Fabrique.

F. The goal of the invasion was "to take the lives of the residents and ruin (the town)" (205v).

L. Handed over as a "tumult maker" by the Indians of Cullcupampa.

61. Mateo Santos/age 40-plus/Guancarama, Challacollo parish, Paria province/captain/16V

A. [He calls them "Ayllus"]: Sicasica, Quelcata, Alcamarca, Amachuma, Vilavila, Conchamarca, Ataraque, Ancoñuño, Machacamarca, Caracollo, Sillota, Arita? Querarani, Umaocollo, Pongo, Condoriri, Rodeo.

B. Asencio Figueroa (captain of war), Mateo Mamani (captain major), Crispín Mamani, Marcos Mamani, Simon Cuba, Silvestre Choque.

C. "that the haciendas [of the Creoles and Spaniards] become the property of the Indians and that from then on there would be nothing in the Kingdom that was not theirs" (208).

F. "The goal of their coming to this village [Oruro] was to do away with all the residents" (208).

I. [the foregoing] "according to the order of their king Tupamaro" (208).

L. Betrayed "by his own people," accused of being a collaborator in the tumults and a principal *caudillo* of the invasions on this town (206v).

62. Ramón Colque/age 40-plus/Calapata, Paria/*caudillo*/16V

B. Lorenzo Mamani.

C. The goal of the invasion was "for all the haciendas to belong to the Indians" (209v).

E. [In particular] "to take the property [of the residents of Oruro]" (209v).

F. "taking the lives of the owners" (209v)

I. "Thus it was commanded by their king Tupamaro" (209v).

L. Betrayed "by his own people," accused of being a collaborator . . . (same as 61).

63. Vicente Quispe/age 30/Poopó-Paria/*caudillo*/16/V

A. Poopó, Sorasora, La Venta, Challapata, Condocondo, Venta, Guari.

E. The goal was "to take control of the riches [of the town]" (211).

L. Betrayed "by his own people," accused of being a collaborator (same as 61).

64. Xavier Guanca/Venta y Media-Paria/*caudillo*/16/V
    B. Mateo Cruz-Lucas Choque.
    L. Same as 61.
65. Crispín Mamani/age 50/native of Sicasica/captain, *alcalde*/18V
    A. La Joya, Sicasica, Pacajes, Paria, Carangas.
    C. "The spoils and haciendas of the Spaniards have to be given to the
       community of Indians" (213v).
    I. [The Indians of La Joya read to the Indians of Sillota] "an edict that
       they said was from Tupamaro, to whom they had to pay only a third
       in tributes which was for San Juan in which belief they all resolved
       to continue with their sedition and by a communication of said Edict
       each *estancia* had to pay 4 pesos" (213v).
    L. Denounced by the Indians of Sillota, Caracollo parish, as "head of
       the uprising and captain in the rebellions and attacks on this town"
       (212v).
66. Nicolás López/age 40-plus/native of Irooma-Paria/captain/18/V
    A. Challapata, Sicasica, Quirquiari, Macha, Pocoata.
    C. [The people from Sicasica assumed that all the haciendas] "had to
       belong to the community" (216v).
    E. [Everyone agreed about the invasion] "because they were interested
       in taking possession of all the haciendas" (216v).
    F. "It was the people of Ichoca who proposed annihilating all the in-
       habitants of Oruro" (216v).
    I. [Tupamaro assured them that the haciendas would be returned to
       the community] (216v).
    L. "Presented" by the Indians of Laquepalca (or Irooma?) as captain of
       his *estancia*.
67. Juan Marca/*est*. Querarani
    A. *Est*. Pongo.
    B. Bartolomé Choque.
    L. "Presented" by the Indians of the *estancia* of Querarani.
68. Agustín Choque/age 50-plus/native of Ayllu Uravi, Corque/sergeant
    B. Sucas Ala, Nicolás Choque.
    C. [The goal was] "to be owners of the haciendas that the Spaniards
       possessed" (222v).
    D. [and] "to be free of taxes" (222v).
    J. [He took part in] "gathering the Indians for the invasions of Oruro
       and La Paz in support of Tupacatari" (222v).
    L. Denounced by the people of Corque, Garangas.
69. Tomás Calle/age 40 – plus/native of Ayllu Uravi, Corque/soldier/25/V
    C. [The Indians promised] "to be lords of all the haciendas the Span-
       iards possessed and that it was time now to be done with the gov-
       ernment of Spain" (224).

E. [They were confident] "that they would take possession of its [Oruro's] riches" (223v).

F. [and] "destroy this town" (223v).

I. [and] "wait for their supposed King the rebel Tupamaro [with whose coming they would accomplish all the foregoing]" (223v).

L. Same as 68.

70. Melchor Cuisara/age 40 – plus/native of Challapata-Ayllu, Andamarca/ soldier/25/V

B. Santos Puma.

E. [The goal was] "to take possession of all the riches of Oruro" (224v).

I. "and to wait for their King Tupamaro to whom they first desired to subject themselves which was the principal intent of the uprising" (225).

L. Betrayed by the Indians of Challapata.

71. Cristóbal Choque/age 30/*est.* Las Peñas-Paria/soldier/25/V

A. Las Peñas, Taraquira, Iturmiri.

E. [The goal was] "to take over the riches [of Oruro]" (226v).

F. [and] "to destroy it" (226v).

H. [In Poopó] "to kill a twelve-year-old boy who they said was the son of Juan de Dios Rodríguez" (226).

L. "Presented" by the Indians of Poopó.

72. Pedro Choque/age 40/*est.* Las Peñas-Paria/soldier/25/V

A. Paria, Chamanta.

B. Bartolomé Achacollo.

C. "All the haciendas of the Spaniards would belong to the Indians" (227v).

D. [and] "they would be free of the burden of tributes" (227v).

I. [The cause of the uprising was] "because they were waiting for the *cacique* Tupamaro who they regarded as their king" (227v).

H. "The principal project of said uprising was to free the provinces from the tyrannical government of the *corregidores*, *caciques*, and *alcaldes* and that this could be done only by an Indian captain who was appointed by the community" (228–228v).

L. Same as 71.

73. Lucas Flores/age 30/Querarani-Sicasica/26/V

A. *Est.* Pongo.

B. Bernabé Cruz, Bartolomé Choque.

E. [The goal of the invasion was] "to take possession of all the riches" (229).

D. [In this way] "they would be free of tributes and all service" (229).

I. [He did it all because] "it was what was ordered by the King Inga Tupamaro" (229).

L. He was also "denounced" but it is not clear by whom.

74. Manuel Cruz/age 40-plus/Querarani-Sicasica/26/V
    A. Sicasica, Ichoca.
    B. Bartolomé Choque.
    D. "In this way they would be free of paying the tributes and all service to the Spaniards" (230v).
    H. "and also of the tyranny of the *corregidores* and *caciques*" (230v).
    L. "Presented" by the *mayordomo* of the *estancia* of Querarani.
75. Antonio Colque/age 40/*est*. Calapata, dist. Paria/26/V
    A. Iruuma, Sillota.
    B. Lorenzo Mamani, Ramón Colque.
    F. [He came to this invasion] "wanting to see the ruin promised by [the Indians assembled] come to pass" (232v).
    L. "Presented" by the Indians of the *estancia* Calapata, Paria parish.
76. Santos Mamani/age 50/Challapata, Ayllu Andamarca/captain and *alcalde*
    A. Machacamarca, Quirquiabi.
    B. Tomás Catari, Lope Chungara, Carlos Cañaviri, Joseph Quispe, Gregorio Ari, Julián Condori.
    C. [On the advice of the people of Challapata] "they had agreed to become absolute lords of whatever there was, assigning to the community the mines, mills, and whatever was in sight" (237).
    D. [Tomás Catari had spread the order not to pay the *repartos* to the *corregidores* any more] (234).
    L. Delivered prisoner by the *alcaldes* of Challapata and those of Poopó, "stating that he was the main force behind the uprisings of that people and of the invasions against this town" (233).

Appendix B

Testimonies of inhabitants of the city

The witnesses were interrogated with the following questions:

1. "Tell if you know, you were told, or you had news that in the Time of the Rebellion in this City, many individuals lived here, both secular and ecclesiastical, with jobs and positions as vicars, priors, *alcaldes*, *regidores*, administrators of rents, and other public posts; specify their names and addresses excluding those who have been ordered arrested in this cause."
2. "If you know that the cited employees have made any efforts to calm and quiet the anger of the rebels, or if on the contrary they lent encouragement and support to [the rebels'] operations."
3. "Also if you know that during the time in question, even if they did not participate, they manifested later in private or public meetings any sentiments indicating their earlier manner of speaking."
4. "Tell if you know or have been told that with motive of that rebellion large assets were taken from the dead and persecuted Europeans."
5. "If you know or heard tell among which persons the said assets were distributed."
6. "If you know or heard tell of purchases, acquisitions or investments of these assets, specify which subjects made these purchases, the investments they made in those assets, and how much they considered suitable to reveal their whereabouts, existence, and exploitation."
7. "If you know or heard tell that in the places of this [illegible] or outside of it there were sent any [charity?] of the [illegible] for the criminals apprehended and the other inhabitants of this vicinity informing you that any other remittance that has preceded will be very relevant to your individual information, to which end you may express and dictate who have been these confidants put in charge of their receipt and everything you consider appropriate and suitable for this clarification."

In the City of Oruro, August 23, 1784

Source: "Testimonio del Quaderno Segundo de Autos Criminales obrados por Don Sebastián de Segurola sobre la rebelión de la Villa de Oruro." Buenos Aires, 1789. Sala IX-7-4-3 Legajo 2, no. 2.

1. **Miguel de Llanos,** *abogado* of the *real audiencia* of La Plata. Resident and *alcalde ordinario* of Oruro (Oruro, August 23, 1784)

1. Dr. Isidoro Velazco (priest of Sorasora), Dr. Agustín Quebedo (environs of Oruro), Dr. Vicente Vericochea (?) (Chayanta), *Licenciado* Diego Olivares (of Panacachi), Maestro Joseph Calancha (La Joya), Dr. González (Choqueota), Dr. Teodoro Zeballos (Poopó), Dr. Pedro Antezama (Caracollo), *Licenciado* Manuel Amezaga (Challacollo), *Licenciado* Zierra (Corqui). And the prelates of the religious orders: Fray Joseph Quadros (San Agustín), The Prior of San Juan de Dios (name unknown). Ramón de Urrutia y Las Casas (*corregidor* and *justicia mayor*), the same (*alcalde ordinario de primer voto*), Don Manuel de Murguí (*alcalde de segundo voto*), Don Gregorio Aldave y Salamanca (*alguacil mayor*), Don Domingo Urquieta (*regidor*), Don Isidro Rodríguez (*regidor*), Don Joseph Antonio Ramallo (*regidor*), Don Santiago Royo (?) (*procurador general*), Don Nicolás Caro (?) (replacement for the previous, deceased), Blas Mariano Vargas (royal scribe), Manuel Montesinos (royal scribe), Don Salvador Parrilla (treasurer), Don Pedro Vicente Vargas (accountant), Don Diego Antonio Portillo (postal administrator), Don Joseph Álvarez Martínez y Catacoro? (his replacement) (3–3v).

2. Yes, the *alcalde* Murguía (it says "*corregidor*"), the treasurer Parrilla, and himself. For the rest, he doesn't know (3v).

3. He doesn't know (having left the city as a fugitive) (4).

4. He knows and was told that the houses of the dead Europeans were sacked and that "most of the neighborhood" took advantage of these robberies (but he gives no names) (4v).

5. Don Jacinto Rodríguez (on the sacking of the house of Rubín de Celis): ". . . that he ordered it to be done with the deceased Don Domingo Galleguillo, Bernardo Pinedo [his Negro] and other agents in the quantity of 30 to 40 thousand pesos; likewise the priest of the city with a bar of silver that said Don Jacinto sent him for the burial of the Europeans . . . ; Father Fray Joseph Fernández Dávila with 2 or 3 bars that he brought to the city of Cochabamba and Don Manuel Herrera with 600 marks of silver in *piña* belonging to the deceased Don Vizente García" (5).

6. He doesn't know.

7. He doesn't know.

2. **Basilio Andrade,** townsman of Oruro (Oruro, August 23, 1784)

1. Army Captain Don Ramón de Urrutia y Las Casas (*corregidor*), M. Llamos and M. Murguía (*alcaldes*), G. Salamanca (*alguacil mayor*), Domingo Urquieta (*regidor*), Joseph Manuel Herrera (*regidor*, already deposed), Isidro Rodríguez (*regidor*), Salvador Parrilla (treasurer), Pedro V. Vargas

(accountant for the *caja real*), Juan A. González de Quiroga (tobacco administrator), Diego A. Portillo (postal administrator), Jose Álvarez (his official *mayor*), Blas M. Bargas and Jose M. Montesinos (royal scribes), Nicolás Caro (attorney), D. Agustín Quebedo (priest in the environs), D. Isidoro Velazco (priest of Sorasora), D. Vicente Vericochea (of Chayanta), Don Joaquín Barron (priest of Chayanta), D. Manuel Amezaga (priest of Challacollo), D. Anselmo Carrasco (priest of Cabari), D. Diego Olivares (priest of Panacachi), D. González Curo (of Choquecota), P. Fray Justo de Peñaloza (Hostal San Juan de Dios), the prior of San Agustín, P. Camiroaga (guardian of San Francisco), Alejo Barnata (*Teniente* of *alguacil mayor*).

2. He knows only what Ramón Urrutia did, who "made several efforts to calm down the soldiers in the barracks (6v). For the rest, he heard news that they took refuge in the monasteries.

3. He doesn't know.

4. He knows and was told that the stolen assets were very large and that in this matter "the townsfolk participated in proportion to what the thieves could snatch" (7v).

5. A lot was robbed by the *cholos*. A shoemaker took a silver *piña* from the house of the *corregidor* and broke it into pieces with the help of two women (whom he does not know). Also, Fray A. Lazo de la Vega proposed to him that he speak with his brother-in-law so he would buy a bar of silver of 800 pesos from him, which he said was one of the stolen ones; the deal was never made (7v). Two days after the revolt a man from Cochabamba went back to his city leading Negro slaves, mules and other stolen property and with him went Fray Fernando Carreño, a Mercedarian monk who had a bar of silver taken from him in Cochabamba, but he doesn't know if it was done by the *justicia real* or his own superior. Also, he heard it publicly said that Fray Santiago Calatayud, of the order of Our Lady of Mercy seized a bar of silver from a Negro slave woman belonging to Joseph Calvete. In the days following the uprising, he saw that A. Quiróz and Domingo Herrera y Galleguillos (now deceased) were asking for the stolen goods in the houses, by order of Jacinto Rodríguez. But this effort was suspended due to the uproar it caused among the people. Jacinto Rodríguez gave D. Patricio Menéndez a bar of silver for the burial of the dead Europeans. He also knows that the troops who came from Cochabamba bought part of the stolen goods (8). The most notorious was the purchase made by *muleteros* (drivers of mules) from Tagna (?), who came to the city on business with *aguardiente* (8).

6. He heard tell that Casimiro Delgado and the deceased Miguel Portilla bought "secret specie."

7. He doesn't know.

3. **Luisa María Calvete**, black slave of D. Joseph Calvete (called to verify Basilio Andrade's statement)

> She is accused of having taken a bar of silver from Fray Santiago (Calatayud or Calatarpio?). Her version is that on the night of the rebellion, "risking her person with enough fatigue she seized said bar from an Indian and considering the obligation to return it to its owner she then handed it over to the said Calatarpio so that as a priest he would find out to whom it belonged and give her a little aid in the form of money; that although later she appealed to said priest in the matter, she got nothing but threats of maltreatment" (10), so she went to the *justicia mayor* of the city and to the Superior who came from Cuzco, but that she still was unable to secure the return of the bar or any aid.

4. **Fray Marcos Gregorio del Rivero**, monk of San Juan de Dios

1. Don Ramón de Urrutia y Las Casas (*corregidor*), Don Miguel Llano y Don Manuel Mugurusa (*alcaldes ordinarios*), Don Domingo Urquieta and Don Joseph Ramallo (*regidor*), Don Fernando Gurruchaga (captain of one of the militia companies), Don Salvador Parrilla (royal treasurer), Pedro Vicente Vargas (accountant), Don Diego A. de Portillo (postal administrator), Juan A. González de Quiroga (tobacco administrator), Dr. Anselmo Carrasco (priest of Cabari?), Dr. Vicente Verecochea (priest of Chayanta), Dr. Joaquín Barras (priest of Chayala), Dr. Juan Francisco González (priest of Choquecota), D. Diego Olivares (priest of Panacachi), D. Manuel Amezaga (priest of Sorasora), Fray Baltasar Campos (prior of Santo Domingo), P. Caminoaga (guardian of San Francisco), Fray Joseph Quadros (prior of San Agustín), Fray F. de Peñaloza (elder brother of San Juan de Dios), D. Quebedo (priest of city environs), D. Teodoro Zeballos (priest of Poopó), the priest of Totora.

2. He does not know what anyone did; but he heard tell that Don Ramón de Urrutia tried to calm down the soldiers; that Father Caminoaga organized a procession on the second day of the rebellion, to pacify the enemy; that D. Salvador Parrilla worked hard to pacify and avert the rebellion; that D. Anselmo Carrasco preached on the second day of the rebellion with the goal of calming the rebels; that Fray Joseph Quadros ordered a mass said for the Indians, commanding them not to sack the houses.

   For the rest, he heard that they took refuge to save their lives, and neither helped nor had any effect on the defense (iiv).

3. He doesn't know.

4. He knows and was told about the great sacking which, using the rebellion as an excuse, the townsfolk made of the wealth accumulated by the dead Europeans (12).

5. Because the imprisonment of Fray Fernando Carreño was widely known, ordered by the superiors of his religion, he knew that [the priest] brought to the city of Cochabamba 2 bars of silver belonging to the stolen booty and that one of them was placed in the *cajas reales* of that city; that he had heard it publicly said that a woman named Teodora, alias La Cantarrana, took part of the wealth of J. R. Celis in collaboration with a lad named Terlintín; that Jacinto Rodríguez assigned several persons to pick up the stolen goods from the houses, during which task they collected much wealth, until because of the threat of new uprisings this operation was suspended; that all the rebels participated in these robberies and that the witness saw "that many *cholos* in the most public places were openly playing with gold quoits" (12v–13).

6. He heard tell that the troops from Cochabamba bought most of the secret loot; and so did the businessmen from the coast, who brought *aguardiente* to the city (13v).

7. He doesn't know.

5. **Felipe Aseñas**, no origin given (Oruro, August 23, 1784)

1. He gives the same names as the previous witness.
2. He knows "by common and public report" that all those named tried to pacify the seditious feelings.
3. He doesn't know anything.
4. That "by public report he knows that the dead and persecuted Europeans in that rebellion were robbed of great wealth, of which the people of this town availed themselves" (15).
5. That a Negro slave woman of Joseph Calvete told him she had acquired a bar of silver and that having brought it to the convent of La Merced, they hid it without giving her 50 *centavos* as a finder's fee which she asked for; that the *cholas* of the city had and spent much of the stolen money (but he doesn't know individual names) (15v).
6. He knows that the deceased Miguel de la Portilla bought a quantity of iron and *piñas* of silver at a very low price (but he does not know who the sellers were).
7. He doesn't know.

6. **Bernardino Ibáñez**, prisoner in the veterans' barracks

1. He mentions the same names, but he mentions (perhaps mistakenly) "José M. Herrera" as *regidor*.
2. He does not know, because after hearing the news that the plaza was "full of dead Creoles," he shut himself in his house and didn't see anything.
3. He doesn't know.

4. He knows that loot was taken from the dead Europeans.
5. He saw that many individuals of the community were spending money extravagantly and gambling in the plaza, each of them showing off their loot; that a servant of his named Vicente Aramayo told him that having helped to bring a bar of silver to a house next to the chapel of Casimiro Delgado, they shared it among themselves and did not give him any share; the servant asked him to go in his company to ask for his share, which he agreed to do and got them to give him 2 silver marks (17v).
6. He admits having bought 6 *arrobas* [150 pounds in all] of steel and 10 or 12 *quintales* of iron of the loot; he also picked up at a roadside inn some stolen goods being held by men from Cochabamba.
7. He doesn't know if loot was taken from the place. He heard tell that Casimiro Delgado bought a bar of silver from rebel Indians, in exchange for liquor.

7. **Miguel Azeñas**, prisoner in the veterans' barracks

1. He names the same people; he also mentions Joseph M. de Herrera as *regidor*.
2. He knows and was told that Don Ramón de Urrutia offered to sleep with the soldiers in the barracks to assure them of his loyalty and "so they would be sure that lies had been told by some women and a monk; and that he did not know why the *chapetones* wanted to kill them" (19v). Others who tried to pacify the anger were D. Salvador Parrilla, Fray J. Quadros, and Fray Marcos de Rivero.
3. He doesn't know.
4. It is true that the property of the Europeans was robbed.
5. He remembers that a group from Cochabamba left the city with stolen goods. He was told that Fray Lorenzo Espinosa had declared that any rich person who bought stolen property would not be absolved by him; but that he would absolve the poor; in light of this, he decided to buy stolen property up to 16 silver marks worth (22v). He presumes that many purchases were of the property stolen in the mines of this area and that at this time they were selling a silver mark at 5, 4, or even 3 pesos (22v).
6. He agrees with what was already said.
7. He doesn't know.

8. **Ventura Aseños**, prisoner in the veterans' barracks (Oruro, August 27, 1784)

1. He names the same people.
2. He doesn't know.
3. He doesn't know.

4. It is true (that the estates of the Europeans were robbed).
5. He knows that Sebastián Díaz handed over to Fray José Bustillos, commander of the monastery of La Merced, some silver *piñas* and that, having asked the said monk for its return, he refused it on the pretext that the Indians who entered the town robbed him of that which had been entrusted to him; that likewise he said he had given to the Hospital of San Juan various goods from Castile, which he sold in his store, and other medicinal drugs, all that he handed over for safekeeping to two monks of that hospital named Fray Marcos de la Rivera and the other a Fray Francisco whose surname he did not know, who gave him the same account as the previous one; that a woman of this town he does not know, a widow of a "little Gallego" had in her house many goods that had been robbed in the rebellion; that in the store of the cobbler Manuel who lives in front of the Cathedral a pouch of stamped silver was distributed (25v–26).
6. He doesn't know.
7. He doesn't know.

9. **María Quirós**, prisoner in the case of the rebellion (Oruro, August 28, 1784)

1. She names the same people and adds D. V. Alarza, *alcavalero* [*sic*] and Anselmo Carrasco, priest of Catari (?).
2. She remembers only the priest of Choquecota, Juan Fco. González who on one of the days of the rebellion urged the *cholos* in the plaza to do no harm.
3. She doesn't know.
4. According to what she was told, the thefts amounted to 300,000 pesos.
5. She knows nothing about the distribution of this booty; she presumes it was distributed among the people, among whom were many patricians of Cochabamba and other outsiders and plantation Indians (28).
6. She knows only that Melchora Barrosa bought stolen goods, especially a mark of silver; a piece of bar worth 3 pesos (28v).

10. **Francisca Orozco**, prisoner in the case of the rebellion (Oruro, August 28, 1784)

1. She names the same people and Diego Azero, commercial judge, and D. Juan M. de Soto, militia officer.
2. She doesn't know.
3. She doesn't know.
4. She knows that great booty was robbed from the Europeans.
5. She knows that the people from Cochabamba who entered the place with food and other goods bought and carried off a large part of the booty;

that on the night of the rebellion, as she stood in the doorway of her house, she saw a silversmith named Juan carrying a parcel underneath his poncho, very heavy, and [as] he continued his trip with his wife and an employee of his, she had reason to presume that package was from the sacking, which at that moment was taking place in the house of the Europeans; that she heard it said that a Negress of Calvete had a bar of silver, and she didn't know the fate it had met; that because of the common distribution that the people made of those thefts among themselves, she could not specify the portions allotted nor to whom (29v–30).

6. She doesn't know.
7. She doesn't know.

11. **María Francisca Goya,** no information (Oruro, August 28, 1784)

1. She names the same people.
2. After the rebellion she saw a procession formed by all the religious and she presumed it was with the object of pacifying anger and placating the tumult (32v).
3. She doesn't know.
4. She knows that they robbed huge booty from the persecuted Europeans.
5. She does not know among whom the booty was distributed. Various Indians whom she did not know came to her store to sell her stolen merchandise, but she did not wish to get involved with such purchases.
6. She doesn't know.
7. After the rebellion, a miner in her store said he had taken into the monastery of La Merced six bars of the stolen silver and that they did not reward him with any money, at the notice of which the husband of the witness took the boy to make a declaration to a competent authority (33v).

12. **Mariano Miranda,** alias Lupercio, master tailor.

1. He names the same people.
2. That of all the individuals he named, with the exception of the priest of the town, who did not have the slightest consideration to pacify the anger of the rebels, all the other *regidores* and priests, especially those of Chayala, Chayanta, and Cabari (?) continuously and effectively warned the rebels to cease in their excesses; that of the prelates of the religious orders, that of San Francisco was notorious for his inaction and P. Quadros, prior of San Augustín, ordered a mass of thanksgiving said for the Indians who entered this town, advising them and telling them to kill the *cholos,* which doubtless he did because he was outraged about the homicides and havoc that the *cholos* perpetrated against the persons of several Europeans (35).

3. He does not know.
4. That the thefts that were made of the great resources of the dead Europeans are well known and notorious.
5. That the greater part of the booty seized came to rest in the house of Fco. (?) Rodríguez, "on whose orders several emissaries went out, such as Bernabé Pineda, Clemente Menacho, officers, and sergeants; Pedro Asquas, Miguel Portilla, and one commonly known as "El Terlintín" (and others) (36). He likewise knows that several men (among them a saddlemaker), two of his officers from Aullagas district, and a hatmaker, at the same time that the house where the goods of the Europeans were kept was set on fire, they entered it and robbed clothing, stamped silver, and other things; he knows that a blacksmith took a bar of silver and distributed it among other companions; he also knows that a brother-in-law of Pedro Asquas and a blacksmith named Julián Molina, took part in the deaths and thefts, with the goods on which they to this day support their commerce and business in this town; that after eight days of rebellion he saw Ambrosio Medrano outside the town dividing up a bar of silver that he had robbed with a group of people who surrounded him; he also knows that the presbyter D. Melchor Quevedo bought a piece of gold from an Indian drummer in town for four pesos; that in the possession of this same cleric he saw a cloak made of a piece of silk from a robbed store; that Don Miguel de Astorga, who lives in a store in the Plazuela del Regocijo, bought a considerable portion of the stolen worked silver; and that also Father Calatayud, monk of La Merced, on the night of the uprising seized a bar of silver from some *cholos* who had stolen it, and he believes that after some time it was taken to the house of Jacinto Rodríguez, "that finally the stealing was so general that in those days the most ragged *cholos* went through the streets raising a ruckus with gold doubloons, with their wives also carrying a portion of the silver and other goods, which in many places was sold to people from Cochabamaba who had come under the command of Lt. Coronel Joseph de Ayarza."
6. He knows that Pedro Asquas, with what he had stolen, bought a hacienda in the vicinity of Mohoza; and that a barber named Domingo Callejas, resident of this town, also redeemed a tax charged against his estate and it was said he had done it with the spoils he had taken (38–38v).

13. **Manuel Cayetano Sorrosa y Larrea** (Oruro, September 2, 1784)

1. He names the same people.
2. Urrutia, Parrilla, and Fray Ignacio Ulloa (of Santo Domingo), and also Captain Gurruchaga, attempted to calm people down.
3. He does not know.

4. The robbery in which the entire neighborhood participated to the extent that each one was able to steal is notorious.

5. Ambrosio Medrano, one of his debtors, participated in the sack of the house of the Spaniards, taking possession of a great quantity of booty; he also knows that Fray Santiago Calatayud and Padre Carreño, of the same order, passed two or three of the stolen bars; that days after the invasion he saw that the priest of the Cathedral carried off one of the bars that Jacinto Rodríguez had given to the priest to say masses for the souls of the dead Europeans; that he saw Clemente Menacho and others leaving the house of D. Jacinto Rodríguez to gather stolen goods; that he had heard that a woman known as La Cantarrana participated in the sack of the house of R. de Celis and that by order of said Don Jacinto his goods came to rest at the house of the latter (41–42).

6. Only by guessing he infers that Pedro Asquas robbed the hacienda of Oputañe (?), inasmuch as before the uprising he had not the means to make this and other purchases; he also heard it said that the people from Cochabamba who arrived under the command of Lt. Coronel J. de Ayarza bought the greater part of the stolen property (42v).

7. He doesn't know.

14. José Vicente Montesinos (Oruro, September 2, 1784)

1. He names the same people.

2. Urrutia, Llano, Ramallo, Captain Sorsano, Father Montesinos (his uncle), and *alcalde* Mugurusa did the services required to calm spirits. Moreover, Salvador Parrilla put 1,000 pesos in his purse for the garrisoned soldiers. As for the lawyer Nicolás Caro, days later he told him about the *chapetones* and that in his view they were well dead; and he heard it said that the guardian of San Francisco, Fray Juan Camiroaga, did not wish to make room in his monastery for Pedro de la Graba and other persecuted Europeans (44–44v).

3. He refers to what he said in the previous paragraph.

4. It is known as published that during the rebellion the goods of various Europeans were sacked.

5. A few days after the rebellion he heard it said that Ambrosio Medrano had robbed certain bars and had distributed them among *cholos* and Indians.

6. He heard it said publicly that Casimiro Delgado bought a bar from an Indian and also various pieces of silver from the one that A. Medrano distributed; and that the soldiers from Cochabamba bought at very low prices various pieces of worked silver and other stolen goods (45).

15. Tomás Carpio, master silversmith, resident of Oruro (Oruro, September 3, 1784)

1. He names the same people.
2. He does not know because he had taken refuge in the houses of Llanos and Jacinto Rodríguez.
3. He does not know.
4. That is true (that the goods of dead Spaniards were robbed).
5. He heard about Fray Sgo. Calatayud and F. Fernando Carreño, of La Merced, that they had taken two bars of silver, but he doesn't know where they ended up.
6. He heard it said that Miguel Parrilla made various purchases of goods stolen from Europeans; that Pedro Aigua bought an estate in the same fashion.

16. Francisco Solano Polo (Oruro, September 3, 1784)

1. He names the same people.
2. He knows nothing of those named or he states that they may have done something to calm the rebellion, except for Fray Joseph Echevarría, about whom he heard it said that he preached to and exhorted the rebels. On the other hand, his wife told him that Dr. N. Caro went to spur on those who set fire to the house of the Europeans; that the priest of Challacollo, Dr. Manuel de Amezaga, and Fray Antonio Lazo de la Vega, of San Agustín, were present at a meeting in the house of Casimiro Delgado when the first notices that *chapetones* wanted to kill the Creoles arrived; they went out to spread and propagate this in the streets and barracks; that Fray Camiroaga did not wish to give refuge to many Europeans and that he even pushed them out violently.
3. He refers to the above and adds that the late Dr. Caro, several days after the rebellion, said in his presence in a shocking way that he felt sorry that the *cholos* and Indians had not finished off all those who lived in this town and only had killed the best people, leaving the worst alive (50–50v).
4. There was a great sacking and each one took what he could.
5. He hid himself because of news that they wanted to finish him off because they considered him "a bootlicker of the *corregidor*"; but from his hiding place he could see how they sacked the flaming store, with the possessions of the Europeans; he saw various monks from the monastery of La Merced entering it, removing what they could; that when he was hidden in the house of Jacinto Rodríguez he saw various Negroes and Indians carrying there many silver *piñas* and cases and packages of whose contents he was ignorant. Bernabé Pineda told him that they came from the house of R. de Celis and that they were brought on the order of Jacinto Rodríguez. Six or seven days after the rebellion, Jacinto Rodríguez ordered that everything that had been robbed be recovered from the houses of the district, he having been one of the commissioners

appointed for that task, along with Bernabé Pineda, D. Urquieta, D. Galleguillo, Menacho Quiróz, Nicolás Herrera, the royal scribe J. M. Montesinos, among others; that thus they were able to recuperate "much iron," various pieces of clothing, pieces of velvet and other kinds of cloth, together with a bar and another piece of worked silver, all of which passed into the house of J. Rodríguez; but when the interested parties asked for the restitution of their goods thus recuperated, Jacinto Rodríguez said that the *cholos* wanted to rebel again and therefore they had to return everything. He had everything brought out to the patio and kept all the valuable goods for himself (51–53). Moreover, a few days after the invasion, the official silversmith Juan Robles offered to sell him a bar of 213 marks, because he lacked the wherewithal to have it smelted, which he refused to do on the advice of P. Echeverría and B. Pinedo; that same day, Francisco Riva wanted to sell him some "gold quoits" at 15 pesos per ounce, to which he replied that since it was stolen gold it was not usual to sell it at so high a price; he knows that this same individual took from the town more than 5,000 pesos and several suits of clothing (54–54v). He also knew that Ambrosio Medrano participated in the looting of the house of the Europeans and afterwards the house of Pantaleón Martínez; from the latter and from Nicolás Herrera he heard that they took advantage of a great part of the property sacked; also a silk dealer of the town, Domingo Rojas, was one of the robbers, and today he sells normally in his place of business (54v).

6. He knows that Domingo Salamanca, nephew of Padre Bustillos, improved his fortune with the purchase of stolen goods; the same thing happened to Bernardino Ibáñez, nephew of Miguel Portilla, about whom it was said he had purchased a bale of local silk cloth, at the scant price of 14 pesos; and Casimiro Delgado, of whom it was publicly said that he bought several stolen bars for 200 pesos each; that the purchase made by those from Cochabamba of these stolen goods meant that the prices at which they were sold were ridiculous, such as 3 *reales* paid by those from Cochabamba for a yard of cloth, as it was told to him.

17. **Melchor Saavedra**, resident of Oruro (Oruro, September 6, 1784)

1. He named the same people.
2. Except for Urrutia, Vicente Berecochea, D. Diego de Acero and himself, he does not know whether others tried to pacify anger.
3. Although at the time of the rebellion they supported and thought well of the killing of the Europeans, he had no proof that any of those named above had contributed to those excesses (57).
4. It is true that they robbed the riches of the dead Europeans.
5. He heard it said that most of the people participated in the removal of the riches; that much of this loot went into the house of the Cantarranas;

that they said that Pedro Asqua and M. Portilla were the main participants in those thefts (57v).

6. He cannot give names because he knows them only by sight; but he saw many people bustling about doing things they never did before, and then disappearing from the place, some of them going to live in Aullagas, others to Potosí, and others to La Plata, besides the people from Cochabamba who turned up in those days (58). He also supposes that Jacinto Rodríguez had a bar of silver that had been bought by Casimiro Delgado.

18. Antonio Montesinos (Oruro, September 6, 1784)

1. He gives the same names (he adds Santiago Arroyo, procurador of the town).
2. The *corregidor*, the *alcaldes ordinarios*, the royal officials Don Santiago Arroyo, the *escribano* Montesinos (his brother), the two militia captains and the priest of Choqueota, did what they could to pacify the anger. On the other hand Dr. Caro (of this he was a witness) encouraged the traitors to continue their rebellion; he urged them on with these words: "(to the Spaniards locked up in the store), yes, round them up like sheep, so we can see if the officials or anyone else will liberate them from the treachery that the *corregidor* means to do to them tonight" (60v). He also heard it said that Fray Joseph Quadros, Prior of San Agustín, rebuked a group of people of the place for having expelled the Indians and saying that that was no way to thank them, that they would see the consequences later.
3. He refers to the preceding.
4. It is true and evident (the looting of the Europeans' property).
5. In addition to the general sacking in which everyone participated, he knows of a "Fulano" Espejo, who made himself *caudillo* of the rebels and who robbed a lot of gold from the Europeans' belongings, also taking all the mules and a Negro from the deceased Juan Blanco; that the principal looters were Vicente Luna, Isidro Quebedo, Joseph Álvarez Martínez Catacora, (and) Gaspar Porras, and that together with others they formed a group under the name "the 12 pairs" and that they bet the money in card games, *fandangos*, and other diversions. Also with them were Pedro Aguas and the hatmaker Bernardino Ibáñez (61). Later his brother, with others, recovered a large part of the stolen property on a tour of inspection authorized by Jacinto Rodríguez, "these individuals (the looters), as well as the rest of the robbers, having testified before Jacinto Rodríguez that they ought to have returned to them all the money taken since it had been acquired fairly in wartime; the said Rodríguez being on his balcony with his lawyer Dr. Caro y Mejía, on their advice it was ordered that all that had been collected be returned again" (61v–62). In the house of one of the saddlemakers he saw on this

same day a lot of merchandise and effects that he recognized as the property of the "deceased Salinas," and these officials presently live in La Paz.
A few days before he met a blacksmith named Evaristo, who was going
to La Plata with several loads of locally produced clothing; he assumed
he was a trader going to sell what he had stolen, since he was told that
on the night of the looting they put a bar of silver in the blacksmith's
shop (62v–63).

He was told that Calvete's Negress went around announcing in the
street that Father Calatayud, a priest of La Merced, had taken a bar of
silver from her; he also heard that Father Carreño, a priest of La Merced,
had taken two bars to Cochabamba; that the priest of Challacollo had
taken another bar of silver from a servant; that Jacinto Rodríguez had
given one or more bars, of those he had taken for himself, so their value
could be applied toward masses for the dead Europeans; that also it is
publicly known that the soldiers from Cochabamba who came under the
command of Joseph de Ayarza took part of these stolen goods, through
purchases, trades and other contracts they made with the robbers (64).
He also knows that a barbarian named Domingo Callejas has brazenly
made improvements to his hacienda in Aique since the time of the
rebellion.

19. **Pedro Asquas**, criminal apprehended and imprisoned (Oruro, September 7, 1784)

1. He gives the same names.
2. He remembers the pacifying action only of Urrutia.
3. He does not know.
4. It is true (that they looted the property of the dead Europeans).
5. The only thing he knows is that a woman named María, married to
   Esteban Salamanca, offered to sell him a bar of silver at a very good price;
   that immediately he informed his captain Menacho, who advised him
   not to buy it (66v).
6. He does not elaborate.
7. He heard that a religious of La Merced, Brother Antonio Carreño, took
   a bar of silver to Cochabamba and that it was taken from him in that
   city; also, that a man from Cochabamba named Pedro Espejo took several mules and a Negro from the town and that they were all taken from
   him in Cochabamba (67).

20. **Melchor de Saavedra**, resident of Oruro (Oruro, September 9, 1784)

[He adds to his previous statement, see No. 17]
He says that his family and especially his wife Isabel Delgado saw during the night of the devastation the weaver Matías Pinto, of Cochabamba,
where he lives now again, make several trips carrying big, heavy bundles

on his back; they also saw on the following day this same Pinto and another official named Siro "washing their hands, which were bloody, and because of this they thought that said official and his master collaborated in the killings and robberies that took place that night"; that his family also saw, the night of the rebellion, the brother-in-law of Pedro Asquas, known as "El Lanchi," carrying heavy objects; that Pedro Asquas was known by him to have scarce resources before the uprising and that a little later they found out he had bought a hacienda, and they supposed that he was one of those who profited from the looting that night (68–69).

21. **José Segarra**, resident of Oruro (Oruro, September 9, 1784)

1. He gives the same names.
2. He knows that the *corregidor*, the *alcaldes*, royal officials, and militia captains are dedicated to their duties; that of the priests "he heard that generally they tried to make peace with their sermons and admonitions; that as for the prelates of the religious orders he heard that in La Merced and San Agustín they cleared the way to the doors of their churches, making way for the Europeans in refuge there to be taken; that in Santo Domingo they were protected; that the guardian of San Francisco did not want to give shelter to any of the refugees" (70v).
3. He does not know.
4. It is true (that they looted the property of the dead Europeans).
5. He says that it is publicly and widely known that Pedro Asquas, his brother-in-law Siro known as "El Lanchi," Ambrosio Medrano, two saddlemakers, Joseph Montesinos and a blacksmith named Evaristo, were accomplices and participants in the sacking and robbery perpetrated on the night of the rebellion; that Asquas bought a hacienda after the rebellion when before he had no money for that and that Montesinos was richer than before the uprising (70). With respect to Father Calatayud, accused of having kept a bar of silver given to him by a Negress, he says that the same religious told him that the commander of the convent, Brother Joseph Bustillos, ordered him to leave the bar in a cell or chamber, from which it disappeared; that he heard that Brother Carreño was arrested in Cochabamba but that he admitted to having taken only one bar of silver; that Casimiro Delgado bought two bars of silver and other property from the looting; that the deceased Miguel Portilla bought gold quoits, bars, and *piñas* of silver that had been stolen; that he knew that a servant named Terlintín and Nicolás Herrera also participated in the theft (72).

22. **Domingo Dalenza**, *cabo* of the Infantry Regiment of Saboya (Oruro, September 9, 1784)

He is called to testify and ratify what Montesinos said, in addition to his declaration. Montesinos testified that having been in Sica Sica during the rebellion with a company of soldiers from Oruro under his command, there was a dispute between him, Azurdún, and Menacho, and for this reason all the soldiers of his company fought against Menacho's men and several servants from the house of Juan de Dios Rodríguez; the latter said on this occasion that they did not fear any reprisal since Juan de Dios Rodríguez had one hundred thousand pesos in Spain and that the scribe Esteban Deheza, Menacho's lawyer, also promised them this declaring that the events in the town had been nothing more than "a fight between one man and another" (64v). Dalenza states "that the argument reported by Montesinos really did take place in Sica Sica; that he does not remember that the servants of Rodríguez had said that Juan de Dios Rodríguez had 100,000 pesos in Spain," but that the rest happened as Montesinos said (78).

23. **Juan J. Artajena**, responding to a notification (no date)

"Having been notified, by order of Col. Sebastián Segurola, present *Gobernador Intendente* of La Paz and its district, that I give information and account of the property looted and robbed in the rebellion in this town, that by way of restitution or return I have in my power as Receiver, which I was named among others for this purpose; and giving the most complete cooperation I say: that since the day of my appointment until the present I have not been given anything except two tablecloths of woven cotton, and the giver of these said that they belonged to Pantaleón Martínez, now a grain merchant, who recognizing them as his own and giving the corresponding receipt on which my signature appears, he took them with him. But I expect the rash malice of some, who being convicted of robbery might, quickly evading justice, excuse themselves by declaring falsely that they had delivered stolen goods to me and therefore in my absence raised suspicions about my honor. I beg your lordship and the Judge whose commission applies in this matter, that you compel them in the case of similar excuses to exhibit my receipt and signature and if they do not have it then you should not believe them at all" (79).

24. **Manuel Amezaga**, responding to a notification (no date)

He responds to the notification made by the royal scribe that he give information about the stolen property. He declares that he delivered everything to the president of the *audiencia* of Charcas, with the exception of 230 pesos, a silver box, a small candlestick, and two account books (which he delivered?) to the accountant Joseph Bustillo and to Juan A. Martínez.

Table B.1. *List of prisoners in the rebellions of Oruro*

Name	Held until*
Bernabé Pineda	September 3, 1790
Sebastián Rodríguez Crespo	May 25, 1790 (left prison)
Isidoro Larriva (de la Riva)	?, 1785 (died)
Casimiro Delgado	?, 1787
Joseph Azurduy	end of 1790
Jacinto Rodríguez	end of 1790
Antonio Quirós	end of July 1795
Nicolás Iriarte	end of July 1790
Diego Antonio Flores	end of July 1790
Juan Gualberto Mejía	end of July 1790
Juan de Dios Rodríguez	end of July 1790**
Clemente Menacho	end of July 1790
Felipe Aceñas	end of 1787
Isidro Quevedo	end of 1787
Bernardino Ibáñez	end of 1787
Miguel Aceñas	end of 1787
Pedro Ascuaz	end of 1787
Francisco Navarro Velazco	end of July 1790
Ventura Aceñas	end of 1787
Mariano Bernal	end of July 1790
Santiago Calatayud	July 12, 1788
Marcos Rivero	July 11, 1788
Manuel Amazarraga	July 13, 1788
Joseph Bustillo	July 12, 1788
Patricio Meléndez	March 27, 1790
Doña María Francisca Goya	July 1790
Doña Francisca Orozco	July 1787
Doña María Quirós	May 1787
Fr. Bernardino Gallegos	July 1788
Nicolás Herrera	November 1787
Miguel Portillo	no date
Manuel Herrera	no date

*The dates given in the "Held until" column are taken from accounting records. This means that until the date shown they were charged expenses in prison. It is not known if this date also indicates the moment they were set free (except in three cases where there is express indication).

**Beside this entry it says that he left prison, and that the viceroy ordered that he be given a 100-peso coin "to get himself cured."

Source: "Lista de Asientos de los Presos de Oruro donde se les carga lo que la Real Hacienda les ha suplido desde el año de 1784 que llegaron a la prisión, hasta. . . ." AGN Sala XIII CVIII A:6, no. 7 (Oruro, legajo 30, book 7).

Appendix C

Table of public jobs in Oruro, 1730–1784

This appendix shows, in addition to the names of the persons occupying the most important municipal jobs, the recurrence of apointments.

The names are numbered, with the same number appearing again in parentheses when an official has been reelected. The periods beside some numbers indicate repetition of the same family name, allowing recognition of the most conspicuous families of officeholders. After the year of election and the name, the job is indicated according to the following list of abbreviations:

Al	=	*Alguacil Mayor*
Amm	=	*Alcalde Mayor* of Mines
Ao	=	*Alcalde Ordinario*
Ap	=	*Alcalde Provincial*
Ar	=	*Alférez Real*
CC	=	Accountant of the *Caja*
Ci	=	Captain of Infantry
Co	=	*Corregidor*
Dep	=	*Depositario Real*
Ec	=	*Escribano* of the *Cabildo*
Ehr	=	*Escribano* of the Royal Treasury
Em	=	*Escribano* of Mines
FEB	=	Foundryman, assayist, and weigher
OC	=	Senior officer of the *Caja*
Pi	=	Protector of Indians
Pn	=	Protector of natives
Pr	=	*Procurador General*
R	=	*Regidor* of the Cabildo
TC	=	Treasurer of the *Caja* itself
Tes	=	Treasurer
Ve	=	Overseer of Mines

Jurisdiction of the *corregimientos*

Co 1 (Oruro)
Co 2 (Carangas)
Co 3 (Paria)
Co 4 (Cochabamba)
(i) interim
(s) auxiliary

Table C.1. *Public jobs in Oruro, 1730–1784*

No.	Date of election	Name	Office
1	1730	Joseph Moreno	Ao
2		Sebastián de Espino	Ao
3		Pedro de Mier	Pr
4	1731	Carlos Puriceli	Co
5		*Cont.* Diego de Otalora	Ao
6		Salvador de Alvarrasín	Ao
7		Antonio Zegarra	Pr
(6)	1732	*Sto. M* Salvador de Alvarrasín	Ao
(5)		*Cont.* Diego de Otalora	Ao
8		Melchor de Herrera	Ap(1)
9	1733	*Gral.* Luis Ibañez	Pr
10		Joachín Mayer	CC
11	1734	Lucas de Traslaviña	TC
12	1735	Silvestre Sentellas	Ao
(8)		Melchor de Herrera	Ao
13		Simón Rodríguez	Pr
14		*Gral.* Jph. Montes de Oca y Zalsedo	Co (3)
15		Gaspar de Miranda	Pn
16		*Gral.* Joseph Rodríguez Carrasco	Co (2)
17	1736	Antonio de Miranda	Ec
(6)		*Sto. M* Salvador de Albarrasín	Ao
18		*M. Cpo* Joseph Imblusqueta	Ao
(6)		Salvador de Albarrasín	Co
19	1737	*M. Cpo* Antonio de Toledo	Ap
20		*M. Cpo* Jph. Fco. Alserreca	Ao
21		Fco. Santos de Alborta	Pr
22		*Gral.* Manuel de Villavisencio y Granada	Co
23	1738	*M. Cpo* Fco. García de Ayllón	Ao
24		Andrés Ortiz de Uriaste	Ao
25		Joachim Calvette	Pr
26		Fco. García Picado	Em
27		Pedro A. Zabala	Co (2)

Appendix C

Table C.1. (*cont.*)

No.	Date of election	Name	Office
28		*Gral.* Martín de Espeleta y Villanueva	*Co*
29	1739	Pedro de Eulato	*Ao*
(20)		Joseph de Alserreca	*Ao*
(5)		Diego de Utalora (dif.)	*Ao*
30		Fco. de Horeña	*Pr*
31		Juan de Albarrasín	*FEB*
32		Antonio M. Barranco	*CC* (i)
(8)	1740	Melchor de Herrera	*Ao*
(7)		Antonio de Zegarra	*Ao*
33		Lorenzo Rodríguez	*Pr*
34	1741	Nicolás de Camisares	*Co* (2)
(19)	1742	Antonio de Toledo	*Ao*
(33)		Lorenzo Rodríguez	*Ao*
(29)	1743	Pedro de Eulate	*Ao*
35		Manuel de Herrera	*Ao*
36		Melchor Rodríguez	*Pr*
(28)		Martín de Espelato y Villanueva	*Co*
37		Juan Perez Inclán	*Co* (3)
38	1745	Juan Manuel de Agüero y Santibañez	*Tes*
(18)		Joseph de Imblusqueta	*Ao*
39		Manuel de Jáuregui	*Ao*
(7)		Antonio Zegarra	*Pr*
40		Martín de Mier y Terán	*Co-Amm*
41	1746	Joseph de Herrera	*Co* (3)
42		Joseph de Helguera	*Ao*
43		Diego Hidalgo de Cisneros	*Ao*
44		Ignacio Barona	*Pr*
45		Juan de Landaeta	*Co*
46		Fco. de Ugalde	*Co* (2)
(38)		Juan Manuel de Agüero	*TC* (i)
47		Nicolás Lescano Bernal	*R*
48	1747	Manuel Gallegos	*Co* (4)
		" "	*Tc*
(29)		Pedro de Eulate	*Ao*
49		Blas de Jáuregui	*Ao*
50		Diego de Jimenos	*Pr*
51		Eugenio Lerdo de Tejada	*Tc*
52		Thomás de Villanueba	*Pi*
53		Thomás de Landaeta	*TC*
(51)		Eugenio Lerdo de Tejada	*Tc*
(38)		Juan Manuel de Agüero	*Tes* (i)
54	1748	Fco. Navarro	*Ao*

55		Mathías de Uriarte	*Ao*
56		Isidro de Eulate	*Pr*
		Nicolás Joseph de Armenta y Zarate	*Ebr*
(55)		Mathías de Uriarte	*Ci*
	1749	Pedro de Eulate	*Ao*
(54)		Juan Fco. Navarro	*Ao*
		Manuel de Plantarrosa	*Pr*
	1750	Eugenio Lerdo de Tejada	*Ao*
59		Juan del Zerro	*Ao*
		Manuel de Plantarrosa	*Pr*
	1751	Melchor de Herrera	*Ao*
(18)		Joseph de Imblusqueta	*Ao*
		Manuel de Plantarrosa	*Pr*
		Lorenzo Rodríguez	*Co* (3)-
		" "	*Amm*
	1752	Pedro Alcántara Gritta	*OC*
(41)		Juan Joseph de Herrera	*Ao*
(58)		Manuel de Plantarrosa	*Ao*
		Tomás de Echeverría	*Pr*
52		Miguel de Landaeta	*Co-TC-*
		" "	*Amm*
	1753	Joseph Fernández de Palazuela	*Ci*
		Pedro de Eulate	*Ao*
		Fco. Santos de Alcorta	*Ao*
55		Joseph Galleguillos	*Pr*
	1754	Juan de Landaeta	*Co*
		Juan Helguero Palacio	*Ao*
57		Domingo Vironso	*Ao*
		Andrés Cavanero	*Pr*
	1755	Salvador Parrilla Espinosa de los Monteros	*TC*
		Melchor Rodríguez de Herrera	*Ao*
		Joseph Mathías de Uriarte	*Ao*
		Francisco Tirado	*Pr*
		Martín de Espeleta y Villanueva	*Co*
		Fco. Jph. León y Incorano	*Ec*
		Juan de Helguero Palacio	*CC* (i)
73	1756	Antonio de Urquieta	*Ao*
74		Isidro de Uriarte	*Ao*
75		Juan de Uriarte	*Pr*
(66)	1757	Juan de Helguero Palacio	*CC* (i)
(47)		Nicolás Lescano Bernal	*Ao*
76		Melchor de Herrera y Medrano	*Ao*
77		Melchor Carreño	*Pr*
78	1758	Juan del Castillo	*CC*
79		Gregorio de Aldave y Salamanca	*Al* (1, 2)
80	1759	Manuel de las Platas y Plantarrosa	*Ao*
81		Matías Ortíz de Uriarte	*Ao*

Appendix C

Table C.1. (*cont.*)

No.	Date of election	Name	Office
82		Isidro de la Riva	*Pr*
83		Bernardo Ruiz de Tagle	*Co-Amm*
84		Lorenzo Rodríguez	*Co-Amm*
(73)	1760	Antonio de Urquieta	*Ao*
(74)		Isidro Ortíz de Uriarte	*Ao*
85		Ventura Santiso	*Pr*
(35)	1761	Manuel de Herrera	*Ao*
(65)		Joseph Galleguillos	*Ao*
86		Cayetano Sanes	*Pr*
(66)	1762	*Gral.* Juan de Helguera Palacio	*Ao*
87		Domingo de Herrera	*Ao*
88		Joseph N. de Salamanca	*Pr*
89		Gaspar Hurtado de Villagomer	*Ve*
90		Joachín de Guerola	*TC*
(35)		Manuel de Herrera	*Co* (3)
		" "	*Amm* (3)
91		Joseph Soto	*CC* (i)
(58)	1763	*M. Cpo* Manuel de la Plata y Plantarrosa	*Ao*
(36)		Melchor Rodríguez	*Ao*
92		Juan de Dios Rodríguez	*Pr*
93		Antonio de Santander	*OC*
(65)	1764	*M. Cpo.* Joseph de Galleguillos	*Ao*
96		Juan Antonio Gonsales de Quiroga	*Ao*
95		Joseph N. de Aldave y Salamanca	*Pr*
96		Blas Garcón	*CC*
(91)	1765	Joseph de Sota	*CC* (i)
97		Domingo de Herrera y Galleguillos	*Ao*
98		Xavier de Bosa	*Ao*
(99)		Juan Antonio González de Quiroga	*Pr*
99		Alejandro Morillo	*Co* (3)
100		Bernardo Ruiz de Tagle	*Co*
(80)	1766	Manuel Plantarrosa	*Ao*
(92)		Juan de Dios Rodríguez	*Ao*
101		Nicolás de Herrera	*Pr*
102		Juan Leonardo	*Co-Amm*
103		Jacinto Rodríguez	*R*
104	1767	Juan de Guzman	*Ec*
(65)		Joseph Galleguillos	*Ao*
(103)		Jacinto Rodríguez	*Ao*
105		Diego Flores	*Pr*
106	1768	Juan Fernando Pacheco	*Co*
		" " "	*TC*

107		Domingo de Pavia	*OC*
108		Isidro de la Riba	*Pr*
109		Diego Antonio Torres	*Ao*
110		Ventura Helguera	*Ao*
(92)		Juan de Dios Rodríguez	*Ao*
111		Joseph Manuel de Uriarte	*Ao*
112		Manuel Serrano	*Pr*
(110)	1769	Ventura Helguero	*R*
113	1770	Benito Domingo Medrano	*Ec* (3)
(69)		Salvador Parrilla	*TC*
(103)		Jacinto Rodríguez	*Ao*
114		Joachín Ruvin de Celis	*Ao*
115		Joseph Manuel de Herrera	*Pr*
116		Isidro Rodríguez	*R*
(109)		Diego Antonio Flores	*AR*
(81)		Manuel Mathías Ortíz de Uriarte	*FEB*
117	1771	Sebastián Fernández de Medrano	*TC*
(109)		Diego Antonio Flores	*Ao*
(94)		Diego Antonio González de Quiroga	*Ao*
118		Manuel de Echaus	*Pr*
(92)	1772	Juan de Dios Rodríguez de Herrera	*Ao*
(97)		Domingo de Herrera y Galleguillos	*Ao*
119		Manuel de Aurrecoechea	*Pr*
120		Domingo de Urquieta	*R*
121	1773	Manuel J. Cabello de León	*Co* 3(4)
(92)		Juan de Dios Rodríguez de Herrera	*Ao*
(97)		Domingo de Herrera	*Ao*
(119)		Manuel de Aurrecoechea	*Pr*
(103)	1774	Jacinto Rodríguez de Herrera	*Ao*
122		Francisco Sorzano	*Ao*
123		Jph. Fdo. de Gurruchaga	*Pr*
124		Juan Gelly	*Co* (i)
125		Fdo. Ramiro y Tena	*Ec*
(115)		Jph. Manuel de Herrera	*Dep*
(112)		Manuel Serrano	*R*
(79)	1775	Gregorio de Aldave y Salamanca	*Ao*
(112)		Manuel Serrano	*Ao*
126		Jph. Antonio Ramallo	*Pr*
		Id (*Of. vendido*)	*R*
(92)	1776	Juan de Dios Rodríguez	*Ao*
(97)		Domingo Herrera	*Ao*
127		Pedro de Urquieta	*Pr*
128	1777	Joachín Cabezas y Escalante	*Co* (3)
(103)		Jacinto Rodríguez de Herrera	*Ao*
(122)		Francisco Zorsano	*Ao*
(120)		Domingo de Urquieta	*Pr*
(126)	1778	Jph. Antonio Ramallo	*Amm*

Table C.1. (*cont.*)

No.	Date of election	Name	Office
129		Manuel de la Bodega	*Co* (3)
(103)		Jacinto Rodríguez de Herrera	*Ao*
(94)		Juan Antonio González de Quiroga	*Ao*
130		Juan Antonio Martínez	*Pr*
(128)	1779	Joachín Cabezas y Escalante	*Co* (i)
(129)		Manuel de la Bodega y Llano	*Co* (3)
		Id.	*TC*
		Id.	*Amm*
131		Pedro Vicente de Vargas	*CC* (i)
132		Thomás Antonio Ayarza	*Co* (i)
(92)		Juan de Dios Rodríguez de Herrera	*Ao*
(97)		Domingo de Herrera y Galleguillos	*Ao*
133		Juan Manuel Soto	*Pr*
(128)	1780	Joachín Cabezas	*TC*
134		Ramón de Urrutia y Las Casas	*Co*
		Id.	*TC*
		Id.	*Amm*
(129)		Manuel de la Bodega	*Co* (3)
		Id.	*TC*
		Id.	*Amm*
(79)		Gregorio de Aldave y Salamanca	*Ao*
(123)		Jph. de Gurruchaga	*Ao*
(134)	1781	Ramón de Urrutia y Las Casas	*Co*
		Id.	*TC*
		Id.	*Amm*
135	1782	José Manuel de Bustillo	*CC*
136		Manuel de Hornera	*Ao*
137		Isidro de Larriba	*Ao*
138		Clemente Menacho	*Pr*
(115)	1783	Jph. Manuel de Herrera	*Ao*
(122)		Fco. Ruiz de Sorsano	*Ao*
139		Diego de Urquieta	*Pr*
(134)		Ramón de Urrutia	*Co, TC, Ao*
140	1784	Jph. Miguel de Llano	*Ao*
(123)		Jpf. Fdo. de Gurruchaga	*Ao*
141		Manuel de Urquieta	*Pr*

Bibliography

Primary sources

Archival material

Archivo Nacional de Bolivia (Sucre)
   Actas del cabildo de Oruro, real audiencia de Charcas, expedientes coloniales (docs. 5862, 5986).
   Archivo de la Corte Suprema, escrituras notariales, Oruro.
   Juicios, Oruro (exp. 1753).
   Expedientes de minas, real audiencia de Charcas (vol. 21, doc. 749).
   Colonia, real audiencia de Charcas, cédulas reales (1580–1817); Libros de Acuerdos (1561–1822).
Archivo General de Indias (Sevilla)
Audiencia de Charcas (leg. 591, 592, 593, 594, 595, 596).
Audiencia de Cuzco (leg. 30, 35, 38, 39, 40, 41).
Audiencia de Lima (leg. 633, 634, 635, 636, 637, 1545, 1619).
Indiferente General (leg. 411, 1713).
Archivo General de la Nación (Buenos Aires)
   Intendencia de Potosí (leg. 6; IX-6-3-3-6).
   Oruro (Leg. 1, 9-7-6-4; leg. 2, 9-7-6-5).
   Caja real de Oruro (1700–91), Sala III.
   Libro real común de la caja de Oruro, Sala XIII-VIII-A6.
   Potosí (leg. 26, libro 4, Sala XIII-6-5-3).
   Informe sobre los tumultos occurridos en Oruro entre marzo y abril de 1781; Testimonio del expediente de diligencias practicadas para averiguar los tumultos meditados contra Oruro; Testimonio del Cuaderno Segundo de Autos criminales obrados por don Sebastián de Segurola sobre la rebelión de la Villa de Oruro (leg. 2, nos. 2–3, Sala IX-7-4-3); Carta de Fco. de Paula Sanz al Virrey Loreto (leg. 3, Sala IX-5-5-4).
   Cartas de Ignacio Flores (al Virrey Vértiz y a Ramón de Urrutia, leg. 190–1, Bibl. Nac.).
   Derrotero de Postas, Caminos y Leguas desde Buenos Aires a Potosí y otras varias noticias curiosas (1775), (Bibl. Nac., leg. 314, doc. 5126).

Publications

Actas capitulares de Santiago del Estero. Academia Nacional de la Historia, Buenos Aires. 1946.
Alcedo, Antonio de. *Diccionario geográfico–histórico de las Indias occidentales o América: Es a saber de los reynos del Perú, Nueva España, Tierra Firme, Chile y Nuevo Reyno de Granada,* 5 vols. Madrid, 1786–89.

Amat y Junyent, Manuel de. *Memoria de gobierno*, Sevilla, Publicaciones de la Escuela de Estudios Hispanoamericanos, 1947.

Ballivián y Roxas, Vicente. *Archivo Boliviano. Colección de documentos relativos a la historia de Bolivia en la época colonial*, Paris, A. Franc, 1872 (Vol. I).

Blanco, Pedro Aniceto. *Diccionario geográfico de la República de Bolivia*, Departmento de Oruro, 1904.

Cañete y Domínguez, Pedro V. *Guía histórica, geográfica, física, política, civil y legal del gobierno e intendencia de la provincia de Potosí (año 1791)*, La Paz, 1952.

Carrió de la Vandera, Alonso (Concolorcorvo). *El lazarillo de ciegos caminantes desde Buenos Aires hasta Lima, 1775*, Paris, 1938.

Carrió de la Vandera, Alonso. *Reforma del Perú*, Lima, Pablo Mancera, 1966.

De Angelis, Pedro. *Colección de obras y documentos relativos a la historia antigua y moderna de las provincias del Río de la Plata*, Buenos Aires, Plus Ultra, 1971.

"Diario del tumulto acaecido en la villa de Oruro en 10 de febrero de 1781 con motivo de la sublevación de Tupaj Amaru," in *La Revista de Buenos Aires, Historia Americana, Literatura y Derecho*, 22 (1870).

Guirior, Virrey. "Memoria de Gobierno," in Lorente (ed.), *Relaciones de los virreyes y audiencias que han gobernado el Perú*, Madrid, 1872.

Helms, Anton Zacharias. *Tagebuch einer Reise durch Peru von Buenos Ayres an dem grossen Plataflusse, ueber Potosi nach Lima, der Haupstadt des Koenigsreichs Peru*, Dresden, 1798.

Memorias de los Virreyes que han gobernado el Perú durante el coloniaje español, Lima, Bailly, 1859.

"Monografía de la Industria Minera en Bolivia," *Dirección general de estadística*, La Paz, 1910.

"Parecer que dió Don Miguel Feyjóo de Sosa," *Biblioteca Nacional*, Madrid, Ms. 13.368.

Recopilación de leyes de los reinos de las Indias, mandadas imprimir y publicar por la magestad católica del Rey Don Carlos II, 4 vols. Madrid, Boix, 1841.

Real cédula de incorporación del Banco del Potosí a la real hacienda, Madrid, Benito Cano, 1795.

"Relación trágica de los funestos y ruidosos acaecimientos de la Villa de Oruro," in *La Revista de Buenos Aires*, Historic American literature y derecho 22 (1870).

Segurola, Sebastián de. "Diario de los sucesos del Cerco de La Paz," in Ballivian y Roxas, Historic American literature y derecho 22 (1870).

Ulloa, Antonio, and Juan, Jorge. Noticias secretas de América, Buenos Aires, Mar Océano, 1953.

Secondary sources

Books

Bargalló, Modesto. *La amalgamación de los minerales de plata*, México, Cía. Fundidora de Fierro y Acero de Monterrey, 1969.

Bayle, Constantino. *Los cabildos seculares en América española*, Madrid, Sapientia, 1952.

Beneyto, Juan. *Historia de la administración española e hispanoamericana*, Madrid, Aguilar, 1958.

Bertrán Ávila, Marcos. *Capítulos de la historia colonial de Oruro*, La Paz, 1925.

Jacinto Rodríguez y Sebastián Pagador: el 10 de febrero y el 6 de octubre. Opiniones (debate with Adolfo Mier), Oruro, M. C. Gamarra, 1944.

Brading, D. A. *Miners and Merchants in Bourbon Mexico, 1763–1810*, Cambridge University Press, 1971.

Campbell, Leon G. *The Military and Society in Colonial Peru (1750–1810)*, Philadelphia, American Philosophical Society, 1978.

Cañete Y Domínguez, Pedro. *Guía histórica, geográfica, física, política, civil y legal del gobierno e intendencia de la provincia de Potosí*, 1787, Editor Armando Alba, Potosí, 1952, vol. 1.

Carr, Raymond. *Spain*, Oxford University Press, Clarendon Press, 1966.

Cervera, Manuel. *Historia de la ciudad y provincia de Santa Fe*, Santa Fe, 1907.

Cole, Jeffrey A. *The Potosí Mita*. Stanford, Calif., Stanford University Press, 1985.

Cornblit, Oscar. *Cambio político en Cuzco y Oruro a fines del siglo XVIII.* Un estudio comparativo de simulación, Buenos Aires, Centro de Investigaciones Sociales, Instituto Torcuato Di Tella, 1970.

ed. *Dilemas del conocimiento histórico: Argumentaciones y controversias*, Buenos Aires, Editorial Sudamericana, 1992.

Crespo Rodas, Alberto. *La guerra entre Vicuñas y Vascongados*, La Paz, Juventud, 1975.

Dalence, José M. *Bosquejo estadístico de Bolivia*, Sucre, Imprenta de Sucre, 1851.

Del Valle de Siles, M. Eugenia. *Historia de la rebelión de Tupac Catari, 1781–1782*, La Paz, Don Bosco, 1990.

María Eugenia. *Historia de la rebelión de Tupac Catari, 1781–82*, La Paz, Don Bosco, 1990.

Di Tella, Torcuato S. *Sociología de los procesos políticos*, Buenos Aires, Grupo Editor Latinoamericano, 1985.

Eguiguren, Luis A. *Guerra separatista*, Lima, 1952.

Fisher, J. R. *Government and Society in Colonial Peru: The Intendant System, 1784–1814*, London, Atolone, 1978.

Silver Mines and Silver Miners in Colonial Peru, 1776–1824, University of Liverpool, Centre for Latin American Studies, 1977.

Forbes, David. *The Aymara Indians*, London, Taylor & Francis, 1870.

García, Juan Agustín. *La ciudad indiana: Buenos Aires desde 1600 hasta mediados del s. XVIII*, Buenos Aires, 1900.

Golte, Juergen. *Repartos y rebeliones*, Lima, Instituto de Estudios Peruanos, 1980.

Hagen, Everett. *On the Theory of Social Change*, Homewood, Ill., Dorsey, 1962.

Halperín Donghi, Tulio. *Guerra y finanzas en los orígenes del Estado argentino (1791–1850)*, Buenos Aires, Editorial de Belgrano, 1982.

Halperín Dongui, Tulio, ed. *El ocaso del orden colonial en Hispanoamérica*, Buenos Aires, Sudamericana, 1978.

Haring, Clarence. *El Imperio Hispánico en América*, Buenos Aires, Solar/Hachette, 1972.

Helms, Anthony Zachariah. *Travels from Buenos Ayres by Potosí to Lima*, London, 1806.

Herr, Richard. *The Eighteenth-Century Revolution in Spain*, Princeton, N.J., Princeton University Press, 1958.

Jacobsen, Nils, and Puhle, Hans Jurgen (eds.). *The Economics of Mexico and Peru during the Late Colonial Period, 1760–1810*, Berlin, Coloquium Verlag, 1986.

Konetzke, Richard. *América Latina: la época colonial*, Madrid, Siglo XXI, 1974.

Kossok, Manfred. "Commentary," in Jacobsen and Puhle (eds.), *The Economics of Mexico and Peru*, pp. 341–56.

Levene, Ricardo. *Historia del Derecho Argentino*, Buenos Aires, Kraft, 1946.

Levillier, R. *Antecedentes de política económica en el Río de la Plata*, Madrid, 1915.

Loayza, Francisco. *Juan Santos, el invencible (manuscritos del año 1742 al 1755)*, Lima, 1942.

La verdad desnuda, Lima, 1943.

Lohmann Villena, Guillermo. *El corregidor de indios en el Perú bajo los Austrias*, Madrid, Cultura Hispánica, 1957.

Los americanos en las órdenes nobiliarias, 1529–1900, Madrid, 1942.

Lorente, Sebastián. *Relaciones de los virreyes y audiencias que han gobernado el Perú*, Lima–Madrid, 1867–72.

Lynch, John. *Administración colonial Española*, Buenos Aires, Eudeba, 1962.

MacLachlan, Colin. *La justicia criminal del siglo XVIII en México*, México, Septetentas, 1976.

Mendiburu, Manuel de. *Diccionario histórico–biográfico del Perú*, Lima, 1931–35.

Moore, John Preston. *The cabildo in Peru under the Hapsburgs: A study in the origins and powers of the town council in the viceroyalty of Peru, 1530–1700*, Durham, N.C., Duke University Press, 1954.

The cabildo in Peru under the Bourbons, Durham, N.C., Duke University Press, 1966.

Moreno Cebrián, Alfredo. *El corregidor de indios y la economía peruana en el siglo XVIII*, Madrid, Instituto Gonzalo Fernández de Oviedo, 1977.

O'Phelan Godoy, Scarlett. *Un siglo de rebeliones anticoloniales*, Cuzco, Centro Bartolomé de las Casas, 1988.

Ots Capdequí, José María. *Manual de historia del derecho español en las Indias y del derecho propiamente indiano*, Buenos Aires, Fac. de Derecho y Ciencias Sociales, 1943.

Instituciones, Barcelona, 1969.

Priestley, Herbert I. *José de Gálvez, Visitor-General of New Spain*, Berkeley and Los Angeles: University of California Press, 1916.

Purser, W. F. C. *Metal-mining in Peru, Past and Present*, New York, Praeger, 1971.

Sahuaraura Titu Atauchi, Rafael. *Estado del Perú, año de 1784*, Lima, 1944.

Sánchez Albornoz, Nicolás. *La población de América Latina. Desde los tiempos precolombinos al año 2000*, Madrid, 1973.

Indios y tributos en el Alto Perú, Lima, IEP, 1978.

Stern, Steve. *Resistance, Rebellion and Consciousness in the Andean Peasant World, 18th to 20th Centuries*, Madison, University of Wisconsin Press, 1987.

Villalobos, Sergio. *Comercio y contrabando en el Río de la Plata y Chile, 1700–1811*, Buenos Aires, Eudeba, 1965.

Whitaker, Arthur P. *The Huancavelica Mercury Mines*, Cambridge, Mass.: Harvard University Press, 1941.

White, Hayden. *Metahistory*, Baltimore, Johns Hopkins University Press, 1975.

Wightman, Ann. *Indigenous Migration and Social Change: The "Forasteros" of Cuzco, 1520–1720*, Durham, N.C., Duke University Press, 1990.

Articles, periodicals, and other publications

Acevedo, Alberto. "El viaje del Contador Navarro entre Lima y Buenos Aires en 1779," *Revista de Historia Americana y Argentina*, 3, nos. 5–6.

Aiton, Arthur S. "Spanish Colonial Reorganization under the Family Compact," *Hispanic American Historical Review*, 12, 1932.

Bakewell, Peter. "Registered Silver Production in the Potosí District, 1550–1735," *Jahrbuch fuer Geschichte von Staat, Wirtschaft und Gesellschaft Lateinamerikas*, 12 (1975).

Brading, D. A. "Las minas de plata en el Perú y México colonial: Un estudio comparativo," *Desarrollo Económico*, 2, no. 41 (April–June 1971).

Brading, D. A., and Cross, Harry. "Colonial Silver Mining: Mexico and Peru," *Hispanic American Historical Review*, 52 (1972).

Buchler, Rose M. "Technical Aid to Upper Peru: The Nordenflicht Expedition," *Journal of Latin American Studies*, 5, no. 1 (1973).

Carretero, Andrés. "Importancia de la revolución de Tupac Amaru" (prólogo) in: Pedro de Angelis, *Colección de obras y documentos relativos a la historia antigua y moderna de las provincias del Río de la Plata*, Buenos Aires, Plus Ultra, 1971.

Céspedes del Castillo, Guillermo. "Lima y Buenos Aires: repercusiones económicas y políticas en la creación del Virreinato del Río de la Plata," *Anuario de Estudios Americanos*, 3 (1946).

Cobo, Bernabé. "Historia del Nuevo Mundo," in M. Bargalló, *La amalgamación de los minerales de plata*, México, Cía. Fundidora de Hierro y Acero, 1969.

Cornblit, Oscar. "Acontecimientos y leyes en la explicación histórica," *Análisis Filosófico*, 8, no. 2 (1988).
"Debates clásicos y actuales sobre la historia," in Oscar Cornblit, *Dilemas*, pp. 7–77.
(ed.), *Dilemas del conocimiento histórico: argumentaciones y controversias*, Buenos Aires, Sudamericana, 1992.
"Levantamientos de masas en Perú y Bolivia durante el siglo XVIII," in Tulio Halperín Donghi (ed.), *El ocaso del orden colonial en Hispanoamérica*. Buenos Aires, Sudamericana, 1978. [Translation of "Society and Mass Rebellion."]
"Society and Mass Rebellion in Eighteenth-Century Peru and Bolivia," in Raymond Carr (ed.), *Latin American Affairs*, Oxford University Press, 1970.
"Acontecimientos y leyes en la explicación histórica," in Cornblit (ed.), *Dilemas*, pp. 253–78.
Cortés Conde, Roberto. "Historia económica: nuevos enfoques," in Cornblit (ed.), *Dilemas*, pp. 123–44.
Crespo Rodas, Alberto. "La mita de Potosí," *Revista Histórica*, 12 (1955–6).
"El reclutamiento y los viajes en la mita del cerro del Potosí," in *La minería hispana e iberoamericana*, VI Congreso Internacional de Minería, León, España, 1970, vol. 1.
"Fundación de la villa de San Felipe de Austria," *Documentos orureños*, colección dirigida por Condarco Santillán, Oruro, Pregor, 1977, vol. 2.
Di Tella, Torcuato S. "La formalización teórica en ciencias sociales," in Cornblit (ed.), *Dilemas*, pp. 199–228.
Fisher, John. "Silver Production in the Viceroyalty of Peru, 1776–1824," *Hispanic America Historical Review*, 35, no. 1 (1975).
Gallo, Ezequiel, and Sigal, Silvia. "La formación de los partidos políticos contemporáneos: la UCR (1890–1916)," in Di Tella, Germani, Graciarena (eds.), *Argentina, sociedad de masas*, Buenos Aires, Eudeba, 1965.
"Lo inevitable y lo accidental en historia," in Cornblit (ed.), *Dilemas*, pp. 145–63.
Guariglia, Osvaldo. "Para una metahistoria del narrativismo," in Cornblit (ed.), *Dilemas*, pp. 229–52.
Halperín Donghi, Tulio. "La historia social en la encrucijada," in Cornblit (ed.), *Dilemas*, pp. 79–121.
Hernández Sánchez Barba, Mario. "La sociedad colonial americana del siglo XVIII," in J. Vicens Vives, *Historia de España y América*, Barcelona, V. Vives, 1961, vol. 4.
Imana Castro, Teodisio. "De lo pasional en la vida de los caudillos indígenas de 1780," in *Historia y Cultura; Revista del Instituto de Estudios Bolivianos*, 1 (1973).
Kahle, Louis G. "The Spanish Colonial Judiciary," in *Southwestern Social Science Quarterly*, 32 (1951–2).
Konetzke, Richard. "Die Enststehung des Adels in Hispanish Amerika waehrend der Kolonialzeit," in *Vierteljahrschrift fuer Sozial – und- Wirtschaftgeschichte*, 39 (1952).
Lenski, Gerhard. "Status Crystallization: A Non-Vertical Dimension of Social Status," *American Sociological Review*, 19, no. 4 (August 1954).
Lohmann Villena, Guillermo. "El corregidor de Lima," Anuario de estudios Americanos 9 (1952).
Mesa, José, and Guisbert, Teresa. "Oruro: orígen de una villa minera," in *Documentos Orureños*, 1977.
Mink, Louis O. "Narrative Form as a Cognitive Instrument," in R. Canary and H. Kosicki, (eds.), *The Writing of History: Literary Form and Historical Understanding*, Madison, University of Wisconsin Press, 1978.
Mora y Araujo, Manuel. "Teoría y verificación en las ciencias sociales y en la historia," in Cornblit (ed.), *Dilemas*, pp. 165–77.
Morner, Magnus. "The Spanish American Hacienda: A Survey of Recent Research and Debate," *Hispanic American Historical Review* (1973).

Noble Cook, David. "La población en el Perú colonial," *Anuario de Estudios de la Universidad Nacional del Litoral*, 8 (1965).

O'Phelan Godoy, Scarlett. "Las reformas fiscales borbónicas y su impacto en la sociedad colonial del Bajo y Alto Perú," in Nils Jacobsen and Hans Jurgen Puhle (eds.), *The Economics of Mexico and Peru during the Late Colonial Period, 1760–1810*, Berlin, Coloquium Verlag, 1986.

Paz, Melchor de. "Diálogo sobre los sucesos varios acaecidos en este Reyno del Perú, los cuales pueden servir de instrucción y de entretenimiento al curioso Lector. Año de 1780," in Luis Antonio Eguiguren (ed.), *Guerra Separatista*, Lima 1952.

Pereyra, Carlos. "La necesidad en la historia," in Cornblit (ed.), *Dilemas*, pp. 307–26.

Pike, Frederick B. "Religion, Collectivism and Intrahistory: The Peruvian Ideal of Dependence," *Journal of Latin Americas Studies*, 10, no. 2 (1978).

Pincione, Guido M. "Generalizaciones y explicación en la historiografía," in Cornblit (ed.), *Dilemas*, pp. 179–97.

Rodríguez Casado, Vicente. "Huancavelica en el siglo XVIII," *Revista de Indias*, Madrid, 1941, Vol. 2.

Salomon, Frank. "Ancestor Cults and Resistance to the State in Arequipa, ca. 1748–1754," in Steve J. Stern (ed.), *Resistance, Rebellion and Consciousness in the Andean Peasant World, 18th to 20th Centuries*, Madison, University of Wisconsin Press, 1987.

Sánchez Albornoz, Nicolás. "Migraciones internas en el Alto Perú. El Saldo acumulado en 1645," *Historia Boliviana*, 2, no. 1 (1982) 11–19.

Santamaria, Daniel. "Potosí entre la plata y el estaño," *Revista Geográfica* 79 (1973).

Seda Reyda, Gladys. "El asedio de la ciudad (basado en el informe del tesorero de la Real Hacienda Miguel Antonio de Llano)," in *Aportes documentales sobre la rebelión de Tupac Catari*, La Paz, UMSA, 1972.

Simpson, Thomas M. "Cuando Marx se identifica con la historia," in Cornblit (ed.), *Dilemas*, pp. 279–306.

Stern, Steve. "The Age of Andean Insurrection, 1742–1782: A Reappraisal," in Stern (ed.), *Resistance, Rebellion and Consciousness in the Andean Peasant World, 18th to 20th Centuries*, Madison, Wis., University of Wisconsin Press, 1987.

Tandeter, Enrique. "Forced and Free Labour in Late Colonial Potosí," *Past and present*, 93 (November 1981).

Zulawski, Ann. "Wages, Ore Sharing and Peasant Agriculture: Labor in Oruro's Silver Mines, 1607–1720," *Hispanic American Historical Review*, 67, no. 3 (1987).

Index

CAMBRIDGE LATIN AMERICAN STUDIES